THE REBELS

ALSO BY JOSHUA GREEN

*Devil's Bargain: Steve Bannon, Donald Trump,
and the Storming of the Presidency*

The Waxman Report: How Congress Really Works
(with Henry Waxman)

THE
REBELS

Elizabeth Warren,
Bernie Sanders,
Alexandria Ocasio-Cortez,
and the **Struggle** for
a **New American Politics**

JOSHUA GREEN

PENGUIN PRESS
NEW YORK
2024

PENGUIN PRESS
An imprint of Penguin Random House LLC
penguinrandomhouse.com

Copyright © 2024 by Joshua Green
Penguin Random House supports copyright. Copyright fuels creativity,
encourages diverse voices, promotes free speech, and creates a vibrant culture.
Thank you for buying an authorized edition of this book and for complying with
copyright laws by not reproducing, scanning, or distributing any part of it in any
form without permission. You are supporting writers and allowing Penguin
Random House to continue to publish books for every reader.

Portions of this book have appeared, in different form,
in *The Atlantic* and *Bloomberg Businessweek.*

LIBRARY OF CONGRESS CATALOGING-IN-PUBLICATION DATA
ISBN: 9780525560241 (hardcover)
ISBN: 9780525560258 (ebook)

Printed in the United States of America
1st Printing

DESIGNED BY MEIGHAN CAVANAUGH

For Chloe and Nick

CONTENTS

THE REBELS

PROLOGUE

I f you were to go looking for one event that shaped recent American politics more than any other—fueling the anger and contention that now feel endemic, eroding the nation's faith in its leaders, and elevating radical alternatives in their place—the 2008 financial crisis would be a strong contender.

It was the point at which America broke down, political consensus went up in smoke, and long-standing assumptions about how society should be organized, and for whose benefit, came under scrutiny. Millions of people were toiling away at careers, raising families, saving for retirement, or going to school in anticipation of these things, when, practically overnight, the global financial system blew up. Then, substantially as a result of that explosion, their own lives and careers and future possibilities began to come apart, too. Major government agencies like the Treasury and the Federal Reserve moved heaven and earth to ensure that banks held together. But most people didn't get that kind of attention. Before long, a realization set in that their elected leaders weren't looking out for them. For many people, it shattered the faith in the democratic ideal we're all taught as schoolchildren, that government serves the common good and that everyone has a fair shot at a life of decency and honor.

Suddenly that seemed like a mirage.

The sweeping totality of the financial collapse, and politicians' failure to engineer a satisfying recovery for all but the best-connected Wall Street financiers, generated an intense anger among the millions of people who wound up on history's receiving end. Not just the deindustrialized Rust Belt factory workers who would become staples of Trump-era journalism, but also students, teachers, civil servants, homeowners (especially Black and Latino ones), and small-business proprietors were left to fend for themselves amid the deepest recession since World War II. Many began to view their elected leaders less as instruments of their salvation and more as the cause of their distress. The great onrushing force of their anger upended American politics in a way that disfavored established politicians in both parties, whom voters understandably blamed for the crisis, and instead created an explosion of interest in outsiders with unorthodox ideas.

The clearest expression of this popular discontent came, of course, on the political right with the election of Donald Trump. I told the story of the rise of Trump's toxic right-wing populism and how it drove the greatest upset in U.S. presidential history in my last book, *Devil's Bargain: Steve Bannon, Donald Trump, and the Storming of the Presidency.*

But the 2008 financial crisis also produced a new strain of populism on the left. Or, rather, it revived an old strain of economic populism that would have been familiar to Democrats of the New Deal era but had fallen dormant in the decades before the crisis, when enthusiasm for regulating financial markets and suspicion of Wall Street banks were pushed to the margins. The crash brought it roaring back and, in so doing, raised a series of bedrock questions: How had the Democratic Party, traditionally the champion of workers, come to identify so strongly with Wall Street? Who made this happen and why? What could be done to return the party to its working-class roots? And who should lead the transition to a new era?

This book tells the story of the new left-populist movement that emerged from the ashes of the financial crisis to become an important force in the Democratic Party. The narrative follows three major characters—Elizabeth Warren, Bernie Sanders, and Alexandria Ocasio-Cortez—each of whom was critical to the movement's rise and carries the book's story in chronological succession. All three played fateful roles in the 2020 Democratic presidential primaries, which were supposed to mark the triumph of left populism but didn't turn out to do so—at least not in the form that most people were expecting.

Big, epoch-defining shifts don't happen just because of charismatic politicians. Out of the public eye, people in politics are constantly building up the party apparatus and jockeying for advantage over their opponents. Winning elections and maintaining control require money and manpower. Sometimes the pursuit of these things has contingent effects that don't show up for many years. Democrats' turn toward Wall Street in the 1980s is one such example. One man's effort to build a Democratic machine to compete with Ronald Reagan lit a long fuse that helped detonate the economy almost forty years later.

At other times, though, these party-building efforts succeed beyond even the hopes of their progenitors. Democrats' ability to harness the "Resistance" protests that arose to counter Trump, and eventually helped restore the party to power, owed a great deal to a group of tech-focused upstarts whom most Washington insiders couldn't pick out of a police lineup. Their stories are interspersed here, too, because each helped bring about a transformation of the party that shaped American political life—sometimes for better, sometimes for worse—first in the 1980s and then again after Trump was elected in 2016.

PART OF WHAT made the 2008 financial crisis so jarring was that it came after a long bull market and an economic expansion that appeared to produce a number of benefits. In the years prior, unemployment fell to near-record lows, easy credit flowed, and consumer confidence drove annual spending above $10 trillion for the first time. Homeownership soared, including among those who had been shut out in the past due to poor credit, racism, or other obstacles. In 2006, minority home-ownership reached 52 percent, a rise widely accorded great social significance because homes are usually families' greatest repository of wealth. Now, at long last, Blacks and Latinos were being cut in on the deal thanks to the miracle of subprime lending. Surely these positive trends would only continue.

The period before the housing bubble burst marked the pinnacle of what Gary Gerstle and other historians call the "neoliberal order"—the idea, then widely accepted by people in power positions in both parties, that America's political economy should be organized around freeing markets from government regulatory constraints because it seemed obvious to them that this was the surest, fastest way to increase everyone's wealth and well-being. It was true that anyone who cared to listen for them could find dissenting voices: in the Seattle street protests against the World Trade Organization in 1999 and the

Million Worker March for better wages and an end to outsourcing in 2004; in the warnings of liberal government officials like the economist Joseph Stiglitz and the labor secretary Robert Reich, who served Democratic presidents and left disillusioned; and also in Elizabeth Warren's academic research and Bernie Sanders's political speeches, although neither was yet well known.

These objections and other flashing danger signs were generally ignored or dismissed as naïve carping from people who had not yet grasped the full wonder of the market's power. It was more congenial to believe that the economic arrangements governing American life were working splendidly and that the dream of an equitable, multiracial, prosperous democracy was closer at hand than ever before.

Both parties were thus culpable for the ensuing crash. But it was more damning for Democrats. Republicans had always been champions of light-touch, free-market capitalism for its own sake. But valorizing businessmen and bankers, elevating them to the highest positions of government, and heeding their judgments on how to run the economy—both before and after the 2008 crisis—were breaks from the party of Andrew Jackson and Franklin Delano Roosevelt that didn't sit well with many of its voters.

What made Warren, Sanders, and later Ocasio-Cortez so captivating in the years after the crash was that each conveyed the sense of having a fully worked-out understanding of how the Democratic Party had lost its way and been captured by Wall Street. A big part of their appeal lay in their knowing exactly who was responsible for the mess and being unafraid to call them out. They satisfied the public's suspicion that bankers and politicians had, in fact, betrayed them, such that people became willing to demolish the existing political order in both parties to express the depth of their displeasure.

————

THERE REALLY IS a backstory that illuminates the Democratic Party's embrace of finance in the years leading up to the crash. Understanding this history helps explain the rise of left populists like Warren, Sanders, and Ocasio-Cortez, who were reacting against the financialization of the party and its subsequent ill effects on American life. Although this book focuses mainly on the years after the Great Financial Crisis, the best way to begin the story is not with the collapse of Lehman Brothers or the frantic midnight efforts of Treasury and Fed officials to keep the economy from imploding. Those were distant effects of decisions made decades earlier.

Instead, it's to go all the way back to 1978. At the time, Democrats were still reliable partisans of the New Deal, but the steady economic progress of the American middle class was coming to a turbulent end. Jimmy Carter was president. He was struggling, without much success, to manage an economy buffeted by inflation, oil shocks, and recessions—problems for which his party had no answers. A conservative countermovement of business groups and Republican politicians was beginning to gather force. One of history's critical inflection points arrived that fall, when Wall Street made its first deep incursion into the Democratic Party in a way that would have lasting significance, although it passed mostly unnoticed at the time.

The great irony of this early conquest is that it began with Carter's ambitious attempt to change the tax code to favor workers at the direct expense of Wall Street investors. Instead, Carter and his fellow reformers suffered a defeat so thorough that the financial lobby not only got to preserve its favorable tax treatment but was able, with Democratic help, to rewrite the rules of the economy in a way that gave Wall

Street an enduring structural advantage at the expense of the middle class—the opposite of what Carter had set out to do.

As much as anything, the story of this fight and how Carter lost it captures the tectonic shift that took place in America as the New Deal era was ending and a new one was being born. It set the party on a path that would transform it into something Democrats of an earlier generation would hardly recognize.

1

THE THREE-MARTINI LUNCH

t is October 14, 1978. Jimmy Carter is sitting in the Oval Office about to make what he knows will be one of the pivotal decisions of his still-young presidency. He is deeply unhappy. The economy is souring. Inflation has picked up again. The midterm election is three weeks away. And it is now clear that his own party's congressional leaders have betrayed him on a matter he considers of great moral importance and in a manner designed to humiliate him personally. Across from him sits a young aide in horn-rimmed glasses, Stuart Eizenstat, who is furiously scribbling Carter's complaints onto a yellow legal pad. If you want to locate the moment when the Democratic Party first turned toward Wall Street, when the party of the New Deal quietly switched tracks and started steaming off in a different direction, it's right now, and its initial rationale is laid out in the tale of futility that Eizenstat is recording in his yellow pads.

Carter's charmed run for the presidency was propelled by the strength of his personal story: farmer, governor, southerner, born-again Christian, his rectitude and modesty—the very image of him in blue jeans and work shirts—were antidotes to the national nightmare of Nixon's Washington. Carter was a populist. The societal rot that produced Watergate, he told voters, grew out of a corrupted value system that powerful business interests had enshrined in the federal tax code—"a disgrace to the human race" and "a welfare program for the rich" that warped every aspect of American life. As he traveled the country campaigning, he'd catalog its grotesque injustices: deductions for yachts, sports tickets, country clubs, and first-class airfare; preferential treatment for capital gains so investors and the idle rich paid less than ordinary workers. At the same time, he'd note, the middle-class tax burden was rising as inflation pushed those workers into higher brackets.

Carter had a favorite illustration that gave vivid dimension to his message that inequality was rampant: the deductibility of "the three-martini lunch." As a populist symbol of elite self-dealing, it was hard to beat. The thought of well-heeled businessmen and lobbyists getting plastered in the middle of the day—at taxpayers' expense!—was infuriating to voters, especially in the wake of the 1974–75 recession. "When a business executive can charge off a $55 luncheon on a tax return and a truck driver cannot deduct his $1.50 sandwich," Carter would say, "then we need basic tax reform."

That his attack elicited howls from its targets only added to its broad popular vitality. "You're taught there's virtue in working hard," one banker griped to *The New York Times*. "So you work hard, and just when you get to where you're about to enjoy some of the reward, you're hated and punished." Another complained, "Who are these people, a bunch of Bolsheviks? It took me all my life to get into the eating class and now they want to take it away." The National Restaurant Association briefly considered launching a march on Washington but seemed to sense that saving the businessman's lunch deduction wouldn't quite measure up, in the public's estimation, to causes such as advancing civil rights and ending the Vietnam War that had spurred earlier Washington marches. Finding the most fatuous example of Wall Street outrage at Carter and crafting a story around it became a kind of sport among national media outlets. "We're in a hyper-tense, high-pressure business," a Wall Street stockbroker huffed to *The New York Times*, "and if it weren't for these lunches, some of these people would be dead."

Along with his diagnosis of what ailed the country, Carter had offered a solution: Zero out the tax code, wipe the slate clean, and start anew. He'd tax capital gains at the same rate as income to put workers back on equal footing with their bosses. He'd eliminate the obscene loopholes through which the middle class subsidized the extravagances of the wealthy. Through determined effort, he would impose his own values—his simple Baptist decency—on the travesty of the federal tax code, ushering it through the Democratic Congress, from whence it would emerge, reborn. To Carter, questions of dollars and cents were secondary to the moral dimension of the problem. When informed that killing the business entertainment deduction for the three-martini lunch wouldn't bring in much government revenue, he shot back, "I don't care if it brings in revenue or not—it's wrong."

Tax reform was front and center when Carter had stood before the bunting and stage lights in Madison Square Garden to accept his party's nomination at the 1976 Democratic National Convention. "The powerful always manage to find and occupy niches of special influence and privilege, and an unfair tax structure serves their needs," he declared. "Unholy, self-perpetuating alliances have been formed between money and politics, and the average citizen has been held at arm's length." He continued, "It is time for a complete overhaul of our income tax system. I still tell you: It's a disgrace to the human race. All my life I have heard promises about tax reform, but it never quite happens. With your help, we're finally gonna make it happen." Then, with a broad smile, he shouted, "You can depend on it!"

Now Carter is no longer smiling. As he sits with Eizenstat venting his frustrations, his grand plan to reform the tax code has just collapsed and divided his own administration, some of whose members have been trying to influence him by sending him private memos quoting his campaign promises to remedy the tax code in favor of working people. His party is likewise divided, and so is the president himself. Carter doesn't know what to do. He laments to his aide, "Tax reform is so screwed up."

He's right about this, and he's also right to sense that his decision will be a turning point in his presidency because the powerful business interests he campaigned against are on the verge of achieving a victory that Carter has the power to stop. What he doesn't know is that it will also be an inflection point in the history of the Democratic Party, one that Eizenstat and other administration officials will come to rue even before they leave the White House. Decades later, Eizenstat will dig up his old yellow notepads and wish he'd counseled Carter differently at the time.

Carter had, in fact, already made an honest stab at reform. At the beginning of his presidency, things even looked auspicious. To spearhead the effort, Carter had lured to the Treasury a superstar named Laurence Woodworth, the longtime director of Congress's professional tax policy staff, who was trusted and admired by both parties and, though forbidden as a civil servant to express political views, was known among reformers to secretly be one of their own. Woodworth liked to dazzle congressmen and reporters by scrawling complicated figures on his chalkboard and then explaining them in plain English; in turn, they lionized him as "a walking encyclopedia of tax law" and Carter's secret weapon on reform.

But things had quickly gone awry. Upon taking office, Carter's advisers had decided that the economy looked weak and prevailed on him to delay tax reform and first pursue a stimulus, which had bogged down in Congress and finally been dropped. Then rising oil prices necessitated an energy bill. That, too, got stuck in Congress and further damaged the deteriorating relations between the White House and Democrats on Capitol Hill.

Carter's habit of ignoring Congress and keeping his own counsel—his "Jesus in the wilderness mode of decision making," as one aide put it—is one of three reasons his reform plan fell apart and opened the door to Wall Street. Carter had no natural aptitude for legislating, disliked horse-trading, and rarely consulted the two critical players who were poised to determine the fate of his tax plan, the Senate Finance Committee chairman, Russell Long of Louisiana, and the House Ways and Means Committee chairman, Al Ullman of Oregon. Carter simply expected them to do his bidding. Chafing at the president's arrogance and having no personal investment in advancing his tax plan, Long later explained, with gratuitous emphasis on his low opinion of Carter, "My advice hadn't been sought. My input's not in it. That's just fine. So I figured I could pretty well do whatever I blessed well pleased about it."

Neither did Carter marshal outside help to advance his cause. He quickly fell out with the most important pillar of the Democratic coalition in the 1970s, organized labor. Because unions were practically nonexistent in Georgia, Carter had no affinity for labor, which he regarded as just another special interest looking for a handout. Further cementing this notion was his personal dislike of the AFL-CIO's cigar-chomping boss, George Meany, and frustration with labor's demands for large wage increases, which Carter felt heedlessly contributed to the inflationary pressures weighing on the economy. The antipathy was mutual. Meany resented Carter's preachy moralism, believed his focus on fighting inflation hurt workers' earning power, and found the president insufficiently committed to pushing labor law reforms that would make it easier to form unions. The first (and last) White House meeting between Carter and Meany went so badly that as Carter was leaving, he muttered to Eizenstat, "Stu, I will never do this again."

The rancor between Carter and Meany was the result of a disagreement over how Democrats should address an economy suffering from high unemployment, low productivity, and inflation. That's what everybody was fighting about in 1978. The inability to reach a consensus on a solution is the second reason Carter's tax bill fell apart.

During his presidential campaign, Carter had emphasized job growth and tax fairness, but once in office he made fighting inflation his priority. These goals demanded different (and countervailing) remedies according to the orthodox Keynesian views held by his economic advisers. Boosting employment through government stimulus and direct job creation, as labor wanted him to do, would increase inflation. But fighting inflation with Nixonian wage and price controls or pushing the Fed to raise interest rates would hurt workers' paychecks, drive up unemployment, and risk tipping the country into recession. The classical economic remedies were no longer working. As Nixon's economic adviser Herbert Stein, himself a committed Keynesian, conceded in May 1977, "We are left now with accumulating criticism of the kind of fiscal policy we have been practicing for the last 20 years, but with no substantial support for any alternative to it."

The Carter administration's inability to steady the faltering economy was the third reason tax reform failed. It left an opening for someone who did have a solution—or at least claimed to. Carter never saw him coming.

CHARLS WALKER WAS THE LIVING, breathing, cigar-smoking embodiment of a three-martini lunch: a jowly, pin-striped Washington superlobbyist and friend to all in power who rode a black limousine between Capitol Hill and Sans Souci, the French restaurant a block from the White House where he held court over glasses of white wine and fillets of sole. Raised poor in north-central Texas, Walker (whose mother dropped the *e* from his name in a failed effort to ensure he wouldn't be called "Charlie") rose to become, in succession, a PhD economist at the Fed, fixer for the American Bankers Association, and deputy secretary of Nixon's Treasury, a position he left in 1973, sensing greater profit and opportunity on the outside. With his rough-hewn charm and gravelly Texas twang, Walker founded the capital's hottest lobbying shop and convinced big business generally, and Wall Street in particular, that he could reverse a decade-long losing streak in Washington that Carter's reforms threatened to extend.

An astute anthropologist of power, Walker had witnessed from his perch at the Treasury how Ralph Nader's army of public interest lobbyists skillfully cultivated grassroots pressure campaigns that bypassed the committee chairmen, who were traditionally the power brokers, and targeted junior members, often in their home districts rather than in Washington, D.C. Walker further recognized, as Nader had, that party rules had shifted after Watergate, opening a path to outsiders like Carter and fragmenting power in Congress in a way that strengthened the rank and file at the expense of the chairmen. Nader's

Raiders exploited this insight to secure a succession of legislative and regulatory victories, several of them in the realm of tax law.

Soon after Carter launched his presidential bid, Walker took over a sleepy financial industry trade group called the American Council on Capital Gains and Estate Taxation and rebranded it as the more exalted-sounding American Council for Capital Formation, a euphemism for the aggressive accumulation of wealth. Walker began pushing the idea that the economy's productivity crisis could be solved if the government changed the way it induced business investment. Since the New Deal, the preferred method had been the investment tax credit, which rewarded companies for building factories. This generally satisfied labor interests, because factories produce jobs. The major business lobbies like the U.S. Chamber of Commerce and the National Association of Manufacturers liked the investment tax credit because many of their members were large industrial corporations. Carter's plan to eliminate the capital gains preference didn't threaten them.

But it terrified Wall Street. Walker's project was to pull off a feat of legislative legerdemain by persuading lawmakers that the solution to U.S. economic malaise lay in shifting the government's focus to encouraging capital formation—a move that would, its backers insisted, revitalize the supply side of the economy by spurring investment, unleashing entrepreneurial energies, and turbocharging productivity. In practical terms, this meant preserving the biggest giveaway to investors in the tax code: the capital gains preference.

It wouldn't look good to run a campaign to preserve a loophole for the wealthiest Americans from the back seat of a limousine. So Walker took a page from the Naderites. Working through local business groups and the newly formed Business Roundtable, which he'd helped launch, Walker arranged for the gospel of capital formation to be spread among the members of Congress and the press. No one was overlooked.

Although he had no idea Walker was behind it, Representative Abner Mikva of Illinois, one of the most liberal Democrats in Congress, and later Barack Obama's mentor, described the uncanny experience of being proselytized to by Walker's forces. "I got phone calls from several people back in my district who had been supporters of mine, and contributors," he recalled. "People who seldom asked for anything. Progressive members of brokerage houses. Public-spirited bankers. First, they asked if we could have lunch. There was no arm-twisting. They were polite, thoughtful, erudite. They had their facts. We have to do something for the economy; look at the low rate of savings. The letters I got were not mass mailings. They were intelligent letters from people who knew me well. Now, obviously, somebody back in Washington was masterminding this, but I'm sure that some of it did sway me." The reason the pitch was so effective, Mikva explained, was its careful framing: "On an issue like capital formation, where you only hear from business, it isn't something for me and nothing for you; it's something for me, and this doesn't concern you."

Throughout Carter's first year in office, as tax reform was repeatedly delayed, the context in which Congress would eventually consider it was undergoing a full-scale change few were aware was even happening. "Within a relatively short period of time," Walker bragged, "'capital formation' has entered the lexicon of 'good' words—not quite equal to 'home' and 'mother,' but still a public policy few would disagree with."

BY THE TIME Carter finally turned his attention to his long-overdue tax bill in late 1977, the economic and political landscape had shifted. Inflation was climbing toward double digits. Discontent was brewing. The public's focus shifted from tax reform to tax relief. The White

House domestic policy staff and Woodworth's Treasury team kept pushing for sweeping change centered on the elimination of the capital gains preference. But skeptics in the administration worried the economy might be too fragile for the shock of major reform. In November, Carter's Treasury secretary, Michael Blumenthal, told Congress that in light of the weakening economy the long-awaited tax bill would focus on tax relief and stimulus—signaling that comprehensive reform was in trouble and Carter was retreating.

Things quickly devolved from there.

Alerted by allies in Congress that support for reform was crumbling, Carter held a news conference to announce an indefinite "time out" for his plan. Then, in December, Woodworth, whom the White House was counting on to sweet-talk the old bulls in Congress, dropped dead of a stroke while attending a tax conference in Virginia. Carter attempted a reboot by finally introducing a watered-down tax bill in his 1978 State of the Union address that aimed to appease all sides by cutting corporate taxes, making permanent the investment tax credit, and sacrificing the bulk of his capital gains reforms. But he found little support, in Congress or anywhere else. Walker's Wall Street contingent was privately stunned: they'd won the battle before the first shot was even fired. And Walker still had an army at the ready. "They were braced for an attack," one congressional staffer explained. "When the attack never came, they decided to invade!"

At Walker's urging, several members of Congress, having fought off a capital gains increase, now turned around and started pushing for a tax cut. Wall Street brokerage houses led by Merrill Lynch and E. F. Hutton bombarded investors with mail telling them of the riches they stood to gain if rates were reduced. As the insurrection mounted over the spring, Ullman stopped work on the tax bill. But the momentum against Carter didn't slow. On June 6, California voters overwhelmingly passed the landmark ballot initiative Proposition 13, which slashed property taxes, made the cover of *Time*, and sparked a nationwide tax revolt. Dozens of antitax measures popped up in states across the country, helping shift the national mood in a more conservative direction and prefiguring the rise of Ronald Reagan.

In Washington, Carter's reformers were overrun like Custer's cavalry. Yet his humiliation wasn't finished. In a remarkable feat of legislative jujitsu, Walker's congressional allies prevailed upon Ullman to swap out the president's tax reform bill for one of their own that, on every major front, was a repudiation of Carter's principles. Instead of raising the capital gains rate to match income tax rates, the new bill slashed it while adding a blizzard of new shelters and exemptions for the wealthy. Practically no one in Congress wanted to go against the national mood and block a bill that cut taxes. In effect, Walker's forces harnessed middle-class rage over inflation-driven tax increases like those that prompted Proposition 13 and redirected that rage to support a windfall tax relief for the rich. Inside the citadels of the right, the mood was triumphant. "Any resemblance between this bill and President Carter's original tax message is purely coincidental," an internal analysis by the conservative Heritage Foundation crowed.

When the bill got to the Senate, Russell Long had no interest in rescuing Carter. Instead, he pushed for an even larger capital gains cut. With the midterm elections looming, Democrats were as eager as Republicans to show they were doing something for the economy. Only ten senators voted against Long's bill. Through it all, Carter watched dejectedly from the White House. "I think the story may well be that not only did we send up a tax package that misread the mood of Congress," one of Eizenstat's deputies wrote to him in a private

memo, "but upon being rebuffed, we retired from the field and became eunuchs."

By October 14, as Carter and Eizenstat waited unhappily in the
West Wing, House and Senate negotiators hashed out a joint bill in a
marathon overnight session. The full measure of Carter's failure now
became clear. One of his defeated soldiers, Representative Pete Stark
of California, used his allotted floor time to read into the *Congressional
Record* a snippet of doggerel he'd composed to mark the bitter occasion
and make one final plea to his president:

> The speaker had sold all the Liberals a Bill,
> And Good Chairman Ullman had swallowed the Pill.
> With loopholes for dry holes,
> And tax breaks for wine,
> The deeds of the lobbyists,
> Were almost a crime.
> They took care of the heirs,
> And built up the shelters,
> But for the poor folks,
> Russell gave us no helpers.
> The rich will have Christmas with ill-gotten gains,
> While others pay taxes with annual pains.
> But Scrolling the people is Washington's credo,
> Now what we need, Tiny Jim, is a veto!!!

And right there, Stark put his finger on the only move Carter had
left. Sitting in the West Wing with his yellow notepad, Eizenstat won-
ders if he has the nerve. This is the decision Jimmy Carter is about to
make: whether to veto the tax bill.

THAT NIGHT, Eizenstat goes home and composes a lacerating assessment of the tax bill now headed to Carter's desk, bluntly laying out the extent of the administration's failure and the consequences of Carter's options.

"The unpleasant facts we have to face squarely are: the House passed a bad bill, the Senate passed a bad bill, and the final bill is not a good bill," Eizenstat writes in a private memo to Carter. "It contains large tax reductions for the wealthiest citizens in our country and small reductions for average working people. It would constitute a setback for tax reform." Incredibly, Eizenstat adds, "the middle class will actually bear a slightly larger share of the overall tax burden under this bill than under present law . . . they will bear net tax *increases*." He goes on, "The bill does not achieve your attempt to achieve greater fairness, progressivity, and simplicity and moves in the opposite direction."

On the other hand, it does include a $20 billion tax cut. The midterm elections are three weeks away, and Democrats want something to run on. Denying them this could imperil Carter's strained relations on the Hill and fatally weaken his public image. "A veto now," Eizenstat warns, "could change the whole tone of the press coverage of the Administration's first two years."

What Carter's advisers agree on is that he needs to make up his mind quickly so Democrats have time to react before Election Day. Instead, Carter waits until the day before the election, November 6, and only then, without fanfare and in the privacy of his office, does he pick up his pen and sign into law a measure that in many respects marks the end of the New Deal era in Democratic political history and the start of a new one.

———

CARTER'S DECISION TO SIGN a bill undermining his own publicly declared principles not only marked a crossroads in his drifting presidency but helped alter the correlation of forces in Democratic politics for a generation to come.

From the end of World War II until the late 1970s, the Democratic Party was a coalition of interest groups in which labor was the senior partner. Unions supplied the organizing muscle for the party's electoral strategy, and improving workers' wages and living standards was the party's chief domestic concern. Democrats emphasized collective bargaining, tight labor markets, and expansionary fiscal policy, which produced a decades-long record of middle-class prosperity: real income for the median family doubled between 1947 and 1973. Relatively stable income distribution between workers and their bosses also produced labor harmony. Historians dubbed this epoch "the Great Compression."

The 1973 oil shock and the recession that followed brought it crashing down. It's easy to share a growing pie, but as productivity fell, inflation spun out of control, labor weakened, and U.S. manufacturers faced stiffer competition from abroad, economic growth slowed, and the old political alignment came apart. It was Carter's misfortune to govern during this period, made worse by the fact that he lacked political skill and his advisers didn't know how to generate long-run economic growth in the face of seemingly intractable problems. Carter got rolled in the 1978 tax reform fight because his supply-side opponents, aided by Walker's deft salesmanship, convinced people that they did know how to fix the economy. As one historian of the era put it, "Carter and his advisers vacated this intellectual space, which was filled by radical new solutions, capital gains reduction and supply-side tax cuts, [replacing] the assumptions that capital and labor should prosper together with an ethic claiming that the promotion of capital will eventually benefit labor—trading factories for finance."

Troubled by growing inequality, Carter had set out to rebalance in favor of the middle class the rewards government allots through the tax code. What he ended up with was a law that further empowered the very forces whose influence he sought to curb. Not only did the Revenue Act of 1978 cut corporate and capital gains taxes—redirecting investment from factories and equipment to financial instruments—but it also established the 401(k) retirement account, which channeled trillions of dollars more directly into the markets and undermined a pillar of middle-class security by eliminating employers' obligation to provide pensions that ensured workers a stable retirement. If you go back to the Great Depression and trace the share of U.S. wealth held by the richest 1 percent of Americans, it falls steadily until 1978, whereupon it reverses and begins a steep ascent that continues to this day:

Top 1% Net Personal Wealth Share in the United States, 1917–2019

Share of U.S. Wealth Held by the Top 1%

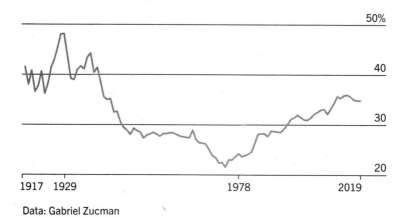

Data: Gabriel Zucman

The law's lasting effect on Democratic politics was that it ended a set of arrangements and a way of thinking about the economy that had held for four decades and replaced them with a new arrangement. Without quite realizing it or intending for it to happen, Carter's signing the Revenue Act marked the beginning of the ascendance of finance capitalism as the major influence on Democratic policymaking. As organized labor declined, Wall Street assumed the role of senior partner in the party coalition. Democratic politicians, in turn, began emphasizing priorities that differed from those of the Great Compression: fiscal austerity, soft labor markets, free trade with low-wage countries, and the further weakening of private-sector unions.

When historians analyze party takeovers, they tend to focus on big changes at the top and how those filtered down—how Donald Trump's hijacking of the GOP, for instance, reversed the party's positions on immigration and trade. Wall Street's takeover of the Democratic Party wasn't like that. It was gradual. It began at the bottom and filtered up. No singular charismatic figure or nefarious master plan was behind it, and even people like Charlie Walker who ushered the process along didn't think of themselves as being involved in a grand ideological project to reshape the American political economy. But the takeover was no less real because of it. And it picked up momentum as soon as Carter lost his bid for reelection.

2

DEMOCRATS FOR THE BUSINESS CLASS

Carter touched off a process that set Democrats on a course that would remake the party, steering it away from the labor-centered liberalism that had prevailed since World War II and reorienting it toward business interests—including those of the growing financial industry. Even before his tax bill, Carter had been moving his party in this direction in fits and starts by deregulating industries like trucking and airlines in response to pressure from Ralph Nader and others on the left who charged that government agencies had been captured by private industries bent on maintaining pricing power by limiting consumer choices. To broaden those choices in the realm of commercial banking, he also made some of the first early moves to unwind the financial regulations put in place after the Great Depression.

While it marked a triumph for Wall Street and Charls Walker, the

Revenue Act of 1978 did little to improve the economy or boost Carter's political fortunes. Two years later, he was steamrolled by Ronald Reagan, and the great liberal stalwarts of the U.S. Senate—George McGovern, Frank Church, Birch Bayh—were ousted as well, leaving the Democratic Party floundering and largely out of power. In politics, when something goes against you on a grand scale that you can't easily rationalize or explain, the instinctive reaction is fear. That's how Democrats responded to Carter's loss. They rejected their association with him. Almost immediately, Carter, with no small help from Republican critics, became a totem of political ineptitude and wrongheaded thinking, someone against whom the rising generation of Democratic politicians would define themselves. The populist inclination that had led Carter to attack the "three-martini lunch" deduction fell out of favor and was replaced by an impulse to valorize the very sorts of people— bankers and businessmen—who were most likely to claim it.

The Democratic coalition that had existed for decades was breaking down. The party's backbone, organized labor, was in steep decline. Campaigns were moving onto television, which was expensive and favored telegenic figures like Reagan who had access to large pools of capital. In the 1970s, Republicans had built up a direct-mail fundraising juggernaut that drew in millions of small contributors with targeted appeals that played on people's fears and anxieties about the direction of the country and the menace of crime, inflation, and communism. Some Democratic officials started worrying that they lacked a comparable source of funding to finance campaigns and build up the party to compete with Republicans. Sensing that a new era was at hand, and feeling compelled by both political and financial necessity, Democrats, in a bid for relevancy, moved quickly to refashion their party into one more willing to accommodate the interests of the business community—not just by supporting capital gains tax cuts, but more broadly by adopting the worldview that put market-friendly policies at its center.

This new era in Democratic politics was driven by a group of ambitious, self-consciously modern, determinedly forward-looking men (they were all men) who dubbed themselves neoliberals. Part branding mechanism, part policy prescription, the neoliberal philosophy was embraced by a post-Carter generation that included Senators Gary Hart, Bill Bradley, and Paul Tsongas, along with Governors Bruce Babbitt, Michael Dukakis, and—soon enough—Bill Clinton. They concentrated their attention on issues like technology, defense, free trade, and economic planning. Purveyors of neoliberal philosophy traded less in concrete proposals that had a direct, measurable effect on the lives of ordinary workers—raising the minimum wage, say, or improving a health-care plan—and instead favored lofty, abstract concepts such as innovation, entrepreneurship, and economic growth that were more in keeping with the Reagan-era zeitgeist. These also functioned as advertisements for the idea that their upstart backers had transcended the stodgy, interest-group-driven liberalism that still defined major party figures like Walter Mondale and were charting an exciting new path toward a future that would universalize prosperity.

The organizing principle of this new brand of Democratic politics was a conviction that market logic should be rigorously applied to all aspects of public policy and that better outcomes for everyone would ensue. This was, of course, what Republicans already believed. It was the argument Walker used to defeat Carter's attempt to produce a more equitable tax code.

Where neoliberalism differentiated itself from Republican thought was that its adherents, who were also called New Democrats, still claimed an allegiance to traditional liberal social goals. The catch was that these goals were now subordinated to the perceived dictates of the market and pursued through market-friendly methods that disfavored activist government and labor unions, the major forces of Democratic change throughout the Great Compression.

As early as 1981, at a dinner sponsored by *Esquire* magazine, Representative Richard Gephardt of Missouri, a rising Democratic star and future presidential candidate, captured the neoliberal ethos by announcing, "I would get rid of government in health care. I would get rid of government in education to a much greater extent than we have. I would discharge those responsibilities either to the private sector or to the states."

These are notes that no Democrat of the prior age would have struck. Similarly novel was the neoliberal emphasis on reducing the deficit and on leaving business largely unfettered in the expectation that doing so would revive the economy and produce greater wealth across society. Traditional liberals, of whom there were still many among the Democrats, objected loudly to what they regarded as a selling out of the party's principles in a misguided effort at political expediency. In words that Elizabeth Warren could have uttered, the historian and stalwart liberal Arthur Schlesinger Jr. lit into the "so-called neo-liberals" who were "fellow travelers in the Reagan revolution" charting a politically futile course for the Democratic Party:

> They have joined in the clamor against "big government," found great merit in the unregulated marketplace, opposed structural change in the economy, and gone along with swollen military budgets and the nuclear arms race. . . . This isn't what a serious opposition party should be about.

Jesse Jackson famously disparaged the Democratic Leadership Council, formed after Mondale's loss in the 1984 election to push New Democrat ideals, as representing "Democrats for the Leisure Class." A less stinging, but more precise, description would have been Democrats for the business class. Neoliberal sentiment was a clear departure from the main currents of liberal thought since the New Deal, which had championed labor, competition, antitrust, and taking a strong hand in regulating the affairs of large corporations. Now that was all being rethought. Rationalizing this break with Democratic tradition, one leading neoliberal thinker declared, shortly after Carter's defeat, "You have to respect what's good about businessmen, while at the same time remaining aware that they can be shits."

The center-versus-left debate carried on for decades. But it wasn't much of a contest. In the battle of ideas inside the Democratic Party, the neoliberal victory was so thorough that by the mid-1990s a New Democrat (Bill Clinton) was president, and not only was traditional liberalism regarded as outmoded and passé, but Wall Street chieftains could comfortably assume top government positions in both Repub-lican and Democratic administrations. Clinton, for one, was heavily influenced by his Treasury secretary, Robert Rubin, the former co-chairman of Goldman Sachs and one of the chief architects of what the modern Democratic Party would become. And while Clinton had campaigned promising a tax cut and stimulus package for "the hard-working Americans who make up our forgotten middle class," he was quickly persuaded to abandon those goals for the market-favored al-ternative of cutting the federal deficit. (That's what prompted James Carville's famous lament about the power that bond traders held over neoliberal politicians. "I used to think that if there was reincarnation, I wanted to come back as the president or the pope or as a .400 baseball hitter," Carville said in 1993. "But now I would like to come back as the bond market. You can intimidate everybody.")

What made it possible for Clinton to reengineer the party into a finance-centric juggernaut was the steady growth of the economy during his tenure in the White House. His timing was propitious. Following the late 1970s upheaval that marked the end of the Great Compression, in 1982 the Federal Reserve chairman, Paul Volcker, engineered a brutal recession that finally broke runaway inflation and ushered in what would be called the Great Moderation, a quarter century of steady growth, low inflation, and rising financial markets that buoyed Clinton's presidency. During his two terms in office, real GDP growth averaged nearly 4 percent, while unemployment fell steadily. By the time Clinton left office, neoliberal precepts about the importance of deficit reduction, small government, free trade, and deregulation were the established canon of the Democratic Party.

This economic arrangement didn't work well for everyone, however, even before the 2008 financial collapse laid bare the full extent of its shortcomings. Neoliberalism produced a way of looking at the world through a market lens that had the effect, not always intended, of hiving off issues that didn't pertain in a clear and direct way to the market and treating them as separate, wholly unconnected concerns, when in fact they were intimately interwoven with, and affected by, changes in the broader economy: issues such as race, poverty, criminal justice, education, and the environment. From the outset, it was clear that in the neoliberal agenda these matters would be subordinated to economic concerns. And to ensure the economy's robust good health, it would not be guided by government officials. "Our proposals," Tsongas wrote in 1983, "presuppose that the economy will work best when private industry leads the way." These views, though rarely so bluntly stated by high-level Democratic politicians, carried across the next three decades.

One problem with gazing at the world through this lens is that despite the market's ostensible success under Clinton, prosperity didn't accrue evenly, or anything close to it. But the neoliberal faith in the market's unerring ability to provide for all made this difficult for its proponents to see. Looking at the American economy in terms of its robust top-line growth masked the fact that people at the top of the income scale were capturing almost all of the gains, while the middle and lower classes were experiencing something entirely different, struggling to keep pace or falling behind. This was true in terms of both income and wealth, and the problem worsened over time. Between 1979 and 2007, income growth in the United States—all of it!—went to the richest 10 percent of earners; the remaining 90 percent saw their income fall. Examining the distribution of gains across income categories, the Congressional Budget Office found that the incomes of the top 1 percent rose by 275 percent between 1979 and 2007, after federal taxes and government transfer payments such as Social Security. Over the same period, the incomes of the broad middle class—the 60 percent of the population in the middle of the income scale—grew by only 40 percent. And the bottom quintile fared the worst, rising by only 18 percent.

Yet this economic disparity didn't cause a political backlash for a very long time. There were three primary reasons why not. First, the focal point of Democratic politics after the New Deal shifted away from banking and financial regulatory matters to issues such as the environment, feminism, and civil rights. The major battles in national politics in the 1990s and early years of the twenty-first century were cultural or geopolitical ones, ranging from the push for national health care and the legalization of gay marriage to the propriety of the wars in Afghanistan and Iraq. Second, both of the Democratic presidents who followed Carter were preternaturally skilled at forging connections with the Democratic base that mitigated material dissatisfaction. "Clinton had extraordinarily versatile cultural competence and emotional intelligence that he was able to employ to get just about any audience to feel like they were being seen," says one prominent labor leader who worked with him. "Toni Morrison's remark that Bill Clinton was 'the first black president' reflected that he was actually comfortable in settings where many white politicians are not. It created a source of trust that gave him license to pursue economic policies that, looked at in the cold light of day, didn't direct most of their benefits to those communities, but to Wall Street." With Obama, those connections were even stronger—enough so that even amid the 2008 financial crisis and its painful aftermath he was able to carry out policies largely favorable to the financial industry without meeting serious opposition from within his own party. Even mild criticisms of Obama from the left, from politicians such as Bernie Sanders, were met with sharp rebukes. It was all but impossible to mount a direct criticism from inside the Democratic Party of a historic and popular Black president.

Finally, too, the growing economic disparity didn't engender more of a backlash because by the time the concentration of wealth and power reached a crisis stage, there was no one left in the Democratic Party with the power and inclination to prosecute the case. The populists had all disappeared. After World War II, Franklin Roosevelt's New Deal banking reforms all but eliminated financial crises; low inflation and steady growth took hold; and large, stable corporations provided lifetime employment and reliable pensions in old age. Big business stopped seeming so scary. By the mid-1960s, fashionable liberal thinkers had abandoned the battlefield, convinced that government regulators had tamed animal spirits. "The public is hardly unaware that the steepest rise in mass standards of living has occurred during the period in which the economy has been dominated by the big corporation," Richard Hofstadter wrote in his 1965 classic, *The Paranoid Style in American Politics*. "Liberals do not often find themselves in a simple antagonistic confrontation with big business, as they did in the past."

Beginning in the 1960s, liberal economic efforts shifted primarily to advancing consumer rights. Charismatic figures like Ralph Nader began pushing liberals to loosen government control of airlines, trucking, and savings and loan institutions in order to foster competition and drive down consumer prices—a position that aligned them with conservatives. As the Great Depression faded into memory, as bank failures and financial crises came to be thought of as problems of the distant past, the deep distrust of financial institutions etched into people with memories of the Depression melted away. Even among Democrats, a faith took hold that markets could discipline financiers more effectively than government regulators could. The gradual dismantling of the New Deal order of regulated capitalism gave way to the rise of unrestrained finance because almost nobody in the Democratic Party—at least nobody with the power to stop it—thought it was a bad idea.

Just how bad an idea it turned out to be became jarringly clear on September 15, 2008, when the failure of Lehman Brothers touched off a financial crisis that blew up the U.S. economy. Millions of Americans lost their jobs, their homes, their retirement accounts, or all three, and fell out of the middle class. Millions more were gripped with the gnawing anxiety that they could be next. All of this happened with sudden force in the middle of a presidential campaign. It was no surprise that voters decided they wanted a change from President Bush, who'd presided over the economy for an eight-year run that culminated in a historic collapse. What seemed odd, at first glance, was how Wall Street reacted: not by maintaining its traditional allegiance to the party of laissez-faire, the GOP, but by backing the Democrat, Barack Obama. In 2008, Wall Street donors gave nearly twice as much money to Obama as they did to his Republican opponent, John McCain.

Why? One could speculate that financiers were as exhausted by the Bush years as everybody else and ready for hope and change. Or one could accept that general premise but add a dose of self-interest: maybe those exhausted financiers didn't perceive Obama as a threat to their well-being. After all, his top campaign economic adviser, Larry Summers, was a protégé of Robert Rubin's. Rubin himself, as hacked Wiki-Leaks emails would later reveal, envisioned himself taking a "Harry Hopkins role" in the future Obama administration, a reference to a man often referred to as FDR's "shadow president." The man organizing Obama's transition hiring behind the scenes, Michael Froman, was another Rubin protégé so comfortably ensconced in the world of finance that he did much of his organizing through his Citibank email account (as WikiLeaks also revealed).

This is how, as the U.S. economy melted down in the fall of 2008, exposing the flaws in the neoliberal management of the political economy, the strangest thing of all happened: the same people who had shaped the old financial system were ushered in to rebuild it once more, because there was still no meaningful left-wing economic critique to provide a compelling alternative vision. But that was about to change.

3

THE SERMON

Elizabeth Warren got the phone call as she was preparing a peach cobbler. It was early November 2008, and Barack Obama had just been elected president. Warren, a notable-but-not-famous professor of consumer bankruptcy law at Harvard Law School, was preparing barbecue for a group of students at her home in Cambridge, Massachusetts, when the call came. The voice on the line was so faint she could barely hear it.

"Who's this?" she asked.

Her caller cleared his throat and spoke louder. "Harry Reid," he said. "I'm majority leader of the U.S. Senate."

"Oh," Warren replied.

"I want you to come visit me in Washington."

Reid was fresh from passing the most difficult bill of his life, the $700 billion Wall Street bailout that narrowly averted a global meltdown.

Buried in the text of the new law, officially the Emergency Economic Stabilization Act of 2008, was a provision stipulating the creation of a five-member congressional oversight panel to monitor how these hundreds of billions of taxpayer dollars were being allotted. In the rush to pass the legislation, the panel was one of several bodies haphazardly assigned the job of policing and analyzing the Treasury's disbursement of the gigantic bailout, but with no clear directive for exactly how it was supposed to achieve this. Along with its meager budget and lack of statutory muscle, the panel was sufficiently unglamorous that its most prominent member, the Republican senator Judd Gregg, quit two weeks into his tenure. This is why Reid was calling Warren: to offer her the chairmanship of a panel whose own members would just as soon be doing something else. She quickly accepted and a few days later headed to Washington with her daughter, Amelia, to meet with Reid and get going.

Years later, Reid and Warren would gild this episode into a meet-cute story of a diligent Senate leader who spotted a promising Harvard talent while perusing a white paper and a provincial law professor startled to be tapped for such a weighty public role. "That's the way he always wanted me to tell it," said Jim Manley, a former Reid aide.

In truth, Reid and the rest of the Democratic Senate caucus had first encountered and been dazzled by Warren three years earlier, in 2005, when she'd made a presentation to them at a private "issues retreat" Senate Democrats held in a historic Beaux Arts hotel in Richmond, Virginia. Still recovering from a devastating loss to George W. Bush in the prior year's presidential election, Democrats were desperate to understand why they'd failed to connect with voters. Party leaders had summoned a broad array of experts, from academics to ministers, to help them divine the electorate's mood and develop new strategies to entice the voters who had spurned them. The fashionable

analysis was that the party had alienated itself from the staunch yeo-
man values of "real" Americans and that the path to renewal lay in
making overt displays of religiosity and deploying other cultural sig-
nifiers that would resonate in red America. (In 2006, Democrats recruited more than sixty military veterans to run for office, and those
"Fighting Dems" helped them win back the House of Representatives.)

Warren's presentation took an entirely different approach, emphasizing economics over culture as the way to connect with voters.
The year before, Warren and her daughter had coauthored a book,
The Two-Income Trap, arguing that the rise in household incomes
since the 1970s—a widely celebrated trend—was fueled almost entirely by the fact that economic pressure was driving women to join
their husbands in the workforce. The robust national growth numbers,
they explained, actually obscured a mounting crisis: as anxious middle-
class families stretched ever further to keep up with rising housing and
education costs, they were putting their families in a state of financial
precarity that often ended in ruin. Recognizing and addressing this crisis in the middle class, Warren told the Democratic gathering, would
allow them to forge the missing connection with voters.

"She gave this incredible speech that blew everybody away about
what had happened to middle-class families as their expenses went up
and their wages didn't, and just how much they were being totally
crushed by the Bush economy," said Mike Lux, a Democratic strategist who met Warren while giving his own presentation at the Richmond retreat. "Her basic point was that Democrats could win the 2006
election by running as populists, because people were really feeling
the pain."

As government leaders raced to contain the 2008 financial crisis,
Reid remembered the ease and fluency with which Warren could
break down complicated matters of finance, stripping away technical

jargon to convey the elemental truth. It was a necessary ability for anyone charged with overseeing—and explaining to the public—a bailout whose myriad programs seemed designed to frustrate attempts at easy understanding and were masked in a blizzard of acronyms (TARP, HAMP, PPIP). The truth about the bailout, as its architects well understood, was that it had been thrown together with such haste that nobody quite knew how it would work. The urgent pressure to pass something big in order to soothe panicked global markets had overwhelmed the normal process of incorporating checks and balances into the legislation. Reid worried about this. "He literally put his head down on the table at one point, because he was being asked to deliver the Senate in three days," Manley recalled.

Now the bailout had been signed into law. Reid knew the U.S. Treasury was forking over the first tranche of $250 billion to troubled banks, to do God knows what with. Officially, this taxpayer money was earmarked to be an "investment" in distressed assets whose inherent value was temporarily depressed by the market panic but would soon recover. Reid had his doubts. "Anytime you have a card game with Wall Street," he said, "they always have an ace up their sleeve. And as is typical, they did better than they should have done in the deal that we made."

Against this, Reid and Nancy Pelosi would set up a small panel that would be comically outgunned both by the financial industry it was supposed to monitor and by the industry's allies in the Treasury. As Damon Silvers, a Pelosi-appointed panel member and labor official at the AFL-CIO, described it, "It was a strange body because it had no authority, no money, no subpoena power, but a lot of obligations—we couldn't swear in witnesses, so people could technically lie to us with impunity. The only thing we had to prevent that was the power of public shaming." When Reid offered Warren the chance to lead the panel, he was surprised that she immediately accepted without preconditions or even many questions. He'd tried to be honest about the enormity of the task and the paucity of resources she'd have to work with. It was not a plum assignment.

Warren didn't care.

What sparked her interest was that this new role would place her at the very center of the government's response to the crisis. It would put her in the arena. And it would give her a tool that even esteemed Harvard professors accustomed to testifying before Congress didn't have: a gavel. Warren's bankruptcy research had long ago radicalized her against the financial industry and the predatory practices it employed that drove so many people to ruin. But identifying abuses and marshaling the political power to rectify them were two different things. As an academic, Warren had not only documented financial industry abuses but spent years knitting together outside advocacy groups to pressure lawmakers to oppose an industry-friendly bankruptcy bill that made it harder for people to get out of debt, a legal change that credit card companies had been seeking for years. Her crusade eventually led her to the witness table at a 2005 Senate Judiciary Committee hearing where she went toe-to-toe on the bill's merits with the credit card industry's great champion, Senator Joe Biden of Delaware.

After Warren described the devastating costs poor families routinely incur from the industry's abuses, Biden jumped in to muddy the waters and redirect blame, summoning the staged outrage that's a familiar senatorial register.

"You make a very compelling and mildly demagogic argument," Biden said, before launching into an extended discourse with himself that eventually landed on the idea that usury, not predatory lenders, was the true culprit.

Warren shook her head vigorously as Biden moved to cut off the debate and press on. "Senator, if you're not going to fix that problem, you can't take away the last shred of protection for these families," she said.

"I got it. Okay," Biden said, flashing a patronizing grin. "You're very good, professor."

Two months later, Warren lost her years-long fight and the bankruptcy bill was signed into law.

Reid's offer presented Warren with a chance to move from the witness table to the dais—a chance to run the whole show. Warren had spent enough time testifying before Congress to understand what every liberal populist of that era eventually came to realize: the process was rigged against them. It wasn't that progressive voices were absent from Capitol Hill. On the contrary, left-wing experts were routinely invited to share their views. But when it came time to set policy, those views were usually ignored—or worse belittled, including by Democrats, just as Warren's had been by Biden.

Although she and her allies in public interest legal groups had spent a decade mounting a battle for stronger consumer protections, the industry's wishes had ultimately prevailed. After 1978, when Congress had last amended the U.S. bankruptcy code, changes to the law were shaped mainly by a cadre of specialist lawyers, academics, judges, and trustees who carefully balanced the interests of consumers and creditors. But in the 1990s, the credit industry had made an aggressive push to displace them, showering Washington politicians with enough money to rival the notorious tobacco lobby. The combination of lobbying money and a diminished opposition gave credit companies a strong upper hand in how new legislation was written. (As Warren lamented in a 1999 journal article, "Liberals and populists from an earlier era, who had regarded bankruptcy as part of a larger package of progressive social legislation, were [now] gone.") Warren was frantic to halt the credit industry's rewrite of bankruptcy laws, believing, based on her research, that the changes would swell industry profits while trapping consumers in debt by blocking them from discharging those debts through a bankruptcy proceeding.

To Warren, the lesson could not have been any clearer: A lack of power in Washington meant that left populists lacked the ability to shape legislation and spotlight issues that might sway public opinion in their favor. Up against corporate interests, Warren knew that consumer interest groups, liberal politicians, the American Bankruptcy Institute (which represented "bankruptcy professionals" such as judges, clerks, and other specialists), and academic experts like herself had little agency to alter the neoliberal consensus that by now dominated both parties.

But in the fall of 2008, as the global economy collapsed, that consensus had started to fracture. What Warren understood about the oversight panel that almost nobody else in Washington did was that Reid was offering her a golden ticket. "She had been delivering the same sermon for years," said Representative Brad Miller, a populist Democrat from North Carolina. "Suddenly she had a pulpit."

IN THE WEEKS BEFORE Reid's phone call to Warren, the world had turned upside down. An American economy powered by its swollen financial industry had seized up, sputtered, and dived headlong into a frightening tailspin.

The first signs of trouble had arrived in the spring of 2007. Real estate prices had peaked the summer before and then had started to fall. As the housing bubble burst, the millions of subprime borrowers who had been fueling the rise began defaulting on their loans, which in turn threatened the financial institutions holding the $1.3 trillion of now-toxic mortgage debt. In February and March, more than twenty-five subprime lenders went bankrupt. In April, New Century Financial, the country's largest subprime lender, also went bust. In June, Bear Stearns was forced to bail out two of its hedge funds that had been nearly wiped out by sudden losses in mortgage-backed securities.

It soon became clear that the fallout wouldn't be limited to shady mortgage lenders—that, in fact, the entire financial system in the United States and Europe was an over-leveraged house of cards built upon a rickety foundation of revolving short-term loans, many of which used mortgage debt as collateral. As lenders suddenly began to worry that this collateral was worth far less than they'd assumed, they stopped making short-term loans. When they stopped making loans, banks and other financial institutions could no longer function and started running out of money. This sparked a chain reaction that threatened the very survival of banks and mortgage lenders in direct rank order of how aggressively they had financed shoddy loans or kept such loans on their books.

The list of institutions suddenly imperiled extended beyond fly-by-night mortgage originators to include many of the country's most prominent commercial and investment banks. What had lured them into the business of risky mortgages was a desire to extend the lucrative refinance boom of the early 2000s. By that time, a thriving industry had developed around the business of making home loans that was spinning off windfall profits to all involved. Banks not only originated mortgages but packaged them into securities and sold them off for handsome fees, usually to the government-sponsored enterprises Fannie Mae and Freddie Mac. In the 1990s, a team at J. P. Morgan had devised an instrument called a credit default swap to protect against the risk of nonpayment. These swaps emboldened banks and hedge funds to massively expand their use of leverage, in the misguided be-lief that they were insured against default; they led insurers on a rav-enous hunt for new pools of mortgages to guarantee, in the misguided belief that writing swaps was tantamount to minting free money. None of it was regulated. By mid-2007, the total value of credit default swaps reached $45 trillion, more than twice the value of the U.S. stock mar-ket and more than six times the value of the U.S. mortgage market.

When banks and mortgage lenders ran out of creditworthy bor-rowers whose loans could be passed on to Fannie and Freddie, they forged ahead into riskier "Alt-A" and subprime loans, packaging them into "private label" securities that were sold to institutional investors or simply kept on their books. The huge fees generated by originat-ing, securitizing, trading, insuring, and servicing loans prompted just about everybody—investment banks, commercial banks, and mortgage lenders—to try to integrate the full supply chain that made up Ameri-ca's turbocharged mortgage machine. Specialized mortgage lenders like Countrywide expanded into securitization. Scrappy investment banks like Bear Stearns and Lehman Brothers acquired originators and ser-vicers to feed their mortgage pipelines and help them scale up in size. Old-line commercial banks like Citigroup that once stuck to plain-vanilla mortgages plunged headlong into "unconventional" loans, which soon came to dwarf the market for standard conforming mortgages. Be-tween 1999 and 2003, 70 percent of new U.S. mortgages were conven-tional loans that could be sold to Fannie and Freddie. Three years later, the market had completely transformed: 70 percent of new loans were now subprime or otherwise unconventional mortgages taken out by far less creditworthy buyers and most likely headed for private-label securities.

This Taj Mahal of financial engineering was the glittering product of the neoliberal revolution, a culmination of three decades of steady deregulatory advances, large and small, pushed by Republicans and Democrats alike. In 1999, the Clinton administration, at the urging of successive Treasury secretaries, Robert Rubin and Larry Summers, did away with the Glass-Steagall Act, the foundational New Deal regulation separating retail and investment banking. This cleared the way for Citigroup and Bank of America to participate in the full spectrum of mortgage activities and grow their balance sheets exponentially. In 2004, Hank Paulson, the head of Goldman Sachs and future Treasury secretary for George W. Bush, led Wall Street's successful crusade to get the Securities and Exchange Commission to loosen its "net capital rule" restricting leverage for large investment banks. Thereafter, firms were effectively permitted to choose their own limit on the basis of their own risk models.

By the time Reid summoned her to Washington, Warren was intimately familiar with all of these developments not just because her academic work focused on the consumers being whipsawed or defrauded by these toxic loans but because both parties kept scaling back financial regulations even after the major New Deal protections had been swept away. As a matter of fact, the 2005 bankruptcy bill that she'd clashed with Joe Biden over had itself helped to supercharge the housing bubble and drive the financial crisis. By giving creditors much stronger protections against defaulting borrowers—as Biden had pushed for—the new bankruptcy law increased banks' willingness to lend, including to people with little prospect of being able to repay their loan. In addition, buried deep within the law's text were two provisions expanding and clarifying the definition of what constituted acceptable collateral for interbank loans to now include mortgage loans and mortgage-related securities. Given this green light, Wall Street soon experienced a surge in short-term lending secured with mortgage-backed assets that drove the cycle even faster.

THE LOGIC BEHIND the deregulation of Wall Street and its esoteric financial engineering was that it would disperse risk to the investors best suited to carry it. Banks could produce many more loans, not just for mortgages, but for auto, credit card, and commercial loans, protected by credit default swaps and an originate-to-distribute lending system that bundled them into securities and spirited them off to outside investors. They no longer needed to limit themselves to what Fannie and Freddie considered safe because they had devised sophisticated tools for measuring credit risk that justified more adventurous forms of lending. And they knew how to market themselves. Champions of the new Wall Street liked to tout the social benefits that were alleged to flow from these innovations. "An increased rate of home ownership has been chosen by our society as a national priority," the Federal Reserve chairman, Alan Greenspan, declared in a speech to an Oakland financial literacy conference for people of color in 2002. "In assessing the opportunity for home ownership in underserved markets, the Census Bureau reports significant gains. The homeownership rate for blacks and Hispanics, between 1997 and 2001, grew at more than double the pace for the general population. Additionally, the homeownership rate among households earning less than the median income increased more than three times the pace for households with incomes above the median."

Greenspan was preaching gospel to the choir back in Washington. To the delight of politicians in both parties, lenders unfettered by the Luddite constraints of government minders were now eagerly extending loans to Black and brown communities previously cut out of the mortgage market and denied their chance to participate in the American dream of homeownership. Here was proof, these politicians insisted, of the magic of the market (and, though this part was left implicit, their own good judgment in enabling it). It certainly must have *seemed* magical to them: Wall Street was driving social changes that Washington had long promised but failed to deliver. A virtuous circle of money and cleverly managed risk would make the world a better, more broadly prosperous place for all.

This is not what happened.

For one thing, not all mortgage risk was dispersed across the financial system. Banks and lenders kept more than $1 trillion of it on their books. The profit incentive to hold on to it was simply too powerful: As long as the housing market was humming, the riskiest bonds yielded the richest payouts. So banks stuffed them into "structured investment vehicles" that were held off their balance sheets or reshuffled them into new bonds that magically earned AAA credit ratings. Even Fannie and Freddie, the pillars of sensible mortgage-lending standards, couldn't resist dipping into private-label securities. When lenders moved beyond the dull fare of conventional thirty-year mortgages, business at Fannie and Freddie began to slow down. This led the agencies to purchase $300 billion worth of "non-agency" securitized mortgages to goose their own portfolios.

As defaults escalated and panic set in, the overnight lending markets froze. The toxic debt embedded throughout the financial system reared up to expose the big firms most recklessly addicted to risky loans. These included the country's biggest mortgage originator, Countrywide, which financed 20 percent of all new home loans in 2006; its fastest-growing commercial banks—Citigroup, Washington Mutual, and Bank of America; and its most aggressive investment banks, Bear

Stearns and Lehman Brothers, which had levered their bets to dizzying heights in a bid for scale. All were rapidly failing.

In January 2008, facing imminent bankruptcy, Countrywide sold itself to Bank of America for a pittance. In March, Bear Stearns collapsed, dodging bankruptcy only when the Federal Reserve arranged a fire sale to JPMorgan Chase by guaranteeing that the government—that is, U.S. taxpayers—would stand behind Bear's bad debts. On September 7, federal regulators seized control of Fannie and Freddie, injecting $200 billion in taxpayer funding to keep the mortgage giants alive and prevent the U.S. housing market from collapsing. "This is like waking up in summer with snow on the ground," marveled one former regulator, as Wall Street giants fell like dominoes.

Doomsday arrived exactly one week later. Discomfited by the prospect of further government bailouts, Paulson and the Bush administration finally stood aside and let the market work its will. On September 15, Lehman Brothers, a Wall Street fixture for more than 150 years, filed for the largest bankruptcy in U.S. history. Chaos immediately engulfed the global markets. Investors around the world, anticipating further bank failures, galloped into full retreat, pulling back their money from wherever they could. As they did, the stock market crashed, bonds went haywire, and private credit all but vanished as banks stopped lending. Paulson's resolve withered a day later as it became clear that the biggest supplier of credit default swaps, American International Group, from which every major Wall Street firm had purchased disaster insurance, couldn't possibly meet its obligations. If AIG went down, it would pull down the entire financial system. It was, in the new coinage, "too big to fail." Seeing no alternative, Paulson arranged for the Federal Reserve to provide an $85 billion loan, while AIG's lawyers, just hours away from running out of money, stuffed stock certificates into briefcases and shopping carts and raced them over to the New York Federal Reserve building to serve as collateral.

More bailouts followed. Washington Mutual was seized by federal regulators. Goldman Sachs and Morgan Stanley were spared bankruptcy only when the Federal Reserve allowed them to convert to bank holding companies and gain access to its discount lending window. It still wasn't enough. Despite the frantic ministrations of Paulson, the Federal Reserve chairman, Ben Bernanke, and the New York Fed president, Timothy Geithner, banks were still too afraid to lend to one another, terrified of what might be lurking on their counterparty's balance sheet. And because the global economy relied almost entirely on interbank lending, the rapid deterioration of the financial system caused productive activity across the whole of the economy to grind to a halt. The grim irony, suddenly apparent, was that a system designed to disaggregate financial risk had instead done precisely the opposite. "What made the crisis more frightening in some ways than the Great Depression was precisely the increased efficiency with which money is now transmitted globally," observed Barney Frank, the acerbic Democratic chairman of the House Financial Services Committee. "Complete interconnectedness has great advantages; it is also a marvelous transmitter of disaster."

Paulson realized, as he later put it, that the government "couldn't keep using duct tape and baling wire to hold the system together." Wall Street's collapse created a vortex that was swallowing up his limited power and resources, along with those of the Federal Reserve. To halt the crisis, he needed enormous sums of money and license to spend it on the unpopular cause of propping up ailing banks. Only Congress could deliver such sweeping fiscal authority. As the ex-chairman of Goldman Sachs, Paulson wasn't an ideal front man to ask for hundreds of billions of taxpayer dollars to help his Wall Street friends. Surmising that his task would be all the more difficult with Democrats controlling the House and Senate, and an election looming six weeks hence, Paulson enlisted Bernanke, whose gravitas and professorial mien he hoped would strengthen his sales pitch.

Bernanke didn't disappoint. "It is a matter of days before there is a meltdown in the global financial system," the Fed chairman told a grim-faced assembly of congressional leaders squeezed into House Speaker Nancy Pelosi's office at the Capitol, late in the evening of September 18. He previewed the horrors to come. As stocks cratered, Bernanke explained, the crisis would spread across the economy. Major corporations like General Motors and Chrysler would slide into bankruptcy, pulling down entire supply chains and producing mass unemployment that would spike to levels not seen since the Great Depression. Congress needed to intervene. Time was of the essence. Paulson was relieved to discover that the leaders of both parties seemed to grasp the dire nature of the emergency.

Contrary to the widespread public perception, during and after the flurry of bailouts, that the powers in Washington were concerned only with rescuing Wall Street and not Main Street, the accounts of those directly involved in the negotiations make clear this wasn't the case—at least not initially. An unintended leitmotif of Paulson's otherwise generous memoir is his annoyance with Democrats in Congress, including Pelosi and Frank, who, as he raced to halt the cascading global crisis, kept pressing him to include stimulus spending, mortgage relief, and limits on bankers' pay in the bill he was demanding from Congress. ("Nancy, we're racing to prevent a collapse of the financial markets," Paulson huffed. "This isn't the time for stimulus.") Geithner openly ridiculed lawmakers clamoring for what he derisively called "Old Testament justice"—their insistence that those responsible for the crisis be held to account. The collective feeling among the principals in Washington and Wall Street battling the crisis was that to raise such plebeian concerns amid a market emergency was to broadcast one's naïveté about complex matters of finance best left to others to sort out.

Paulson's initial ask of Congress put this sense of entitlement to paper. Just three pages long, it sought $700 billion—more than the annual defense budget—to buy toxic mortgages with the aim of "providing stability or preventing disruption to the financial system," a charge so crucial Paulson felt he needn't deign to submit to scrutiny how, precisely, he would spend all that money. His proposal declared, "Decisions by the Secretary pursuant to the authority of this Act are nonrenewable and committed to agency discretion, and may not be reviewed by any court of law or any administrative agency." This was, among other things, a statement of values. Rescuing banks was deemed necessary to stave off another depression; therefore, working- and middle-class interests would have to take a back seat to elite prerogative.

One reason Democratic negotiators were a thorn in Paulson's side is that it was already clear that the avalanche crashing down on Wall Street would not just wipe out banks and mortgage lenders. It would wipe out millions of families, too. Within weeks of Lehman's bankruptcy, the economy was contracting at a Depression-level rate. Unemployment skyrocketed. Foreclosures hit a record high. Within a year, one in eight mortgages in America would be in foreclosure or default. Everyone gathered around Pelosi's conference table understood that the financial precarity of the American family, which had climbed steadily across the 1980s and 1990s, was about to explode and push millions of people out of the middle class. Mitigating that damage and helping people to rebuild their lives was going to be the major work of government for years to come. So lawmakers naturally wanted to claim for them a share of the enormous sum Congress was about to hand over.

And yet Democrats still yielded to Paulson's priorities. There were several reasons why. Many had been persuaded by Bernanke that a depression really was imminent if Wall Street wasn't rescued. They also had won rudimentary oversight measures: the $700 billion would be disbursed in tranches, and they were assured that they'd be kept apprised of how it was spent. Although they didn't advertise it, many Democrats cared a great deal about Wall Street's fate. For all that the GOP was bruited as "the party of business," Barack Obama was in the process of raising more money from Wall Street than his Republican opponent, John McCain.

Buried even deeper, though, was a powerful element of self-interest— of political self-preservation, really. Democrats convinced themselves that Paulson's plan to bail out the banks could in fact become a vehicle to help troubled homeowners, through a clever trick he could perform on the toxic mortgages he promised to take off banks' balance sheets. A provision in the law's text (specifically, Section 109 of the Emergency Economic Stabilization Act of 2008) empowered the Treasury secretary to "facilitate loan modifications to prevent avoidable foreclosures." What this meant for desperate homeowners was that Treasury could change the terms of the mortgages it purchased to rescue people and keep them in their homes. What it meant for members of Congress, as any honest lawmaker would privately admit, was that they could avoid a politically unpleasant vote to bail out undeserving borrowers (or borrowers who could be portrayed that way) by shifting the responsibility for their rescue onto the Treasury.

Despite its elegant design, this was a lousy way to try to help struggling homeowners. Not only did it require an expertise Treasury lacks—emergency mortgage modification—but it presupposed that helping borrowers stay in their homes was a goal that Treasury officials shared and would ardently pursue. It wasn't, for either the Bush or the Obama administration. Instead, as one of Paulson's deputies confessed a year later, Treasury officials believed something like the opposite: "Too many borrowers were in the wrong house, not the wrong mortgage." Paulson, desperate for a large bailout to restore investor confidence and stave off collapse, wasn't about to litigate the matter and risk alienating Democrats. He needed their votes. This became jarringly clear a few days after the September 18 emergency meeting in Pelosi's office, when the $700 billion deal that was hammered out among party leaders was flatly rejected by the House of Representatives—because most Republicans defied their own president (and his desperate Treasury secretary) and refused to vote for it.

It took a second try, four days later, on October 3, for the House to pass Paulson's bank bailout. In the end, it was Democrats who somewhat surreally rescued an unpopular Republican president by furnishing the majority of votes in the House and Senate. The Troubled Asset Relief Program, as the bailout was christened, would indeed help to slow the spiraling crisis in financial markets. But it was built upon a fundamental deception in which Democrats were fully complicit and for which they eventually paid a steep political price. Even as Paulson and Bernanke explained to the emergency gathering in the Speaker's office why Congress needed to bypass the middle class and give hundreds of millions of dollars directly to failing banks, Pelosi had insisted that political leaders mask their true intention. "We have to position this as a stimulus and relief for the American homeowner," she told Paulson, even though that was plainly untrue.

This became the misleading public rationale offered not just for TARP but for the entire crisis response—the combination of loans, guarantees, capital injections, and other measures provided by the government that at their peak totaled nearly $7 trillion: that an un-precedented bailout of Wall Street's most prominent banks and their creditors was in fact a broad-scale rescue of the struggling American middle class. Elizabeth Warren, now armed with a gavel, was about to shoot to fame and spark a populist backlash by showing the world that it really wasn't.

4

ORDINARY PEOPLE

When Warren arrived in Washington in November 2008, the country was in the midst of a paroxysm of anger over the ongoing crisis and bailouts, but still foggy about what exactly had happened and who was to blame for it. Warren made it her business to supply an answer. She revived a liberal critique of Wall Street and big business that had lain dormant since the 1980s and energetically applied it to explaining the chaos engulfing people's lives as the economy collapsed. She seemed to know whom to blame, who should be fixing things and how, and when the people in charge were obfuscating or falling short. She didn't suffer fools. She named names. Within months, she would become the country's unlikely populist tribune.

In early November, the national furor briefly ebbed as America celebrated the election of its first Black president. But Obama's victory complicated the economic rescue effort in two ways. It raised expectations, particularly among Democratic partisans, that the "change" Obama campaigned on and embodied would be swift in arriving and would encompass the increasingly dire economic situation. It also added a new element of confusion to the government's frenetic crisis response, because President Bush's team would technically be running things until the inauguration.

To say that the public was growing hostile to that response doesn't capture the intensity of feeling toward the perpetrators of the crisis as Obama was taking office. Gallup found that confidence in banks was at an all-time low and that an overwhelming majority of Americans (86 percent) thought economic issues were the country's most pressing problem. What spared legislators the full force of that rage was the promise Pelosi extracted from Paulson to present the Troubled Asset Relief Program as a rescue effort for middle-class homeowners and stimulus for the battered economy. The government's message was, *Help is on the way.*

But a week after Bush signed TARP into law, Paulson abruptly changed his mind about how he would spend the $700 billion. The original plan to buy up toxic mortgages was scrapped in favor of "capital injections"—giving money directly to ailing banks to shore up their balance sheets. Paulson justified his volte-face on the grounds that there wasn't time to set up an auction facility to fairly price the banks' troubled assets. What really spooked him, though, was a sudden drop in the stock market, which suffered its worst week since 1933, with the Dow and S&P 500 falling 18 percent each. "The market was deteriorating so quickly," he later rationalized, "that the asset-buying program could not get under way fast enough to help." So instead of helping banks by relieving them of their bad loans, he decided to recapitalize them in the hope that this would induce them to start lending again and revive the economy.

Paulson's new plan was faster, simpler, more reassuring to markets—and politically toxic. It seemed like a bait and switch that hurt struggling homeowners by cutting out the part of the deal that was supposed to help them: namely, the part where Treasury bought and modified mortgages to keep them in their homes. Instead, it concentrated all its resources on the hated banks. People got angry. Democrats were implicated along with Republicans because they'd supplied the votes to pass the bill. So, too, was Obama, who at Paulson's request pressured his party to get behind it. The whole episode created an indelible impression in the public's mind that politicians in both parties, faced with a generational crisis, had galloped in, commandeered a mountain of taxpayer money, and used it to rescue the bad guys, rather than the good guys.

Against this backdrop, the Congressional Oversight Panel gathered for the first time on November 25, 2008, electing Warren its chair and Damon Silvers her deputy. The panel's remit was to track how the $700 million authorized by the Troubled Asset Relief Program was being spent and to share what they learned through regular reports and public hearings.

From the outset, though, Warren had something much grander in mind. She wanted to change how people measured the effectiveness of the government's crisis response by shifting their focus away from the status of the big banks and the stock market—the measures preferred by most politicians and bankers—and putting it on the well-being of ordinary people. The panel's first report, published just two weeks after that initial meeting, was the beginning of an attempt to reframe public perception along these lines. It began, "The U.S. and the global economy have been in a steadily accelerating downward spiral since the early spring of 2007. The American family is at the epicenter of this crisis."

It may seem strange that Warren and her fellow overseers felt it necessary to remind everyone that families were in peril. Demonstrating reverence for the "hardworking middle class" is a standard political trope in any situation, crisis or not, and amplifying the fears of families hurt, or afraid of being hurt, by an economic catastrophe is a staple of every evening newscast. But Warren's academic work studying the causes of bankruptcy, and her personal experience of trying to derail the bankruptcy bill a few years earlier, jaundiced her view of Washington's commitment to protect American families, even in a crisis. Warren, practically alone, referred to that struggle as "the bankruptcy wars," and the martial imagery conveys her sense of how large she believed the stakes were and how costly the defeat. Her etiology of that loss leaned heavily on the conviction that the basic opacity of what goes on in Washington—including even in high-profile dramas like the TARP bailout—allowed the financial industry to exploit middle-class Americans to an unconscionable degree, just as Paulson seemed to do when he repurposed the TARP funds. Warren sometimes summed up her academic career by saying that she studied "the middle-class squeeze" and later wrote that the bankruptcy wars "taught me that the squeeze wasn't accidental." Her approach to policing the bailout would be shaped entirely by her experience of having been outmaneuvered by financial firms and realizing afterward that it wasn't what was said publicly at hearings or press conferences that determined the outcome, but what transpired behind closed doors when the fanfare ended and it was time to get down to the real business of hashing out the important details—conversations from which Warren and people like her were excluded. "That's how I'd come to under-stand power in Washington," she said.

Warren's plan for the oversight panel, laid out in that first report, was to throw a giant switch and short-circuit the standard Washington process. The plan wasn't complicated at all; it entailed figuring out what was happening with the bailout money behind closed doors and then making a lot of noise about it so that everyone would know, prac-tically in real time, who was being cut in on the deal and who was being excluded.

"We are here to investigate, to analyze and to review the expendi-ture of taxpayer funds," the report continued. "But most importantly, we are here to ask the questions that we believe all Americans have a right to ask: who got the money, what have they done with it, how has it helped the country, and how has it helped ordinary people?"

As Warren herself put it, with characteristic bluntness, "We want to know what's going on, and so we're asking."

Because she was (at best) a minor player, heading a panel with little formal power, almost nobody in Washington noticed or cared what she was doing. With the benefit of hindsight, however, one can read the report as a blueprint for how to generate a populist uprising. For Warren, the document was also a declaration that now the roles were reversed: now she would be the one applying the squeeze.

WARREN WASN'T WRONG to suspect that privately, and notwith-standing the law's instructions, the Bush Treasury wasn't exactly eager to rescue homeowners. After he left the Treasury, one of Paulson's key lieutenants, Phillip Swagel, wrote a surprisingly candid paper giving his insider's view of the crisis. It emphasizes that while they had few qualms about saving failing banks, many of his colleagues had basic philosophical objections to extending the same help to struggling homeowners: "While the Fed staff was focused on underwater borrowers, within the administration—among White House staff in particular, but also within the Treasury—many were unwilling to put public money on the line to prevent additional foreclosures, because any such program would inevitably involve a bailout of some 'irresponsible' homeowners."

Only a few years earlier, Alan Greenspan and prominent Bush officials had hailed the extension of mortgage credit to low-income households as a triumph for civil rights because it rapidly increased the homeownership rate for Blacks and Hispanics. For decades, redlining and denial of credit drove the staggering disparity in home equity between white and minority families that underlies the racial wealth gap. Now that crisis had struck, those same borrowers had morphed from striving chasers of the American dream into an ugly caricature, freighted with racial implication, of irresponsible moochers looking for a handout. As Swagel put it, "Spending public money on foreclosure avoidance would be asking responsible taxpayers to subsidize people living in McMansions they could not afford, with flat-screen televisions paid for out of their home equity line of credit."

Although Bush officials insisted publicly that they were working to limit foreclosures, Swagel confessed that by the time Warren took over the Congressional Oversight Panel, they had privately "ruled out" any such undertaking and decided to punt the whole problem to the next administration.

In January 2009, Obama and his Treasury secretary, Timothy Geithner, inherited the financial and foreclosure crises, along with what they soon discovered was the substantial burden of having to answer to Warren and the oversight panel. The sharp candor of its monthly reports and Warren's willingness to engage with reporters won the panel early notice even before the new administration settled in. But no senior member of the Bush or Obama team had testified before it until Geithner first appeared in April. Warren's clashes with him became the opening scenes in a national drama that would shape the public's impression of Obama's leadership in the financial crisis, often in a way that discredited the White House's claims that it was doing all it could to alleviate the country's worsening economic condition.

FOR ALL THAT Obama represented "change," his approach to addressing the financial crisis and its aftermath was the area where he might have differed the least from his predecessor. Inexperienced in national politics and new to matters of global finance, Obama surrounded himself with the mandarins of Democratic Wall Street, credentialed veterans of the Clinton era whose views largely overlapped with Paulson's. Larry Summers was brought in to run the National Economic Council. Geithner moved over from the New York Fed. Robert Rubin hovered in the background, counseling Obama to stop invoking "the middle class" and instead cast himself as a "pro-growth Democrat" to avoid what Rubin regarded as an upsetting class distinction bankers wouldn't appreciate. From his first days in office, Obama's press handlers worked diligently to try to distance their boss from the failures of the prior administration. But you had to squint to see the difference.

"During the Bush administration," Keith Hennessey, a former director of Bush's National Economic Council, said in 2010, "you basically had three people who were the core in making the policy recommendations to the president and implementing them. And they were Hank Paulson, Ben Bernanke, and Tim Geithner. Now it's Larry, Ben, and Tim, and Tim has moved chairs. What this means is that two-thirds of the core policy group is unchanged from Bush to Obama. The Obama political and communications operations have always wanted to emphasize just how different and transformative the Obama solutions are, relative to the Bush people who—they claim—left them this enormous problem. The reality is, there is remarkable continuity, from a personnel standpoint and a policy standpoint, in what's being done."

Warren recognized this continuity and understood what it meant. The new administration, even though it was run by her own party, was going to proceed much as the old one had. Whatever change Obama brought to Washington wasn't going to alter the calculus at the heart of the U.S. government's crisis response, which Paulson had concluded—and Geithner agreed—began with rescuing the banks at all costs. Only then, once credit was flowing again, could the focus shift to the rest of the economy and the millions of people who were collateral damage.

The trouble for Geithner was that this approach became much harder to defend in the months after Bush left the White House. You couldn't defend it directly, because saying banks should take precedence over American families was political suicide. You couldn't require banks to be fully transparent about how they were using TARP funds without revealing which among them were weakest. "You would not want them exposed to market reaction," a Treasury official admitted. And you certainly couldn't defend the brazenness with which bankers shirked any acknowledgment that they were wards of the state and kept on granting themselves lavish bonuses and other perks, even as job losses soared in less favored sectors of the economy.

In January, news broke that Merrill Lynch's CEO, John Thain, had spent more than $1 million hiring Obama's decorator to outfit his office with a $35,000 toilet and an $87,000 area rug, even as the company was collapsing. In February, Bank of America, which required a $45 billion bailout, sponsored a five-day, multimillion-dollar Super Bowl party, something it defended as part of its "growth strategy." In March, the insurance giant AIG, the largest bailout recipient at $170 billion, and fresh off booking the largest quarterly loss ($61.7 billion) in U.S. corporate history, revealed plans to award bonuses of more than $1 million each to seventy-three employees in its financial products division, the unit responsible for the swaps contracts that destroyed the company and nearly brought down the global economy. Channeling public anger, Obama wondered aloud at a press conference, "How do they justify this outrage to the taxpayers that are keeping them afloat?" On *The Tonight Show*, he vowed to Jay Leno to "do everything we can to get those bonuses back." But the White House quietly snuffed out a bipartisan effort to claw back those bonuses through a targeted tax, fearful that punishing financial firms would dissuade them from participating in government programs. Meanwhile, the net worth of American families had fallen more than 20 percent in the prior eighteen months.

When Geithner showed up to testify before the oversight panel, he walked into a lion's den. Notionally, Warren was a fellow Democrat who'd campaigned with Obama and was presumably rooting for his success. The new president, too, was remarkably popular, including with Republicans: 73 percent of Americans viewed him favorably. But Warren didn't see herself as an ally. "She was a Harvard law professor, she was tenured, and she was pissed off," said Dan Geldon, a close aide who prepped her for the hearing.

Geithner's appearance made for riveting drama. From the moment she banged the gavel to open the hearing, Warren lit into her star witness in a way that dispelled any question about whether she would interrogate the new administration as vigorously as the old one.

"People are angry that small businesses are threatened with closure because they can't get financing from their TARP-assisted banks," Warren said, staring down her quarry. "People are angry that when they read the headlines of record foreclosures, even if they aren't personally affected, they see their own property worth less, and they see their communities declining as a result of the foreclosures around them. People are angry because they're paying for programs that haven't been fully explained and have no apparent benefit for their families or for the economy as a whole, but that seem to leave enough cash in the system for lavish bonuses or golf outings. None of this seems fair."

She put the onus on Geithner to rectify the injustice. "People need to understand why you're making the choices that you're making," she continued. "People want to see action described in terms that make sense to them. They want to see that taxpayer funds aren't being used to shield financial institutions from the consequences of their own behavior. They want to see that money—taxpayer money—is used to advance the public interest and not just the interests of Wall Street."

Geithner's goal was to project an image of crisp competence, of someone who had the crisis firmly in hand (while avoiding uncomfortable details). In truth, he did not. Banks were still dangerously undercapitalized, even after Treasury and the Fed pumped in hundreds of billions of dollars; still viewed with deep suspicion by anxious investors frightened of what might lurk on their balance sheets; and still precariously exposed to the possibility of a sudden, ruinous loss of confidence—one that could bankrupt enough of them to plunge the economy into a full-blown depression. And yet most banks resisted taking government funds because they didn't want to sell their toxic assets at a loss or subject themselves to the oversight and temporary pay constraints that doing so would entail. The flurry of confusingly acronymed rescue plans—SSFI, PPIP, TANF, TALF, CPP, and on and on—was a smoke screen for the government to save them anyway, designed to seem too dull and complicated to arouse public ire. Even so, Geithner existed in a state of perpetual alarm that some event or other would trigger a bank run and bring the whole thing crashing down. That's why it was fine for the government to fire the heads of Fannie and Freddie, and to oust the management of the bailed-out automakers—but not fine to fire, or even sternly upbraid, a bank CEO. Not even one who'd screwed up so royally as to need a bailout. It's also why Geithner was the leading force inside the administration to kill the idea of clawing back AIG bonuses: forcing bailed-out bankers to limit their pay would make them even more determined to resist government aid and perpetuate the risk to the economy.

Peering down from her chairman's seat, Warren conducted a public vivisection of the government's response that highlighted this disparity in a way that gave Geithner and his aides heartburn. Really successful public officials possess an ability to say a lot while revealing very little, aware that plans function best when their inner workings remain opaque. Geithner tried. But all his capework didn't confuse the bull. Warren, in what would become her signature style, drove at precisely the specifics her witness most hoped to avoid:

WARREN: Are you saying that the difference in treatment between how the banks were treated and how the auto industry has been treated is effectively one of timing and that, going forward, the banks will be treated with the same kind of accountability at a minimum that's been demanded from the auto industry?

GEITHNER: Well, I'm trying to be candid. They're different challenges. They require different solutions. But there's less difference than your question suggests. Just to cite a couple examples, if you look at where the government had to act early, in substantial force, in some of the largest and weakest parts of the system, in that context—both in the context of Fannie and Freddie and in the context of AIG—we were very clear that the conditions in that context came with changes in board and management for exactly the reasons you said. Now there has also been—

WARREN: I'm sorry, I just want to make sure I'm following. You're saying there have been changes in management at financial institutions?

GEITHNER: Where the government acted—absolutely.

WARREN: That have received TARP funds?

GEITHNER: Well, as I said, in the context of the interventions taken in Fannie and Freddie and AIG, just to cite three examples—

WARREN: I'm asking about the financial institutions.

GEITHNER: Those are financial institutions.

WARREN: I'm asking about the banks.

What made Warren so insurrectionary in this and other hearings was that she was willing to pinpoint issues Obama officials were eager to obscure, and she didn't hesitate to criticize those same officials publicly when she felt they weren't being forthcoming. Even some of her Republican colleagues were taken aback. "I once told her after a hearing, 'It's hard to believe you and Geithner are in the same party,'" said Ken Troske, an economist appointed to the Congressional Oversight Panel by the Republican Senate leader, Mitch McConnell.

To many insiders, especially Democrats, this was a thrilling breach of intraparty decorum, a spectacle that grabbed your attention and eventually gave way to the realization that Warren was asking sharp questions that merited answers, which the Obama administration was often reluctant to give. Warren's command of financial detail, and her willingness to badger witnesses more pointedly and aggressively than was customary on Capitol Hill, meant she could often pierce the fog of euphemistic spin and extract real information that shaped people's view of the crisis. "One of the great secrets of that era was that Democratic senators and members of Congress had a strong desire to understand the liquidity crisis and the mortgage crisis turning everything upside down, but they really didn't understand it. Very few had even a cursory grasp," said Brian Fallon, then a top aide to New York's senator Chuck Schumer, a Wall Street favorite. One way senators learned about the crisis, he said, was by reading Paul Krugman's column in *The New York Times*. Another was Warren. "Warren's style was considered uncouth, even rude," said Fallon. "You weren't supposed to behave like that, to create conflict—personal conflict—and lean into it. And Wall Street influence wasn't an issue anybody went to the mat for. But all of them paid attention to what she was saying, and some of them learned from it."

Drilling away at bankers' privileged treatment, and the comparatively shoddy handling of middle-class mortgage borrowers, was the seam that Warren and the oversight panel would mine for the next two years, to increasing public notice. Interrogating the kid-glove handling of bank CEOs was the first stage of a rolling investigation that ultimately probed everything from the overgenerous prices government paid to inject money into ailing banks to the mystery of what exactly financial firms did with the hundreds of billions of dollars U.S. taxpayers handed over to them.

Like a sleuth, Warren followed the money. Once Paulson resolved to spend TARP money on recapitalizing banks, the Treasury carried out his orders by purchasing preferred equity shares in the institutions that needed help; that is, the government bought a stake in the banks. Paulson hoped injecting new money would allow them to skirt insolvency brought on by their own bad loans and begin lending again. The idea had a lineage; Herbert Hoover's Reconstruction Finance Corporation used a similar mechanism to limit bank failures during the Great Depression. But buying shares of banks that were effectively busted thanks to their own negligence raised the thorny political question of whether taxpayers were getting fleeced. It wasn't an abstract question, either. Private investors like Warren Buffett were also buying equity stakes in banks—Buffett took a $5 billion stake in Goldman Sachs when it was desperate for capital in September 2008—so there was a benchmark for what a fair deal looked like.

Treasury's stock answer to anyone who inquired was that both parties would benefit: banks by getting a capital cushion, and taxpayers by receiving warrants that they would profit from if markets recovered. But officials went to great lengths to avoid answering the question directly, including to the Congressional Oversight Panel. Rather than let Treasury manage these tensions behind its impenetrable facade, Warren put them on full display. At Damon Silvers's suggestion, the panel hired an international valuation firm, Duff & Phelps, to conduct a study to determine whether Treasury had overpaid for the $250 billion it invested in Bank of America, Citigroup, JPMorgan Chase, Morgan Stanley, Goldman Sachs, and other banks. Duff & Phelps reported back that it had—by a staggering $78 billion. "Unlike Treasury, private investors received securities with a fair market value as of the valuation dates of at least as much as they invested, and in some cases, worth substantially more," the report concluded. U.S. taxpayers, on the other hand, had effectively given those banks a $78 billion gift, without so much as knowing it or even being entitled to an explanation.

Naturally, the attention Warren drew to these sweetheart deals inflamed public opinion. It angered many government officials, too, who felt they were doing their best to stop a crisis and shouldn't be criticized for it or second-guessed by professors. What became clear, though, as the hearings and reports piled up, was that the basic facts Warren's panel was turning up weren't really in dispute. Rather, the fight was over how one interpreted them and the story they told about whom the government had chosen to rescue—and whom it hadn't.

For all Treasury's obstinacy about divulging details of its capital injections, there was no real disagreement (privately, at least) about the fact that banks were taking taxpayers for a ride. Later, Swagel, Paulson's lieutenant, offered this justification: "In a sense, this had to be the opposite of the 'Sopranos' or the 'Godfather'—not an attempt to intimidate banks, but instead a deal so attractive that banks would be unwise to refuse it. The terms of the capital injections were later to lead to reports that the Treasury had 'overpaid' for its stakes in banks, which is true relative to the terms received by Warren Buffett. But this was for a policy purpose: to ensure broad and rapid take-up."

Treasury didn't offer this justification at the time, because doing so would have been politically untenable. It would have illuminated a value hierarchy that put banks above nearly everyone else, even though they'd brought on the crisis and showed no remorse. Paulson, Geithner, Summers, Bernanke, and their intellectual allies in both parties saw themselves as hard-eyed realists making tough calls for the greater good of society. Propping up banks on practically any terms was, in their view, a necessary expediency that they were unhappy to have to explain.

In this way, the crisis response was emblematic of the narrow, finance-centered way of looking at the world and trying to solve its problems that had obtained for three decades, regardless of which party was in power. But this insular consensus of an elect tribe of policy-makers wasn't impregnable. It had formed without public input, and mostly hidden from view, because no one of significant public standing had presented both a compelling alternative vision and an ability to command broad national attention. Warren's chairmanship of the oversight panel, often with Geithner as her foil, began to furnish this public critique of how the world worked and how it could work better for ordinary people.

Warren didn't just reframe the government's response in a way that indicted the elite consensus and shifted Wall Street's role from hero to perpetrator. She used her platform to show how this consensus had attacked and displaced a post–World War II political economy that had held the financial industry in check while at the same time giving rise to a broad and prosperous middle class. Gavel in hand, she literally taught a history seminar. Among the hearings she chaired as head of the oversight panel was one titled "Learning from the Past: Lessons from the Banking Crises of the 20th Century."

But Warren's bigger contribution to the rise of liberal populism was her ability to galvanize public sentiment around ideas that hadn't had much purchase in America since the middle of the twentieth century, when memories of the Great Depression still fostered widespread distrust of Wall Street. She sparked a national movement that almost immediately began to shift sentiment within the Democratic Party and elevated her into a kind of folk hero in the popular culture. Nothing in her background marked her as likely to inhabit such a large public role. Early on, it was difficult to see what she would become. The precise nature of Warren's power on the oversight panel, as it would be in the Senate later, was initially misunderstood or missed altogether. A *New York Times* profile of Warren just after she became oversight chair predicted, wrongly, that the panel's "main source of influence is that it will have the ear of lawmakers who can tighten the bailout purse-strings or rewrite its charter."

The panel's true influence was much broader than that. In short order, it developed the power to shape the public's perception of the crisis and the government's feeble, halting response—a power that owed almost entirely to Warren's performative talents and to her ability to spread a message in ways that nobody had thought of before.

5

THE MEDIUM IS THE MESSAGE

Almost as soon as she got to Washington, Warren did something unusual. The Congressional Oversight Panel was assigned temporary space in the Hart Senate Office Building on Capitol Hill. This location had one notable asset: it was near the Senate TV studio. Because the staff of the oversight committee was classified as employees of the U.S. Senate, Warren had access to the studio. Even before she hired a full staff, she used her access to shoot a straight-to-camera video explaining, in plain language, what the committee was for and what it intended to do. Then she uploaded it to a website that was new in the world of politics: YouTube.

It's difficult to recapture so many years later what an odd thing this was to do. Today, everyone is constantly glued to a screen, and social media suffuses our daily lives. People are bombarded with messages from friends, politicians, and corporate brands—at every moment, on every device—most of them engineered to elicit a specific emotional response. In 2008, the world was simpler and more innocent. The iPhone was brand-new, most people weren't yet on Facebook, and Donald Trump still didn't know about Twitter. YouTube was growing quickly, but it wasn't a domain of politics or public persuasion. It was rather, as one newsweekly put it, a "home for piano-playing cats, celeb goof-ups, and overzealous lip-synchers."

From a distance, Warren, a nerdy professor of bankruptcy law, would not have registered as an obvious candidate to spark a social media movement. But the idea, in embryonic form, had taken root in her several years earlier, after she had decisively lost the bankruptcy fight in 2005. Warren returned to Harvard frustrated and chastened, but with a clearer understanding of the forces arrayed against liberal reformers. "She's back at Harvard licking her wounds, but she's also worried that the economy is going to collapse because of the mortgage market," says Dan Geldon, who was a law student of Warren's at the time. "What she knew she needed to figure out was advocacy. Any issue that came down to a roomful of lobbyists was one where she was going to get rolled. She knew she needed to build public energy around her cause."

Warren was always a relentless popularizer of her own ideas. At the same time her academic star was rising, her ability to translate her scholarship for lay audiences won her media exposure and a public profile beyond that of a typical law professor, even an Ivy Leaguer. She had a protean talent for shaping her public persona in a way that commanded attention. In 2003 she teamed up with her daughter, Amelia Warren Tyagi, to write *The Two-Income Trap*, a book that caught the eye of the daytime television star Dr. Phil, who made Warren a repeat guest on his talk show after she demonstrated a capacity to reinvent herself as an empathetic financial expert and life coach for his troubled guests.

She realized the internet's potential as a lever for policy change when she witnessed up close how the bankruptcy legislation was written—and by whom. In 2005, Josh Marshall, the founder of the influential liberal blog *Talking Points Memo*, was surprised when Warren contacted him offering to write about bankruptcy reform for his website. Nobody had done anything like that before. Warren had deduced that congressional staffers were more digitally inclined than their bosses and instrumental in shaping their views. They wrote the legislative text that congressmen and senators debated and voted on. Most staffers were much younger, often shockingly so, than the elected officials they served. They spent a lot of time online reading blogs. Warren thought that blogging was a way to reach them directly, along with the growing crowd of grassroots activists who had become increasingly vocal during the Iraq War. "She could see that blogs like TPM were having a decisive effect on the evolution of Democratic politics at a time when that wasn't yet clear to the older generation of party operatives and officeholders," Marshall says.

By late 2008, as Warren was unpacking boxes in her new Washington office and scrambling to assemble an oversight staff, the potential of the internet to reshape politics was much clearer. Barack Obama's upstart campaign had just knocked off Hillary Clinton in the Democratic primary and John McCain in the general election, powered by hundreds of millions of dollars and legions of eager volunteers, both of which had arrived mainly through online channels.

Although she was a skilled communicator in her own right, there was a world of difference between Warren and the charismatic young president-elect, destined for history, whose oratory was often compared with Martin Luther King Jr.'s. Warren didn't do soaring speeches. What she had going for her in 2008 was the context of the times, the almost palpable fear people had that something terrible was happening and an accompanying anger that those in charge weren't being straight about it, or even looking out for their interests. Warren, quite intentionally, cast herself in the role of explainer.

When she uploaded her video from the Senate TV studio on December 11, the U.S. economy was in free fall, shrinking at the fastest pace since the Great Depression. The evening news was a steady procession of grim-faced men in suits offering dubious reassurances as everything went to hell. Henry Paulson had abandoned his pledge to buy up troubled mortgages with the $700 billion TARP fund. That morning, as if to confirm the worst suspicions about his motives, a front-page story in *The New York Times* ("Fighting Foreclosures, F.D.I.C. Chief Draws Fire") reported that White House and Treasury officials were attacking the chairwoman of the Federal Deposit Insurance Corporation, Sheila Bair—one of the few people insisting that bailout money be used to modify the loans of homeowners facing default. "White House and Treasury officials argue that Mrs. Bair's high-profile campaigning is meant to promote herself while making them look heartless," the *Times* reported. "As a result, they have begun excluding Mrs. Bair from some discussions."

Anyone disgusted by this high-powered backstabbing who encountered Warren's first YouTube video would have felt that they had discovered an ally. Warren, wrapped in a maroon cardigan and seated in a softly lit office, immediately establishes a direct, personal connection with the viewer. Looking earnestly into the camera, she introduces herself with a folksy smile as a professor who teaches "the money courses" at Harvard Law School. "Two weeks ago, I became the chair of the Congressional Oversight Panel, established to check out how $700 billion of your money"—here Warren jabs her finger at the viewer, like Uncle Sam—"is spent in Washington." Peering through rimless glasses, her hair in a simple bob and tucked behind her ears, Warren exudes the guileless integrity of a Sunday school teacher (which she once had been). Here at last, a frustrated viewer might conclude, was a trustworthy soul who seemed to be driven by something other than her own material interest.

In her video, Warren makes a big show of telling it straight and not putting on airs. "We had our first meeting two weeks ago today—and we don't have much yet," she says, with a sheepish grin. "No phones. No fax machines. No coffeemaker. But we have met with the Treasury Department, the Federal Reserve, and the GAO, and we have put together some questions that we think are important." They're the same questions regular folks wondered about: "What have financial institutions done with the taxpayers' money that they have received so far? What is the Treasury's strategy? What is the big plan here?" Unlike the officials on the nightly news, Warren doesn't speak as if she's been marched out at gunpoint, and she doesn't use confusing financial argot. She strives, a bit too self-consciously, to come across as winningly ordinary. But she seems nice. And she promises to do what no one else in 2008 appeared willing to, which was to figure out what was going on and report back, no bullshit.

Then Warren does something entirely new. She rattles off the URL for the oversight panel's new website and invites viewers to become active participants in a process that so far has excluded them at every stage; it's a primitive version of the cheery call to action that comes at the end of every YouTube video today ("Don't forget to smash that 'Like' button and subscribe!").

Her invitation wouldn't go unheeded.

———

WARREN'S VIDEO DIDN'T LIGHT UP the internet the way that piano-playing cats do. It lit up a specific corner of the internet that has out-sized power to shape what everybody else sees and hears about. Along with the liberals who discovered a folk hero, Warren's video circulated among reporters and cable news producers who were scrambling like everyone else to make sense of the unfolding crisis and running into the same roadblocks she did when seeking answers from the government. In Warren, they discovered a source with prodigious financial knowledge who was in regular contact with all the key players or their deputies and was unusually willing to hop on the phone with them or appear on their shows and talk about it. Despite her folksy affect, she instinctively understood and was willing to inhabit a critical role in modern media storytelling, especially when it comes to big, dramatic, complicated events like the financial crisis. Warren became the plucky, truth-telling underdog who supplies an alternate, populist narrative that frequently clashed with the official one emanating from the White House—a dramatis personae of the crisis. Most people found her not only accessible but viscerally thrilling to watch. She forced a national debate through the means of the questions she asked and the charges she lobbed not just in her regular YouTube videos and oversight hearings but in an ascending series of media appearances that turned her into a bona fide celebrity.

Practically from the moment she joined the oversight panel, Warren was everywhere. She slammed the banks and the Obama administration on Fox News, in the pages of *The New York Times* and *The Washington Post*, and in Michael Moore's documentary *Capitalism: A Love Story*. She had a ready arsenal of newsy provocations and was the rare Democrat willing to go after Obama by name and on the record.

"He meets with bankers," she told the author Ron Suskind. "He doesn't meet with me." Warren was adept at what media people call "flooding the zone": she made herself ubiquitous. "It was the philosophy she had for how she could use the role," says Geldon.

But one appearance stood out above all the others, vaulting her to prominence beyond Washington and equipping her with a kind of power that wasn't proscribed by the limitations of the oversight panel. In April 2009, Warren was a guest on *The Daily Show with Jon Stewart* on Comedy Central.

The booking was a bit of a curveball. Warren's was not a name that would excite viewers of the cult comedy show. But Stewart wasn't a typical comedy host, either. He was closely attuned to the financial crisis (his brother, Larry Leibowitz, cofounded the hedge fund Bunker Capital and was later a top executive at a company that owned the New York Stock Exchange), he knew about Warren, and he shared her moral outrage at the government's seeming indifference toward many of the people faring worst in the crisis. "We're political nerds," says Steve Bodow, the show's executive producer at the time. "Our show was paying a lot of attention, relative to most comedy shows, to the Troubled Asset Relief Program and the lady policing it. We were reaching down further into the Washington bureaucracy than late-night talk shows typically do. But Warren was the approximate opposite of the Wall Street bullet heads. She talked in language you could understand and seemed to have the same concerns normal people had. Jon was an early, loud, and consistent voice [asking], 'Why are you letting all these people lose their homes and funneling money to banks?' She seemed to share our perspective that this was all crazy."

The timing was propitious. In the weeks leading up to her appearance, the Dow Jones Industrial Average bottomed out at 6,469, down more than 54 percent from its October 2007 peak after a grueling eighteen-month-long slide (although this nadir would become evident only in hindsight). The AIG bonus scandal had ignited a national fury. Job losses and foreclosures were now rampant—much worse than in the fall—and the government was still pitchforking tens of billions of dollars at giant banks. Bodow recalls seeing a headline around the time of Warren's booking announcing that the stock price of Citigroup, recipient of a $45 billion bailout, was now less than the price of a can of Pepsi. A full-blown depression seemed not only possible but increasingly likely. "The emotional context of those weeks is important to remember," Bodow said later. "The country was *freaking the fuck out* in a way that's easy to lose sight of now. Everyone and their mom was watching their 401(k) falling apart. The job loss was the most intense in our lifetime. It was a really, really scary moment."

Adding frisson to Warren's appearance was the fact that Stewart had just been burned by one of the more loathsome minor figures in the crisis drama. Rick Santelli, the loudly opinionated CNBC personality whose February 19 rant against struggling homeowners ("losers") is often credited with birthing the Tea Party movement, was scheduled to be a guest on *The Daily Show*. But a few days later, perhaps sensing Stewart's ire, CNBC changed tack and abruptly pulled Santelli from the show.

For all her felicity with the Washington press corps, Warren regarded *The Daily Show* as being more significant, and therefore more daunting, than the public affairs shows she was accustomed to. Overcome by nerves, she vomited in the greenroom while awaiting her summons. "She went through a lot before she ever got out there," says Hillary Kun, a producer who helped Warren clean herself up. Walking out onto the stage, Warren later recalled, she felt "like an astronaut who had just left the space capsule."

At first, things didn't go well. Her halting answers made for stilted conversation. When Stewart asked her about a Treasury rescue program known by its acronym, PPIP, Warren froze up and couldn't remember what it stood for (Public-Private Investment Program). After a lengthy digression about how much taxpayers had overpaid for the equity stakes Paulson had taken in troubled banks, time ran out on Warren's segment without her having articulated any broader criticism of the government's crisis response or how it could be improved.

As the show went to a commercial, Stewart made it known that he wasn't satisfied with what had transpired. Waving off the stage director who came to spirit Warren away, he grabbed her forearm and told her to boil down her message to a single sentence. "You don't have much time," he warned.

When they returned from break, Stewart teed up a question that went right to the heart of the emerging debate over the Obama administration's recovery strategy—to the heart, in fact, of the nature of the American capitalist enterprise. "Why not liquidate the banks that truly should be liquidated and not just keep throwing good money after bad?" he asked.

With that, Warren hit her stride. After agreeing that "capitalism without bankruptcy is like Christianity without hell," Warren shifted into tutelary mode, delivering a brief history of the boom-and-bust cycles that have plagued the U.S. economy since George Washington's time. Basic regulations put in place after the Great Depression had eliminated financial crises for the next fifty years. But Wall Street had chipped away at them until they were gone, and that led directly to the savings and loan crisis; the collapse of the hedge fund Long Term Capital Management, which shook global markets; the rampant fraud at Enron; and finally the great crash that now suffused everything. "And what is our repeated response?" Warren asked. "We just keep pulling the threads out of the regulatory fabric."

A hallmark of Warren's leadership of the oversight panel was that she always kept an eye toward the future, knowing that as soon as the economy stabilized, Washington would turn to writing new rules. For a brief moment, the possibilities for financial regulation would be unusually malleable in a way that they hadn't been in seventy-five years. Warren had spent years preparing for this moment. In 2007, she wrote a journal article proposing the creation of a consumer financial protection agency. The oversight panel's report on the lessons of the twentieth-century banking crises was another bid to shape this process. Both were aimed at a small but influential group of policy insiders who would write the new laws. Sitting onstage at *The Daily Show*, having recovered her wits, Warren knew she was in a prime position to reach a much larger audience that could, along with the man seated across from her, influence the future course of events in Washington.

She took her shot. "We have two choices," Warren told Stewart. "We're going to make a big decision, probably over about the next six months. The big decision we're going to make is that it's going to go one way or the other: We're either going to decide, 'Hey, we don't need regulation, it's fine . . . and good luck with your 401(k).' Or, alternatively, we're going to say, 'You know, we're going to put in some smart regulation that's going to adapt to the fact that we have new [financial] products, and what we're going to have going forward is some stability and real prosperity for ordinary folks.'"

Warren's dichotomy struck a chord. After the applause died down, Stewart turned serious. "That is the first time in probably six months to a year that I've felt better," he told her. "I don't know what it is that you just did right there, but for a second that was like financial chicken soup for me. Thank you. That actually put things into perspective that made a little bit of sense. . . . Good luck with that." Then he added a joking threat that he soon made good on: "And if they don't give you transparency, you tell me, because I'll keep talking about it."

Warren's star turn on *The Daily Show* made her into a household name and her critique shaped the national conversation. Her impatience with the Obama administration's deference to Wall Street, her revulsion at winner-take-all capitalism, and her insistence that federal regulators seize failing banks, fire their managers, and write strict new rules became a template for how millions of people thought about the worsening national condition. Her flair for dramatizing her positions by provoking clashes with her adversaries only added to their appeal; she was easy to root for, provided you weren't a member of the Obama administration.

But the success of Warren's brand of liberal populism from that point forward owed no small debt to Stewart's enthusiastic, ongoing endorsement of it each night on *The Daily Show*. And he was more than willing to give her a regular platform to expound on it.

"We did a debrief after the first show," says Kun. "Jon instantly loved her. She was one of those no-brainers that you know you're going to book again. Sometimes with guests I wasn't sure and I'd have to talk to Jon first, get his reading. With Warren, there was never any question. She became someone we called back again and again."

THE ALCHEMY OF highbrow cable comedy and her viral clashes with Tim Geithner and other Wall Street sympathizers made Warren a cult figure on the left. But Stewart's imprimatur also gave her a kind of soft power that extended further across the political spectrum. *The Daily Show* was just then at the apex of its influence. It was an important opinion setter, maybe *the* important opinion setter, for upwardly mobile young people and the sorts of civically engaged professionals who think of themselves as being dialed into popular culture—in short, the rising Democratic base. At the time, cable shows like Stewart's still commanded real cultural power because their audience had not yet balkanized across TikTok, YouTube, and dozens of streaming services. Stewart himself was a powerful shaper of elite journalistic opinion. During this period, he was routinely lionized by critics and academics for his judgment and probity, and often touted as the Walter Cronkite of his era. That same year, a *Time* magazine poll found that Stewart was America's most trusted newscaster.

Warren's sudden prominence, buttressed by these collective forces, earned her the enmity of Wall Street's allies in the Obama administration and beyond. She became the bête noire of a noisy breed of billionaire accustomed to being celebrated, not vilified, who would pop up on CNBC every so often and make martyred squeals of displeasure, which themselves went viral and fed into the growing sense that Warren was a figure of consequence.

But it wasn't just the populist potency of her message that drew fans to Warren in droves. She was the type of woman whom a certain species of puffed-up male politician or banker couldn't help but patronize, as Biden had done during the bankruptcy fight in 2005. In her role as oversight chair (and later senator), this sexist impulse, far from being a handicap, worked to her advantage, because it tended to produce moments of kinetic drama whenever Warren—who attended college on a debate scholarship—trapped some unsuspecting witness in an awkward evasion or a risible defense of the indefensible. Women especially (but many men, too!) savored these confrontations, and the rapid growth of social media and the proliferation of smartphones suddenly made it easy for them to give public expression to their feelings.

Right around this time, Warren inaugurated a specific kind of online political act that was new but quickly became common among the passionate tribes that sprang up around her: the posting and sharing of video clips of her slashing cross-examinations and beatdowns of various and sundry villains, each slapped with a crackling title brimming with righteous triumph, such as "Elizabeth Warren EMBARRASSES Bank Regulators," "Elizabeth Warren Rips Wells Fargo's CEO a New One," "Elizabeth Warren Destroys CNBC Anchors," "Elizabeth Warren Asks Why Sallie Mae Is Ripping Off Taxpayers to Screw Over Students," and on and on, each clip leading algorithmically to the next in a crescendo of populist fury.

It wasn't fun to be on the receiving end of her public wrath, to find yourself suddenly trending on YouTube, or to learn from your kids that your worst moment from the day's hearing was being brutally dissected by Jon Stewart on *The Daily Show*. Often, the people who wound up in the crosshairs were fellow Democrats or members of the Obama administration. The attacks stung. Geithner would write in his memoir that he felt Warren "was better at impugning our choices—as well as our integrity and our competence—than identifying feasible alternatives."

Other Treasury and White House officials were much harsher. Granted anonymity for reasons of self-preservation, they routinely disparaged Warren to reporters as a "professional critic," "sanctimonious," and a "condescending narcissist." Resentful that she wouldn't give the president and his advisers the deference many of them felt they were owed, they orchestrated a campaign of leaks that aimed, without much success, at tarnishing Warren's heroic image. Venting to *Politico*, one former Treasury aide captured the flavor of the administration's indignity: "We're with Barack. We're the liberals. Why are you pissing in our face?"

Whatever ill feelings she engendered, Warren's gambit was a remarkable success. Using her part-time position on a largely power-less congressional panel, she established a populist beachhead within Democratic politics and quickly amassed a devoted following. She represented a new *style* of politics, too. No prominent Democrat was as willing as Warren was to criticize policies that had gone unchallenged for decades or to attack what she viewed as the formidable misalliance between Wall Street and the Democratic Party. With millions of Americans suddenly broke, scared, and angry, perhaps it shouldn't have been a surprise that Warren's message would resonate to the degree that it did. But harnessing that energy and yoking it to a populist agenda that could break Wall Street's grip on Washington would prove to be a much tougher task.

IN WAYS THAT NEITHER of them could have foreseen, the next decade in U.S. politics would be shaped to an extraordinary degree by the battle that Geithner and Warren were just then waging over how America should respond to the financial crisis.

One way to think about this struggle is to put it into historical context. Practically since the nation's founding, mistrust of banks and bitter disputes over their scale and power have been a venerable theme in U.S. politics. Anyone who's seen the hit Broadway musical *Hamilton* will be familiar with the basic outline of the debate. Alexander Hamilton, the first secretary of the Treasury and the father of the American financial system, favored big merchants and financiers at the expense of artisans and yeomen farmers, who aligned themselves with Hamilton's intellectual rival, the great skeptic of concentrated economic power Thomas Jefferson (and his ally, the costar of *Hamilton*, Aaron Burr). American politics since the eighteenth century can be viewed as a never-ending contest for primacy between Hamiltonians and Jeffersonians. As they battled over the relative power of big banks versus smallholders in the wake of the 2008 financial crisis, Geithner and Warren were just the latest political figures—another Treasury secretary and his chief nemesis and critic—jousting over America's oldest struggle.

But a better way to think about this *particular* struggle is as its being the natural extension of the lived experience of the two people most visibly waging it. Warren's entire life up to that point had conditioned her to see the problems of the financial crisis from the bottom up, whereas Geithner's had taught him to look at it from the top down. Everything that each of them did followed directly from these distinct and opposing perspectives.

Warren grew up in Oklahoma City in modest, sometimes tenuous, circumstances. She was the youngest of four children and the only girl. After her father had a heart attack and lost his job as a carpet salesman, her mother took a minimum-wage job answering phones at Sears to keep from losing the family's home. Warren, even after winning a full scholarship to George Washington University on the strength of her debating skills, didn't escape precarity in her own life. She married at nineteen, dropped out of college, and had her first child at twenty-two. She followed her husband to Houston, where she finally earned a degree and later became a special-needs teacher. She lost that job when she became visibly pregnant with her second child. By then, Warren and her family had relocated once more, to New Jersey. Restless for stimulation, she enrolled at the Rutgers School of Law, where for the next few years she struggled to balance parenting, her legal studies, and a failing marriage.

Later, when she was a politician trying to connect with voters, Warren would often speak about the grinding anxieties of her early life at the ragged edge of the middle class. But the formative experience in her adult life, the thing that shaped who she became and how she reacted to the financial crisis, was the academic research she conducted as a law professor.

In 1978, Warren accepted a job at the University of Houston Law School. That year, Congress passed a major revision of the bankruptcy laws. Warren and two colleagues, curious about its effects, decided to study them. "By happy coincidence, Liz and I were both interested in the law in action, how it actually works in the real world," Jay Westbrook, a University of Texas Law School professor and one of Warren's collaborators, recalled. "That's kind of unusual for law professors, who tend to be more interested in theory and rules."

Warren and her colleagues went out into the world to learn what sorts of people declare bankruptcy, and why. Because there were no electronic records, the team spent years traveling to courthouses all over the country to examine individual bankruptcy cases, hauling along a portable Xerox machine they dubbed R2-D2. The prevailing view at the time held that shiftless people who were profligate overspenders made up the bulk of bankruptcy filings. Warren initially thought the same. The data showed otherwise. One of the first cases she reviewed was that of a middle-class couple whose deep shame over their heavy debt drove them to commit suicide before their first court hearing. Many others involved families hit with the sudden loss of a job, a medical emergency, a divorce, or a bad accident that wiped out their savings and left them ruined. More troubling still was the trend Warren and her colleagues detected in the data. Prior to their research, people thought that bankruptcy was concentrated among "day laborers and housemaids," as Westbrook put it. But the records they were gathering showed that by the early 1980s a growing number of middle-class Americans were coming under severe financial stress and filing for bankruptcy and most of them were homeowners. One of the big drivers was their inability to make mortgage payments. "We were way ahead of the curve on that one," Westbrook said. "Too many people were stretched to the limit to buy as much house as they thought they could afford."

In 1989, after nearly a decade of research, Warren, Westbrook, and Teresa Sullivan published *As We Forgive Our Debtors: Bankruptcy and Consumer Credit in America*, a book that reshaped popular understanding of consumer bankruptcy and established Warren's academic reputation. In addition to showing the triggers of financial failure, the trio included a remorseless dissection of the financial industry's culpability in the rising wave of bankruptcies. "Credit card issuers were willing to give out the fifth, sixth, or seventh bank card and to approve charges after debtors already owed short-term debt so large that they could not possibly pay the interest, much less the principal," the authors wrote.

This calculated recklessness and its devastating toll on families became a focus of their research. In 2000, they published another book, *The Fragile Middle Class*, that drew on further empirical work to document the growing precariousness of middle-class American life and sound a warning about America's impoverished social safety net. "Without universal health insurance to protect every family from the financial ravages of illness and without higher levels of unemployment compensation to cushion the effect of a layoff, each day, in good times and in bad, some families will fall over the financial edge," they wrote.

Warren came to believe—correctly, it turned out—that she and her colleagues were documenting an onrushing catastrophe that nobody else was seeing. Their research didn't just identify what sorts of people were getting wiped out; it showed that whole new categories of people once thought to be safe credit risks were going bust. These bankruptcies were not random acts of fate; they were the inevitable by-products of a predatory financial industry. Politicians weren't just ignoring this behavior; they were actively facilitating it—including prominent Democrats like Joe Biden who presented themselves as, and were generally accepted as being, enlightened champions of the hardworking middle class. But the strain on the American family was hidden behind a facade of rising income and GDP growth because families had adapted to intensifying financial pressures by breaking from the traditional single-earner model and sending both spouses to work. This was the argument Warren put forth in her 2003 book, *The Two-Income Trap*. This new arrangement, she warned, had dangerous implications: it stretched families to the breaking point and left them vulnerable to financial collapse if almost anything went wrong.

Over the years, Warren's voice grew more urgent and angry, especially in her popular writing, which wasn't constrained by the dictates of academic decorum. Her radicalization grew out of her research. "The first book says, 'The system is being used the way that it should. Those people are in real trouble,'" she said. "Second book says, 'And let's tell you something about who those people are. They are surprisingly middle class.'" She continued, "The people who are filing for bankruptcy in increasing numbers every year, it's not the poorest. It's not the people at the economic fringes. It's people who worked hard and played by the rules."

By the time she wrote *The Two-Income Trap*, Warren was fed up and taking direct aim at politicians, including marquee Democrats such as Biden and Hillary Clinton, for abetting what she considered a corrupt and destructive form of laissez-faire capitalism. In the book, Warren recalled briefing Clinton, then the First Lady, about the industry-friendly bankruptcy bill. "It's our job to stop that awful bill," she quotes Clinton as saying. But several years later, when Clinton had become a senator and the bill came up for passage, she voted for it. "The bill was essentially the same, but Hillary Rodham Clinton was not," Warren seethed. As a senator, "she could not afford such a principled position. Campaigns cost money, and that money wasn't coming from families in financial trouble." To Warren, the episode captured everything that was wrong with the modern political economy: a government obligated to protect its citizens from the worst effects of unfettered capitalism instead had been captured and failed in this fundamental duty.

In the months leading up to the crisis, she even singled out the precipitating factor: mortgages. Writing in 2007 in the journal *Democracy*, Warren proposed the creation of a new agency to protect consumers from exploitative financial products. As she put it in her now-famous lede: "It is impossible to buy a toaster that has a one-in-five chance of bursting into flames and burning down your house. But it is possible to refinance an existing home with a mortgage that has the same one-in-five chance of putting the family out on the street—and the mortgage won't even carry a disclosure of that fact to the homeowner."

Warren's academic research gave her a glimpse into the future: she saw what was coming and knew what it would do to middle-class families. When the crisis arrived, her warnings were validated. By Warren's way of thinking, this made her uniquely well qualified to know where the human fallout would be concentrated and what the government could do to alleviate it for the tens of millions of people whose lives and livelihoods were suddenly upended.

To begin with, she thought, any rescue plan should marshal the country's huge capacities for crisis fighting and direct them squarely at the middle class. It should aim to foster the kind of economic resilience that had gradually been leached out of the American family. There were numerous ways to shield people from the worst effects of the crisis: the government could issue stimulus payments, enhanced unemployment benefits, small-business loans, student loan relief, mortgage aid, an eviction moratorium—anything and everything to spare as many people as possible from becoming new case files in bankruptcy court. At the same time, federal regulators could seize insolvent banks. Then, with markets stable and a relief program in place, the country could at last embark on root-and-branch reform to fix the economic problems that had caused—but long predated—the financial crisis. In keeping with her Jeffersonian instincts, Warren wanted not just a consumer protection agency but to break up the big banks, reimpose the Glass-Steagall Act separating commercial and investment banking, and dismantle what she regarded as the political-financial oligopoly that controlled American government to the detriment of working people no matter which party was in power.

She got almost none of it. Instead, the Hamiltonians prevailed. Geithner had a wholly different concept of the crisis and how to address it, and he also had the president's ear, which Warren did not. He won the policy argument in a rout. By embracing Geithner's plan, Obama soothed financial markets and returned the U.S. economy to growth, albeit so meager that it consigned the country to a decade of anemic employment levels. But his plan was politically poisonous because it didn't account for the deep dissatisfaction of the people it left out—the people Warren was focusing on. Democrats came to regret this error. When the COVID pandemic drove the U.S. economy into an even deeper recession in the spring of 2020, both parties quickly agreed to a multitrillion-dollar plan that included almost all of the economic relief measures Warren had advocated for twelve years earlier. Then, for good measure, when Joe Biden became president, Democrats on their own followed up with another nearly $2 trillion relief package that channeled still more cash directly to households and businesses with remarkable success: the U.S. poverty rate actually fell during the worst economic slump since the Great Depression, thanks to these government rescue efforts.

But that was still many years, and a political revolution, away. In the wake of the 2008 crash, Obama, operating under Geithner's heavy influence, committed the country to a course of action that was targeted mainly at financial markets, because that's what a generation of influential policymakers in both parties believed he should do. There was an entire playbook that Geithner himself had helped to develop that dictated how governments should address financial crises. It was based largely on the U.S. experience battling the emerging market crises in the 1990s and the early 2000s, and it represented the collective wisdom of three decades of neoliberal thought about how to manage the global economy. Geithner, whose career coincided almost exactly with this shift in how Democrats think about markets and finance, was instrumental not only in shaping these strategies but in persuading Obama to implement them in the wake of the 2008 crisis. This approach succeeded in helping the United States avoid plunging into another depression. But the actions Obama took were so unpopular that they ended up driving populist rebellions in both parties that in short order would transform America.

If Geithner were a character in a British period novel, he'd be the diligent son of the head servant, someone whose outstanding qualities are noted by the master and who, when the time comes, is unexpectedly rewarded with passage to university and the world beyond. He makes a deep impression on powerful people everywhere he goes.

Geithner grew up in a series of far-flung, exotic locales. Just after he was born in 1961, his father, who worked for the U.S. Agency for

International Development, moved the family to Rhodesia. Later, when his father moved to the Ford Foundation, they lived in New Delhi and then Thailand. Growing up, Geithner was surrounded by people who worked for development organizations such as Oxfam, CARE, the World Bank, and Amnesty International and whose business it was to try to solve big, intractable-seeming problems that governments alone couldn't manage. As a young man, he followed a path strikingly similar to his father's—up to a point. At Dartmouth, he majored in government and Asian studies, then took a graduate degree in international relations, as his father had, from the Johns Hopkins School of Advanced International Studies. He deferred going into government to gain private-sector experience, again like his father, landing a job in 1985 at Kissinger Associates, the consulting firm founded by Henry Kissinger and run by Lawrence Eagleburger and Brent Scowcroft.

For a young man planning a career in the international side of government, this was a stroke of almost unimaginable good fortune. It didn't happen by chance. The dean at Johns Hopkins personally recommended Geithner to Scowcroft. When he arrived, Geithner quickly distinguished himself by writing memos on political and economic affairs and personally briefing Kissinger, who chose Geithner to write a series of longer papers—not for the firm, but for him personally—that became part of the basis for *Diplomacy*, Kissinger's sweeping history of international statecraft.

With Kissinger's backing, Geithner moved on to the Treasury, where he landed in the Office of the Assistant Secretary for International Affairs. At the time, OASIA (pronounced "Oh-asia") was a rich-in-tradition, upper-echelon bureaucracy with a skilled career staff, much like USAID, and an institutional culture that was proudly nonideological, eastern establishment, consensus-driven, and business-friendly. It was here that Geithner had his first experience with financial crises.

In the spring of 1990, he was dispatched to the U.S. embassy in Tokyo, arriving just after the Japanese real estate bubble burst and the Nikkei index began its dizzying fall—the beginning of Japan's "lost decade" of deflation and stagnation. The Japanese government mostly resisted U.S. entreaties to confront the reality that its banks were paralyzed by bad loans, preferring to wait in hopes that its banking system would heal itself. Geithner's job was keeping abreast of all the recondite details, knowing their possible second- and third-order effects, and seeing the whole picture from on high. It took eight years for the Japanese government to relent and fortify its banks with public capital. For Geithner, the Japanese experience underscored the limits of moral suasion and the dangers of taking a gradualist approach to a banking crisis. "These were very capable people," he said later. "They were making a completely conscious choice that they were going to take this strategy, even though it was going to be costly in terms of growth forgone."

Geithner returned to Washington and OASIA in 1992, intending to stick around just long enough to help a new boss settle in and then move on. It turned out to be Lawrence Summers, the brilliant, prickly Harvard economist entering government for the first time. Geithner agreed to stay on temporarily as a special assistant. He never left.

The pair fast developed a symbiotic relationship. Geithner had the rare capacity to withstand Summers's intellectual bullying and thrive; Summers valued his uncanny feel for how power functions in a government bureaucracy. (Geithner's Secret Service code name as Treasury secretary was Fencing Master.) As Summers put it, "Most people, when you ask, 'What should I do about X?' will give you a list of considerations. Tim always gave you a strategy."

In 1995, Geithner's career took another propitious turn when Robert Rubin, the former cochairman of Goldman Sachs, became Treasury secretary. Rubin instituted a new management style that flattened Treasury's hierarchical culture and gave more of a voice to young staffers. Geithner was soon dazzling a new patron. His timing was impeccable. Winning Rubin's confidence gave him a perch at the commanding heights of the global economy at the exact moment when two decades of neoliberal policy were suddenly beginning to destabilize economies around the globe. Policymakers were growing aware of new and esoteric dangers arising from the globalized and deeply interconnected world they had created. The Mexican currency crisis that hit just as Rubin was taking over was typical of these new disruptions in that it was a distant and unanticipated event that nevertheless imperiled American interests and required sweeping action at a national scale. An overriding concern of the Treasury became defending America's long bull market against foreign incursions. OASIA was the laboratory for figuring out how.

As with the U.S. crisis later, Mexico's trouble began with irresponsible borrowing and spiraled when investors panicked. The reason this threatened the United States was that a debt default would frighten investors into abruptly pulling out of emerging markets around the world, wrecking their economies. Because about 40 percent of U.S. exports were purchased by developing countries, the United States would suffer severe job losses, economic contraction, and a sharp rise in illegal immigration. Geithner was part of the Treasury team that put together a response on the fly. The initial plan was to rally investors by providing Mexico with $25 billion in loan guarantees. But after sending early signals of support, Congress refused to fund a "bailout." So the Clinton administration, again foreshadowing what was to come, cobbled together $40 billion in loan guarantees from the International Monetary Fund and the U.S. Treasury. It worked: the crisis subsided, and Mexico repaid its loans early, at a small profit to the U.S. government.

Mexico was the first in a series of crises that would go on to sweep across Asia, beginning in 1997 when Thailand devalued the baht. Thailand, too, had financed itself on unsustainable short-term borrowing, burned through its foreign reserves, and watched helplessly as investors fled. Malaysia, Singapore, the Philippines, and Hong Kong all came under similar pressure. Larger economies were next: Indonesia, South Korea, Brazil, and Russia. Russia's bond default caused the collapse of the hedge fund Long Term Capital Management, which briefly destabilized the U.S. economy. Geithner became a sort of bureaucratic adrenaline junkie, racing between the front lines. By the end of the Clinton era, a basic method had emerged for responding to financial crises: Quickly flood the market with money to restore confidence. Buy time to work out debts by not upsetting investors. Make stringent reform a condition of rescue—shut down weak banks, bust up oligarchies, and clean up corruption. Then withdraw. A view emerged that the U.S. government had more or less figured out how to manage the global financial system, winning those at its helm extraordinary renown. The era's time-capsule-worthy artifact is a *Time* cover touting Alan Greenspan, the Federal Reserve chairman; Rubin, the Treasury secretary; and Summers, Rubin's deputy, as "The Committee to Save the World."

Geithner became Rubin's most trusted aide-de-camp, steadily promoted up the chain of command. When Summers succeeded Rubin as Treasury secretary in 1999, Geithner rose once more, to the job Summers had occupied when they met, undersecretary for international affairs.

After the Clinton administration, he moved briefly to the International Monetary Fund and then landed another plum job: president of the Federal Reserve Bank of New York. Geithner's was an unusual hire. The New York Fed is the most powerful of the twelve regional banks that compose the Federal Reserve System, intended to function as the Fed's outpost on Wall Street. It's the embodiment of everything connoted by the phrase "clubby Wall Street institution." Its shares are owned by the same financial firms it oversees, and its president is chosen by (and reports to) a board of directors typically drawn from top executives of these firms. The presidency of the New York Fed is a job insiders give to one of their own. Geithner wasn't a Wall Street insider. But he had a powerful patron who was: Bob Rubin convinced the New York Fed's board chairman, the billionaire private equity mogul Pete Peterson, that Geithner, at just forty-two, was the right man for the job. "Pete asked me if I had any thoughts," Rubin later recounted, "and I said, 'Yeah, I have a heck of an idea: Tim Geithner.'"

Geithner arrived at the New York Fed in 2003, which means he arrived at the epicenter of finance just as Wall Street was roaring into its unbridled latter-stage boom. He won over his new constituents, Hamiltonians all, with characteristic aplomb, arranging a series of personal meetings with CEOs. In its own way, Geithner's job, like Warren's, gave him an early premonition of disaster on the horizon. Once he'd settled in, he chose to focus on the dangers posed by derivatives, and over the next few years he delivered a series of prescient speeches about their risks. As early as 2004, Geithner was warning of "fat tails," a term that suggests that catastrophic events at the far end of a bell curve are more likely to occur than statistical models imply. "I felt like my entire time in New York," he later recalled, "there was a fear that this was going to end badly."

Unlike Warren, however, Geithner didn't try to sound an alarm. Instead, he worked diligently over two years to build consensus around improving the technical infrastructure that underlay derivatives trading—banks still confirmed deals by fax—to limit the chaos and destruction that unsettled trades would cause in the event that a market crisis were to strike. His efforts paid off in short order. When Lehman Brothers failed, its hundreds of billions in derivatives contracts settled within seventy-two hours, sparing untold amounts of anxiety and money (absent this reform, a panic would have driven down the market even further). But Geithner took no drastic steps to warn the public of the lurking danger. "I don't believe in the Chicken Little stuff," he said. "It wasn't my place."

And yet, when the 2008 crisis broke out, Geithner was paradoxically in prime position to rise once again. His job at the New York Fed made him a chief actor, with Hank Paulson and Ben Bernanke, in the government's rescue of Bear Stearns; its decision not to rescue Lehman Brothers; and its bailouts of AIG, Citigroup, and Bank of America. Public opinion polls showed overwhelming disapproval of these actions. But Barack Obama was billeted for the White House and in need of a Treasury secretary who understood the cascading crisis in all its terrifying detail. Lacking market experience himself, Obama put special stock in the opinions of those who had it. Those opinions coalesced around Tim Geithner.

"Markets are funny animals," Rubin, an Obama confidant, said later. "Tim, through his work on the Asian financial crisis, got a lot of exposure to market psychology and how markets work, and developed a feel for it. Very few people who have not worked in the markets develop a feel for what they're like, but Tim did."

One can imagine the realization dawning on Obama: Here was the man he needed. He had deep knowledge of derivatives. He was an expert discerner of the mystical "market psychology" upon which so much seemed to hinge. He had glowing references from big shots on Wall Street and in Washington. He also had what Obama needed most: a strategy. "Plan beats no plan," Geithner liked to say. What he lacked was a personal relationship with the new president. But his talent for winning over powerful men had its effect on Obama. By most accounts, Geithner won the Treasury secretary job over his old mentor Summers (whom Obama knew quite well) on the basis of a single sixty-five-minute interview with Obama on November 16.

GEITHNER CAME OF AGE in Washington just after the cold war ended, when the country's preoccupation with wealth and protecting the long boom became a focal point of government policy, and the populist impulse that people now associate with the likes of Warren and Sanders didn't factor into public thinking at all. His formative experience, as well as the basis of his glittering career, was figuring out how to contain the upheavals across the international financial system in the 1990s at as little cost and risk to the U.S. government as possible. It was how he'd learned to look at the world.

It became the way Obama looked at the world, too. Wittingly or not, by choosing Geithner as his key economic lieutenant and heeding his counsel above others', an inexperienced, malleable new president was adopting a Hamiltonian, finance-centered outlook that dictated a much different response than he might otherwise have pursued.

Within the context that Geithner viewed the crisis, his plan for how the United States could recover from it was bold, creative, and—judged on the metric by which he measured the problem—a clear success, even as it set off a cascading political disaster that resonates to this day. Geithner saw the 2008 crisis as an off-the-Richter-scale disruption that was much larger than, but not fundamentally dissimilar to, the ones he'd battled in the 1990s—a macroeconomic event that could be solved through a series of aggressive technical fixes. He believed that governments facing a financial crisis typically did too little to respond, rather than too much, and paid a steep price for their caution. The United States couldn't risk becoming Japan, slowly bled of its economic vitality. He told Obama,

> The simplest way to say it is that you have to move quickly with overwhelming force. You'll be able to get out more quickly if you do. You'll solve the problem more cheaply: less cost to the economy, less unemployment, less business failure, less cost to the taxpayer. People do the gradualist approach for two reasons. One is, the politics are terrible, because nobody wants to have to take that consequential act of putting a lot of money behind a financial system and helping a bunch of people that caused the crisis. The other reason is that people tend to hope it will get better, hope they're overestimating the problem, hope it'll heal itself, and that causes them to wait. But ultimately it takes capital in the financial system, and it takes the fiscal cannons of the government to work.

Geithner's plan aligned three cannons. First, the Federal Reserve would lower borrowing costs to nearly nothing. Second, Congress would pass a massive stimulus to fill the gap in private spending. Third was recapitalizing the financial sector so banks could absorb losses and keep lending. All of this was textbook crisis response. The daring break from form—really, the plan's defining feature—lay in where the bulk of the money would come from. Historically, the government supplied it. Geithner's novel idea was that private investors could give banks the money they needed instead, saving taxpayers an enormous sum. Research by the Cleveland Fed estimated that the typical financial crisis cost 5 to 10 percent of GDP, which would leave U.S. taxpayers on the hook for somewhere between $700 billion and $1.5 trillion—maybe more, given the severity of events.

Geithner's was the sort of clever solution that would elicit approving nods in the boardroom of Kissinger Associates or Goldman Sachs—or, as it happened, in the Oval Office. Implicit in this outlook was that aggregate cost was what mattered most, was the measure by which the government's performance would ultimately be judged. Providing direct material aid to people whose lives were destabilized or punishing the transgressors who caused the crisis was a distant second-order concern. "In a crisis, you have to choose," Geithner said. "Are you going to solve the problem, or are you going to teach people a lesson? They're in direct conflict." He had no patience for people who rejected this basic precept. "That's exactly the dilemma," he said. "The stuff that seemed appealing in terms of sharp discontinuity, Old Testament justice, clean break, fix the thing, penalize the venal, would have been dramatically damaging to the basic strategy of putting out the panic, getting growth back, making people feel more confident in the future—solving it without putting trillions of dollars of the taxpayers' money at risk unnecessarily."

By the measure Geithner favored, his plan worked. The economy didn't sink into another Great Depression. No big TARP recipient went belly up. The financial industry quickly recovered. Even AIG survived. Eventually, the U.S. government sold its controversial stake in the banks for a profit of $24 billion. The final cost of TARP to taxpayers wasn't $700 billion or $1.5 trillion. It was $32 billion.

In another sense, however, the cost was immeasurable. Geithner thought the plan's biggest risk was that it might fail to lure private investors and thus ruin the government's credibility with them. What no one quite appreciated was that the far bigger risk was political—that voters, not investors, would lose faith in the government and elected leaders, *even if* cost and risk were held to a minimum. It was a natural blind spot for someone like Geithner to have, one that Obama came to share. For all their experience battling financial crises, "Committee to Save the World" types didn't engage much in the domestic politics of the countries where they intervened. They orchestrated financial regime change from afar—often including painful, politically unpopular austerity measures—and then moved on.

Here there was no moving on. While Geithner's plan neatly solved a budgetary problem, it exacerbated a political one. It was wildly out of sync with the public desire for swift, retributive justice against the banks. Worse, it committed Obama to a position of pleading deference, because any strategy that depended on the financial sector's willingness to invest amid chaos had to tread cautiously or risk scaring off the very people it sought to attract. What was so surreal about this period was Obama's conviction that he needed to protect, rather than punish, those who'd destroyed the economy, in the belief that shielding them advanced a higher purpose. When the White House summoned the heads of the major banks in the spring of 2009, it wasn't to excoriate them or extract concessions, as the bankers feared. It was to implore them to behave better so as to alleviate blowback against the White House. "My administration is the only thing between you and the pitchforks," Obama reminded them. The charge that the White House coddled Wall Street wasn't just true; it was key to the whole recovery strategy.

Geithner in particular became fearful of intervening in any way that investors could perceive negatively, fighting off White House efforts to impose pay caps on banks receiving federal aid and derailing Democratic legislation to permit judges to reduce the mortgage principal of underwater borrowers. When the market crisis abated and stocks began to recover, the Obama administration cheered. But many Americans saw the rising stock market not as a gauge of economic revitalization but as an infuriating reminder that the financial overclass responsible for the crisis not only got off scot-free but also was getting richer in the bargain.

A bigger problem was the narrowness of the recovery. It simply failed to reach millions of people outside the financial sector, discrediting any notion they might have held that the Democratic administration was looking out for their interests. Fearful of sticker shock and longing for bipartisan support, the White House pushed for a much smaller stimulus than was necessary, one Republicans whittled down further. As a result, high unemployment and low job and wage growth persisted for much of the next decade, while household incomes were allowed to fall and debt-burdened homeowners were left largely on their own. Contrary to Geithner's expectation, most people didn't feel more confident about the future. They felt angry and betrayed.

Should this have been a surprise? Should Democrats (and Republicans) really have been blindsided by what happened next? Probably not. In adopting Geithner's plan, Obama understood that he was rescuing the banking system according to terms set out by a sympathetic regulator whose experience had taught him the enormous damage a systemic failure would impose. "With the world economy in free fall," Obama later wrote in his memoir, "my number-one task was not remaking the economic order. It was preventing further disaster. For this I needed people who had managed crises before." Yet Geithner wasn't a politician. His remit didn't extend to worrying about how people who didn't work at an elite level in the financial industry would respond to his bank rescue plan—or to anticipating how negative that response would be at a time when market-oriented liberalism had just failed spectacularly to deliver on its promise to provide Americans with a good life. This compounded people's impression that the basic economic arrangements of recent decades had utterly failed and needed replacing. For most households, the economic gains of the 1990s and 2000s were concentrated in the value of their homes—wealth that had suddenly evaporated. Populist disaffection soon found expression in ways no one expected, unleashing partisan energies on the left (Occupy Wall Street) and the right (the Tea Party) that wiped out the political era of neoliberal consensus and ushered in a poisonous, polarized new one. The critical massing of conditions that led to Donald Trump had their genesis in this backlash. So did the political ascendance of Elizabeth Warren and the populist left.

Somehow, though, this upheaval didn't shake the faith of the president and the Democratic mainstream. They held fast to many of the same ideas that dominated economic thinking before the crash: a fixation on deficit reduction, inflation, trade liberalization, and boosting private investment and financial innovation, even as these ideas were losing appeal with important Democratic constituencies. The crisis helped push thinking about economic inequality and market fundamentalism into the mainstream of American political life. But Obama was slow to embrace it. Instead, his interest turned to trying to strike a "grand bargain" with Republicans that would cut social spending in order to reduce the deficit. He gave no sign that his outlook on the world had changed.

WARREN HAD A STORY she liked to tell to explain why. It was meant to dramatize just how differently Obama and Geithner saw the crisis than other people did. Warren told the story over and over again to reporters, and she also included a version of it in her memoir, *A*

Fighting Chance. It aimed to distill, in a single anecdote, the corrupting influence that the Democratic Party's long embrace of Wall Street has had on its traditional role as defender of the middle class. It functioned for Warren as an all-purpose illustration of how the party had lost its way and what it must confront in order to find it again.

It's the fall of 2009. Home foreclosures are rampant. Geithner has at last yielded to her incessant badgering and invited Warren and the Congressional Oversight Panel to meet with him in the Treasury Building to discuss TARP. The meeting is held in an ornate room filled with antique furniture and rich draperies that looks to Warren "like a room for kings to negotiate over who was going to get what colony." The whole setup is meant to intimidate. Geithner, the savvy bureaucrat, seizes control of the meeting by talking nonstop and daring his guests to be rude enough to interrupt him. Sometimes in telling the story, Warren, who does a mean impression of Geithner, would mimic the way he avoids eye contact and mumbles into his shirt collar.

After a while, Warren sees what's happening. She and her team are being filibustered. So she finally interrupts him to ask about the rising number of foreclosures and what the administration is doing about it. "What does this mean for the country?" she asks him. "How are you thinking about this? And what's your plan to deal with this crisis?"

In Warren's recollection, Geithner looks up and tells her not to worry. He has taken steps to "foam the runway" (a favorite Geithnerism) and prevent disaster. "We've done the calculations," he says, "and figured out that the number of foreclosures will not reach the point that they will sink the big banks."

Then Warren drives home the punch line with a can-you-believe-it? look of incredulity.

"Here were the two of us sitting in this room at Treasury across the table from each other," she says, "and when I'm using the word 'crisis'

I'm thinking about millions of families who are losing their homes, their jobs, their savings, and how that echoes through the whole economy. He's thinking about a handful of giant financial institutions who had sold all those mortgages and whether they were going to get enough cash back on them to keep themselves afloat!"

Warren shared this unflattering glimpse of Geithner because it suited her larger ambition of forcing a reckoning within her party. She wanted to spark a rebellion. She wanted people to gasp at how thoroughly top Democrats had assimilated Wall Street's point of view and then ask themselves: How had things come to be this way and who was responsible for it?

It was the right idea. Millions of Americans trapped in the fallout were furious that banks were being thrown a lifeline while they were being left to drown. It didn't seem right. The Democratic Party was supposed to represent workers. Yet everyone could see that its concern lay elsewhere. The price of this neglect would become horrifyingly clear several years later, when Donald Trump rode the backlash to the White House. But Warren's question about how the party came to embrace Wall Street deserves an answer. It wasn't an accident or the result of some inexorable process that couldn't have been avoided. It happened because of choices Democratic politicians made in the wake of Jimmy Carter's defeat about how the party should rebuild itself to compete with the rising force of Ronald Reagan and the Republicans. One man in particular epitomized this new direction.

6

FOLLOW THE MONEY

The 1980 election didn't just wipe out Jimmy Carter. It also, a bit more unexpectedly, brought an abrupt end to the political career of Representative James C. Corman of California, the head of the Democratic Congressional Campaign Committee, who narrowly lost his bid for reelection.

As it is today, the DCCC was then the chief fundraising organization dedicated to electing Democrats to the House of Representatives. But in 1980 that meant less than it suggests; without much difficulty at all, Democrats had held control of the House since 1954. They felt little pressure to raise money because the prospect that a day might arrive when they *didn't* control the House was too foreign for most of them to contemplate. Reelection campaigns often required little more than billboards and bumper stickers. As a result, the DCCC was a sleepy backwater whose chief fundraising activity was a single gala held annually in Washington. In 1980, the committee struggled to raise $1.8 million and finished the election cycle in debt. (By way of comparison, the DCCC raised about $350 million in the 2020 cycle.)

Reagan's victory shattered the image of Congress as an impregnable Democratic fortress. Along with Carter's anemic performance—he carried just 41 percent of the vote and six states, along with the District of Columbia—Republicans won the Senate in a rout, defeating nine incumbent Democrats and taking control for the first time since 1954. In the House, the GOP gained a net thirty-three seats and managed to oust twenty-eight Democratic incumbents, half of them veterans of at least ten years. Most humiliatingly, one of those veterans was Corman. The DCCC, everyone suddenly realized, was so impotent that it couldn't protect its own chairman.

It was into this situation that Tony Coelho launched himself, a self-anointed savior come to redeem his reeling party. Remaking the Democratic Party to compete in the age of Reagan would be the work of his brief, contentious, scandal-plagued political career. He achieved this primarily by forging financial ties between the Democratic Party and business interests, including, with great consequence, the Wall Street financial firms just then entering their booming 1980s heyday. His influence would long outlive his time in Washington. When people like Elizabeth Warren wondered, in 2009, how the Democratic governing class had come to identify so thoroughly with Wall Street's view of the world, one way to answer the question is through the life and lasting effect of Tony Coelho.

Coelho was a thirty-eight-year-old congressman from California's Central Valley first elected in 1978. Overwhelmingly ambitious, even by Washington's elevated standard, and savvy to the changing nature of modern electoral politics, he quickly distinguished himself by raising more money than just about anybody else, through sheer dint of personal effort. A dervish of energy who took daily doses of phenobarbital to control his epileptic seizures, Coelho became known to all as a tireless, beaming glad-hander whose suit pocket was perpetually stuffed with thin white envelopes bearing $1,000 checks from his personal political action committee, which he doled out like candy to his Democratic colleagues. Amid the carnage of 1980, Coelho might have been the only Democrat who grew in stature: he raised $100,000 for Corman's campaign and another $80,000 for Jim Wright, the House majority leader, astounding sums for a freshman congressman with no personal wealth to speak of.

Coelho was marking himself as a comer because he had an audacious goal that he revealed as soon as the dust had settled from the election: he wanted Corman's old job as head of the DCCC. This was an unheard-of ambition for a second-term congressman. Privately, Coelho was more ambitious still. He viewed the DCCC job as a stepping-stone to becoming majority leader and, one day, Speaker of the House. Though he lacked seniority, Coelho had two advantages. The first was timing: Democrats were shell-shocked. The 1980 elections, as a reporter for *The Wall Street Journal* later noted, "created an atmosphere of fear that would drive Democrats for the next six years." The second was money: In 1978, the cost of the average congressional campaign had suddenly leaped by almost 50 percent, to $128,000, due to the costly new imperatives of having a professional pollster and TV and radio ads crafted by media consultants. Coelho had just proved that he could raise the kinds of sums Democrats would need if they were going to fight off the Reagan juggernaut and keep control of the House. On his way out of Congress after his loss, Corman, a bluff Irishman who had 100,000 reasons to think highly of Tony Coelho, recommended to another bluff Irishman, the Democratic House Speaker, Tip O'Neill, that this eager young upstart would make a fine replacement for him at the DCCC, age and precedent be damned. Coelho made the decision even easier. "I said I could raise $5 million," he later recalled.

What Coelho was really selling to O'Neill and his colleagues was the promise of a solution to the problems Reagan's landslide victory had just exposed. For decades, Democrats had relied on labor unions and urban machines for money and voting muscle, but both were in steep decline. The old methods no longer sufficed. Republicans, it was suddenly clear, had developed powerful new ones and deployed them to devastating effect. Democrats needed to catch up. It was Coelho's fervent conviction that the master organizing principle of the post-Carter Democratic Party should be equipping it to compete with Reagan and the GOP in the new political age that revolved around television—and, because television wasn't cheap, money. Coelho's fascination with Reagan's telegenic appeal bordered on the mystical. "The guy is beautiful," he once marveled. "He's a master. He plays that thing for everything it's worth. The thing about Reagan is that he understands that all he has to be is a grade B actor. Not even a grade A actor—and project truth through that tube."

Lulled into complacency by their long domination of Congress, Democrats hadn't schooled themselves in the methods of the modern campaign or bothered to concern themselves with party building. But Reagan, whom most of them regarded as a dim-witted charlatan, had shown the world what a powerful political force television could be, building a movement that carried him to the White House and brought an army of fellow Republicans to Congress. Coelho offered Democrats the promise of salvation. He got the job.

BEFORE HE WAS A MONEY CHANGER, Coelho wanted to be a priest. Born to a family of poor dairy farmers in Los Banos, California, second-generation immigrants from the Azores, Coelho and his brother milked cows every morning before heading off to school. He studied by taping his notes to the metal partitions of the milking stalls.

He received little encouragement. His father, dubious of formal schooling, told him, "Your hands are more important than your head." In high school and at Loyola University in Los Angeles, a Catholic men's school, Coelho excelled anyway and had designs on attending law school. But in 1963, his life was turned upside down. His father's farm went bankrupt, and that bad news was followed by John F. Kennedy's assassination. Coelho, a serious Roman Catholic, claimed that these events altered his outlook on life so profoundly as to steer him away from law school and toward the Jesuit seminary instead. And then that prospect crumbled, too.

When he was sixteen, Coelho was badly injured in a truck accident on the farm and began suffering from periodic blackouts. His parents, distrustful of modern medicine, took him to a series of faith healers, who poured oils on his head and filled him with herbal teas. The blackouts eventually grew milder, and he learned to live with them. Not until his senior year at Loyola did he receive a formal medical diagnosis of epilepsy. His parents refused to accept it: Portuguese folklore regarded epilepsy as a disgrace and a punishment for past family sins. Coelho grew estranged from them. His doctor imparted the further unwelcome news that medieval canon law forbade epileptics to become priests, dashing Coelho's plan to enter the seminary. Although he soon married a woman and wouldn't publicly disclose his sexual orientation until several decades later, Coelho was also gay, which must have added a further dimension to his challenges as he wrestled with his identity and his uncertain future.

As unhappy children sometimes do, Coelho compensated by developing a superpowered personal force and drive, along with a self-mythologizing origin story that added to his public allure when he got to Washington. As he told it, his epilepsy diagnosis plunged him into a period of heavy drinking and despair, from which he was finally rescued by a close friend, a Jesuit priest, who arranged an unusual opportunity for him. "I have a job for you," the priest told Coelho. "It's a good one. You'll be working for Bob Hope." The legendary comedian and his wife, Dolores, who was active in Catholic charities, were looking for an assistant. Encouraged by the priest, Coelho moved into the Hope household in Palm Springs and found a new path.

Coelho had been living disconsolately in his college fraternity house. He parachuted into the innermost sanctum of Hollywood glamour. Soon he was workshopping jokes with Hope and attending television and movie premieres, sometimes in a Rolls-Royce. In Coelho's telling, Hope was a key figure in his redemption who enjoyed taking midnight drives on the freeway after he finished taping shows and liked to have long, searching conversations with his troubled young assistant. One night, Hope asked him what he wanted to do with his life now that the priesthood was foreclosed to him. "He finally said to me, 'It's obvious you have this burn to help people,'" Coelho recalled.

Coelho wasn't sure what he wanted to do. But Hope had a suggestion—politics. "He said, 'If you're really serious about helping people, if that's your bag, why don't you go to work for a member of Congress?'" Coelho recounted. "'You can satisfy your priestly needs and desires, you're working with people, you're helping people, you're correcting problems for groups of people.'" If the story seems a bit too much like a Hollywood fable, Coelho liked it well enough to adopt it anyway. It not only imbued his biography, undistinguished until then, with a gloss of celebrity; it affixed a beneficent purpose to the next phase of his life, which many people came to view as unseemly.

Through an uncle he landed a job with his local congressman, whom he would eventually succeed, and began his steady rise up the ranks of Democratic politics. A century earlier, George Washington Plunkitt had exclaimed that his Tammany Hall political machine "does missionary work like a church." Coelho brought the same self-serving conceit to his own work raising money for the beleaguered House Democrats.

COELHO TOOK THE HELM of the DCCC in 1981 and immediately set about implementing his vision for how Democrats could recover. On one level, his diagnosis of the party's malady was unassailable. Republicans had built up a substantial money machine in the 1970s, powered by direct-mail fundraising and newly radicalized business interests that channeled money into political action committees. By the time Coelho settled in at the DCCC, the gulf between the parties was staggering. In the 1981–82 cycle, even as Reagan confronted the deepest recession since World War II, the three GOP party committees—the Republican National Committee, the National Republican Congressional Committee, and the National Republican Senatorial Committee—raised $190 million. Their Democratic counterparts managed only $28 million.

Underneath the hood, the problem looked even worse. Republicans were smarter. With brisk efficiency, they were directing their money to the candidates in the most competitive races, including challengers hoping to unseat incumbent Democrats. Democrats, by contrast, allotted money chiefly by seniority, which not only channeled resources to prominent legislators in safe seats but also steered little or nothing to challengers.

Coelho set out to change this. As a staffer and a congressman, he'd seen the fundraising problem up close and exploited it to enable his own rapid rise. Now he wanted Democrats to raise loads more money and impose a measure of rationality on how it was distributed. He had tacit approval from O'Neill and the House leadership, who knew that if Coelho failed, he would make a handy scapegoat. He didn't fail. But he ran into trouble because of the manner in which he succeeded.

By his own admission, Coelho was no innovator. Instead, he copied the Republican playbook. This entailed competing with the GOP for the rich and growing stream of money pouring into national politics from Democrats' traditional nemesis, big business. Between 1974 and 1983, the number of business PACs exploded from just over a hundred to more than two thousand, an upsurge caused partly—and inadvertently—by the federal government's response to the Watergate scandal. In 1975, an advisory opinion from the Federal Election Commission declared that corporations could solicit political contributions from employees and shareholders, so long as they were not "coercive." The FEC aimed to stamp out illegal cash bribes in the wake of Richard Nixon's downfall, but it set off a gusher of new business money— entirely legal—from corporations seeking political influence.

Cozying up to corporate interests presented no ideological conflict for Republicans, but it challenged the basic identity of the Democratic Party. Coelho, a supernal pragmatist, simply denied that any tension existed. He insisted that Democrats had always been great friends and supporters of business, citing the example of his Roosevelt-loving parents and their dairy farm. By his convenient logic, the business community's ardor for Reagan and the Republican Party was an unfortunate and misguided—but temporary—aberration in the natural order of things that he would helpfully set right by restoring the proper "balance" to the corporate world's engagement with Washington. In his more candid moments, Coelho was blunter about what he was up to: "Politics is a business and you have to have revenue."

Coelho was a consummate salesman, unburdened by propriety, with a valuable product to sell: access. He set up an outfit he called the Speaker's Club to target businessmen and their political action committees. Membership was gained by making large donations to the DCCC: $5,000 annually for individuals, $15,000 for PACs. A brochure left no question about what was being purchased. "Members of the Speaker's Club serve as trusted, informal advisors to the Democratic Members of Congress," it read. Lest anyone doubt Coelho could deliver what he was peddling, the brochure featured a self-abasing quotation from Tip O'Neill so naked in its invitation to private influence that it's hard to believe he uttered it: "I have learned to listen. Tell us what you think—at a time and place where we can really hear what you have to say."

With his Zig Ziglar dynamism and high-wattage charm, Coelho put the touch on a class of rich inside players who previously dealt almost exclusively with Republicans and hadn't realized, until he enlightened them, that the Democratic Party, too, was worthy of a sizable financial commitment.

A Texas businessman named James Devlin gave a flavor of the Coelho style. In 1981, Devlin, the chairman of U.S. Telephone Inc., traveled to Washington to lobby congressmen about phone deregulation. As he sat outside the House dining room, Coelho approached him cold and began pitching him on the Speaker's Club, promising access to O'Neill and other Democratic bigwigs. Devlin admired his brio. "Tony had these little index cards he was writing on, and before I knew it, he was saying, 'I'll just put you down for $5,000,'" Devlin recalled. "Suddenly I felt myself in the presence of a businessman."

Coelho developed the ingratiating habit of mirroring the behavior of his quarry. Devlin liked that he had "a style that's engaging to business people. Tony's a guy who makes lists, who summarizes, who gets to the point quickly and then moves on to the next item."

And when the time came, Coelho delivered. To Devlin's delight, O'Neill himself traveled to Texas for a private gathering of wealthy donors who were previously off-limits. "Picture the setting," Devlin enthused. "A palatial Dallas home, a string orchestra performing, Texas Republicans in evening clothes—plus Tip O'Neill. And he charmed them, absolutely charmed them!"

Coelho didn't rely solely on charm. He had no compunction about issuing veiled, and sometimes not so veiled, threats to the major industry groups with business before Congress. Until his arrival at the DCCC, Democrats had largely accepted that business money would, as a matter of course, flow mainly to Republicans. But Coelho bridled at such deference: money was a weapon, and so long as Democrats controlled the House, he felt entitled to a share of it. In the manner of a mafia boss running a protection racket, Coelho reminded the heads of the trade associations that Democrats controlled the key committees and could make life difficult for them. "I'd tell them, 'We control the House,'" he later recalled. "'You folks need to get along with us.'"

Coelho didn't break any thumbs, but he understood the power of instilling fear. To prove he meant business, he singled out what were then the three most important industry groups—the National Association of Home Builders, the National Association of Realtors, and the U.S. Chamber of Commerce—and forbade Democrats to attend their conferences. "Did every Democrat agree with me? No," Coelho later remembered. "But enough did that the Chamber got very concerned, because I was very open and aggressive as to what was going on and why we were doing it." The unsubtle threat was that

Democrats were willing to block the bills and provisions critical to the businesses that composed these groups, whether it was bankers who profited from federal housing subsidies or Realtors pressing to inflate the mortgage interest deduction and drive up home prices.

When Reagan won a landslide, many business executives were genuinely elated and became swept up in the idea that a new era of free-market conservatism was at hand. Coelho did everything in his power to shatter this romantic illusion by reminding them of a basic truth even the lowliest congressional staffer quickly comes to understand: whatever their personal political views, the people who run big businesses must by necessity care more about individual bills, and often obscure provisions within those bills, than any lofty notions of free enterprise or the government's proper role in the economy. Partisanship, Coelho reminded them, is a luxury few executives can truly afford if their business intersects in any meaningful way with the U.S. Congress.

His threats produced the desired effect. After a spell, the chamber's point man in Washington grew so alarmed at the damage his members stood to suffer from a Democratic boycott that he began to panic. "He would call me late at night, drunk," Coelho recalled many years later. "He would plead with me, 'Please stop this because it's hurting us.' And I loved it because I knew I was scoring."

Business money began migrating to Democrats. With organized labor already sending the overwhelming majority of its contributions to Democrats, Coelho didn't have to outcompete Republicans for corporate money (although eventually he did). He only needed to lay claim to enough of it to stop the Republicans' advance. By the time the 1982 midterm elections rolled around, Coelho had managed to steer about one-third of the money from business PACs to Democratic candidates, which had the doubly advantageous effect of helping his party protect its House majority while denying to Republicans resources they had previously considered theirs alone.

By 1982, Coelho had more than tripled the DCCC's fundraising haul. On Election Day, the Democrats won back twenty-seven seats in the House, effectively halting the Reagan incursion. Republicans wouldn't threaten the Democrats' House majority for the remainder of the decade. Coelho further expanded the Democratic margin in the years ahead, buttressed by a source of funding few in either party would have envisioned just a few years earlier.

"It never even occurred to me," Guy Vander Jagt, Coelho's counterpart at the NRCC, later confessed, "that if business formed PACs the great bulk of the money wouldn't go to Republicans."

COELHO WAS HARDLY the only Democrat convinced that the party's salvation lay in aggressively cultivating business interests. The new head of the Democratic National Committee, a rich California lawyer and bank chairman named Charles Manatt, was just as eager to court the corporate classes and established the Democratic Business Council in the mold of Coelho's Speaker's Club that offered membership—and, of course, special access—to those willing to pony up $10,000 for the privilege. Like Coelho, Manatt was part of a new breed of Democrat that would reshape the party, an arriviste in national politics who stepped into the post-Carter void to take a job few were clamoring for and who, lacking attachment to traditional Democratic interests such as organized labor, harbored none of the inhibitions about business that would have been typical for someone in his role. This new generation of party leaders viewed Democrats' historically adversarial position toward business less as a principle than as a needless limitation. So they pushed to loosen the party's philosophical moorings in a quest to burnish its diminished appeal and return Democrats to a position of competitiveness.

To rationalize the pursuit of corporate money these Democrats performed a sleight of hand, reframing the nature of the party's relationship with business from being a matter of ideology to being one of plain, practical common sense: *politics is a business and you have to have revenue.* They happily ignored the contradiction lurking at the heart of Coelho's bargain—the belief that Democrats could fund their campaigns through corporations while governing on behalf of workers, that they could simultaneously represent the interests of capital and labor. As Representative Pat Williams, a rare populist Democrat from Montana, pointedly observed, his party was trying to elide the uncomfortable choice of "being virtuous and losing, or playing the game and compromising our soul." Even skeptics like Williams were conflicted. "We have to have the dollars to be competitive, and Tony figured out how to get them," he admitted. "But if we think we can out-special-interest Republicans, we're in for a big surprise at both the bank and the ballot box. Ultimately the votes are more important than the dollars."

Williams was the rare public critic of his own party. There weren't many. If they had qualms, most Democratic lawmakers held their tongues and quickly reached consensus that strengthening the party's appeal to the corporate world was the surest path back to the kind of power Carter and the Democrats had just lost. "All of those boys went through a whole life change in the 1980 election," William Sweeney, a top DCCC official under James Corman, told the author Brooks Jackson.

Nothing underscored this transformation so much as the Democrats' response to Reagan's signature legislative initiative during his first year in office, his massive tax cut plan. So desperate were Democrats to match Reagan's popularity and advertise their new openness to free enterprise that they engaged in an unprecedented bidding war with Republicans to see who could propose the deepest cuts in business taxes—a legislative arms race they were of course destined to lose. As one writer for *The Atlantic Monthly* quipped, "The party tried to sell its soul and failed."

COELHO WAS A VIGOROUS PURSUER of anyone who he thought might contribute to Democrats. But it's the nature of the business he was in that the most attractive targets often revealed themselves to him. Generally speaking, two kinds of special interests are most eager for access to powerful politicians and willing to pay handsomely to get it: those that are growing rapidly and want to set the rules that govern them and those that are battling for market share and want to set the rules for their competitors. Wall Street financial firms were both of these things in the 1980s, and their importance grew across the decade and into the next one.

From the outset of his tenure at the DCCC, Coelho was keenly aware of finance as a growing political force. In 1980, the American Bankers Association more than doubled its donations from the previous cycle, sending most of that money to Republicans. Ever alert to opportunity, Coelho wanted a bigger piece of the action. But he knew that bankers regarded Democrats as gloomy tax-and-spend liberals inclined toward stifling regulations, an impression that, to Coelho's great annoyance, Reagan reaffirmed every chance he got. What he needed, Coelho decided, was an ambassador to Wall Street. He found one in Robert Rubin.

Rubin was then vice-chairman of Goldman Sachs and a proud Wall Street Democrat willing to use his Rolodex to help politicians. Even before he led a financial drive for the 1984 Democratic presidential nominee, Walter Mondale, that reaped $3 million—nearly 20 percent of the ticket's privately raised funds—Rubin had clout in financial circles. Coelho booked him to be the centerpiece of the DCCC's annual fundraising gala, to send the message to Wall Street that Democrats were no longer the enemy.

"The reason we asked him," Coelho later explained, "is because he represented the fact that we weren't anti–Wall Street, we weren't anti-banking. My whole perception then was that we needed to convince that element—the banking element—that we weren't against Wall Street, and we used Bob as one of the vehicles to get that done." The gambit worked well enough that Rubin became a regular speaker, further cementing his status as the Democrats' point man on Wall Street.

In the grand scheme of things, Coelho didn't regard bankers as especially important. The Big Three—Realtors, home builders, and the Chamber of Commerce—occupied most of his energy because he thought they set the tone for business generally. But Coelho was also a big believer in charging onto enemy turf to assert Democratic claims, and Wall Street counted as hostile territory. The salesman in him seemed to relish the challenge. And Rubin's endorsement had its intended effect. As he did with so many industries, Coelho succeeded in raiding the financial sector's war chest, by tapping into not only the banks and brokerage houses but also the savings and loan industry. He established the DCCC as the largest recipient of political contributions from Drexel Burnham Lambert, the notorious Beverly Hills brokerage firm run by his "good friend" and faithful contributor Michael Milken.

To Coelho, it was all of a piece: in the buccaneering world of 1980s high finance, everyone wanted something from Congress. Sometimes it didn't even involve banking. One day, his liaison to the business community, Tom Nides, passed along a juicy bit of Wall Street gossip: John Mack, a top executive at Morgan Stanley (and future CEO), was furious that his local congressman, a Republican named Joseph Dio-Guardi, wouldn't stop a postal storage facility from being built behind Mack's home. Coelho contacted Mack to propose a fix: Why not back the Democrat, Nita Lowey, who was running against DioGuardi? Mack, a Republican, agreed and enlisted enough contributors to make Lowey one of the best-funded candidates in the country, which enabled her to narrowly beat DioGuardi. "I didn't do anything for Morgan Stanley," Coelho later boasted. "Morgan Stanley did something for me."

But this was dissembling. The symbiosis of Wall Street money and Democratic candidates' needs was plain to see, even if Coelho chose not to. As the financial industry grew larger, the symbiosis deepened. Coelho was an early, propulsive force in the alliance, but it grew and spread long after he left the stage. The people closest to him went on to exert a profound influence on the Democratic Party, steering it in the direction big banks and other financial firms were pushing for. John Mack's grudge notwithstanding, the driving force wasn't bankers' personal pique but a growing desire among competing financial sectors to manipulate, and eventually dismantle, the regulatory regime that had governed Wall Street since the New Deal. That was a task, Coelho liked to remind people, that couldn't happen without Democrats.

WALL STREET'S LOBBYING push had its genesis in the economic doldrums of the late Carter years. In the 1970s, when inflation shot up, people started moving their money into mutual funds, where it might grow fast enough to keep up with rising prices, and away from banks, where the government capped interest rates well below the level of inflation. The declining profits of the big commercial banks prompted them to push Congress and the Reagan administration to unwind the Glass-Steagall Act, the New Deal law separating commercial and investment banking, in order to gain entry into the lucrative fields of securities and insurance underwriting. In the early 1980s, the chief obstacle to financial deregulation wasn't just skeptical Democrats but investment banks and insurance companies, which didn't want new competition. They argued—presciently, it turned out—that repealing Glass-Steagall would force taxpayers to fund huge bailouts if federally insured commercial banks were allowed to underwrite securities and took on too much risk. But they were hardly pro-regulation: investment banks and insurance companies both wanted to ease restrictions that prevented them from expanding into the other's line of business. All three groups donated aggressively to politicians in both parties in an effort to protect and grow their turf. What ensued was a three-way standoff that had the effect, in Congress at least, of freezing the regulatory regime in place, even as things were shifting dramatically beneath the surface.

Year after year, commercial banks renewed their push in Congress, filling campaign coffers, while insurance and securities firms buttressed their defenses, filling them more. Democrats took umbrage at any suggestion that campaign contributions colored their views. But their voting record told a different story. In 2015, two political scientists studying the history of deregulation matched congressional votes with financial industry contributions and found that partisanship effectively disappeared early in Coelho's tenure. "After 1982," they concluded, "there is no discernible difference between the two parties with regard to their effect on financial deregulation." When it came to Glass-Steagall specifically, the correlation between money and voting was even stronger: as finance contributions increased, Democrats became even more likely than Republicans to support repeal.

Yet repeal kept failing, not because Democrats had too much integrity to go forward, and not because the special interests were too weak, but in fact because they were so strong. By design, the fractured nature of the banking regime that had emerged from the New Deal—insurance companies, commercial banks, and investment banks were separately regulated and forbidden to compete with one another—prevented the harmonization of interests. So the ongoing objections of insurance and securities firms caused the fragile stasis to endure through Ronald Reagan's presidency, through George H. W. Bush's, and well into Bill Clinton's, even though all three presidents and congressional leaders in both parties were convinced that blowing up Glass-Steagall was a wise thing to do. With the financial sector divided against itself, Congress simply wouldn't act. As the Republican majority whip, Tom DeLay of Texas, remarked, with Coelho-like candor, in 1995, "We are not interested in a bill this year if it is this controversial and we have to pick between our friends."

The cracks in the foundation of the New Deal order that broke the stasis and finally led Congress to act came via the Federal Reserve and the Supreme Court. In 1987, the Fed, over the objection of its chairman, Paul Volcker, granted a petition from Citicorp, J. P. Morgan, and Bankers Trust allowing them to engage (through subsidiaries) in certain investment banking activity, such as underwriting mortgage-backed securities, so long as it didn't constitute more than 5 percent of their gross income. The Supreme Court upheld the Fed's decision. In 1989, the Fed upped the limit to 10 percent, and then, in 1996, to 25 percent. Investment banks, wary of this growing incursion, pushed to be allowed to merge with commercial banks. Another Supreme Court ruling let commercial banks enter the insurance business. So anxious insurance companies, seeing the writing on the wall, decided that *they'd* like to be allowed to merge with commercial banks, as a defensive maneuver. At this point, all sectors were in alignment and the dismantling of the remaining major banking restrictions could proceed. Amid great fanfare and mutual acclamation, with the confident imprimaturs of everyone from Alan Greenspan to Robert Rubin to presidents from both parties, an overwhelming bipartisan majority in Congress—90–10 in the Senate, 362–57 in the House—passed the Financial Services Modernization Act repealing Glass-Steagall, and on November 12, 1999, Bill Clinton signed it into law.

There were dissenting voices, mostly Democrats. Senator Paul Wellstone of Minnesota said Congress "seemed determined to unlearn the lessons from our past mistakes." Senator Byron Dorgan of North Dakota predicted, "We will look back in 10 years' time and say we should not have done this, but we did because we forgot the lessons of the past, and that that which is true in the 1930s is true in 2010." (His prediction was off by only a year.) Bernie Sanders was one of fifty-seven votes in the House against repeal and presciently warned of "taxpayer exposure to potential losses should a financial conglomerate fail." Warren, then at Harvard Law School, was deeply immersed in the bankruptcy fight and didn't publicly weigh in on repeal, although her opposition can be assumed. Ocasio-Cortez was ten years old and had other interests. But that same year, Representative Joe Crowley, the Queens Democrat whom she would one day dethrone, was sworn into Congress for the first time and voted yes on repeal.

But these dissenters were outliers. Most of the reactions betrayed no trace of doubt that doing away with landmark banking laws could have anything but a salutary effect on America. At a time when Republicans and Democrats were growing steadily more polarized on nearly every issue—when partisan acrimony had just led to Clinton's impeachment—it was striking that both parties managed to find accord on financial deregulation while adopting, essentially wholesale, the outlook, the policy priorities, and even the language of the banking industry. As the Democratic senator Bob Kerrey of Nebraska declared in a regrettable fit of post-bill-signing euphoria, "The concerns that we will have a meltdown like 1929 are dramatically overblown."

BY THAT TIME, Coelho was long gone from Congress. He'd become a casualty of the Washington money culture he'd done so much to pioneer—done in, particularly, by his close ties to some of the financiers he'd cultivated and the promiscuity of his fundraising techniques.

In the 1984 elections, Democrats held on to their House majority, even as Walter Mondale was trounced by Ronald Reagan, thanks in no small part to Coelho's success raising money. That year, remarkably, business PACs showered more money on congressional Democrats than on Republicans.

Two years later, in 1986, Democrats expanded their majority, and Coelho finally gained a measure of the power and recognition he craved. His colleagues elevated him to majority whip, the third-ranking position in House leadership. This placed him on the path laid down by Democratic titans such as Lyndon Johnson and Tip O'Neill, who had both used the DCCC to vault themselves into leadership positions— in O'Neill's case, to majority whip and ultimately to House Speaker. The brass ring was closer than ever. In the triumphant afterglow of the election, Coelho appeared to feel that he was invincible. Speaking to a Realtors conference a few days after the election, he declared, "Special interest is not a nasty word."

Coelho was a gifted reader of donor psyches, but his contention could not have been more sharply at odds with the views of the American public. People were growing fed up with Congress and its unremitting parade of scandals. Before long, Coelho's aggressive tactics and his penchant for seeking favors for his biggest contributors caught up with him.

In the span of just a few months, Coelho was caught using, free of charge, the private Lear jet and 112-foot yacht of a corrupt savings and loan operator (soon to be imprisoned for fraud) to host lavish fundraisers; borrowing money from another wealthy thrift proprietor to fund a sweetheart deal on a $100,000 junk bond without disclosing it to the IRS; and boasting to the *Los Angeles Times* about his exploding personal wealth: "I'm earning more money than I ever dreamed of making."

What made this petty grifting so politically poisonous was that it came to light just as the high-flying savings and loan industry was collapsing. People who ordinarily didn't pay any attention to banking laws were learning about the unseemly private world of Washington favor trading, what people today call "the swamp." Over the years, Coelho and his colleagues facilitated a raft of bipartisan rules changes that unwound the restraints on financial institutions—the sorts of changes nobody who isn't directly involved even notices. Now everybody found out and got angry. As the thrifts began failing, the same owners Coelho cultivated and championed sought help from Congress. The losses the industry generated required federal bailouts that would eventually cost taxpayers $131 billion.

The stories of excess jumped off the page, populated with cartoon villains enjoying hedonistic lifestyles filled with Lear jets and Cadillacs, parties and prostitutes, all of it seemingly perpetuated through private payoffs and sweetheart deals that enriched members of Congress like Coelho. It gave the impression that the seedy exchange of money for political favors was the driving factor behind the legislative and regulatory changes that fueled the rise and fall of the savings and loan industry.

But there was more to the story. Democrats were also primed to accede to the financial industry's demands because the suspicion of bankers and the hostility toward organized capital that distinguished liberalism in the decades following the New Deal had all but disappeared by then. During the 1960s and early 1970s, a time devoid of major financial crises, domestic liberalism turned its focus to the environment, race, and gender. By the 1980s, you could be a liberal in good standing without holding a particularly liberal position on economics. As the journalist Robert Kuttner lamented of the party's new donors, "Their liberalism tends to take the form of everything *but* economic populism." And these wealthy contributors not only weren't populists; many were financiers and ardent believers that Democrats should move rightward on matters of economics and financial regulation. Absent a strong labor movement, the countervailing force in mid-century, there wasn't much resistance.

While the Democratic Party had always had rich supporters, including financiers, their politics had fit comfortably with the party's prevailing, labor-focused ethos. In a wonderfully titled 1972 book, *Fat Cats and Democrats: The Role of the Big Rich in the Party of the Common Man*, the political scientist G. William Domhoff noted that these donors typically were outsiders: Jewish or Catholic, rather than white Anglo-Saxon Protestant; self-made entrepreneurs, rather than manor-born inheritors of great wealth; wildcatters and real estate developers rather than the Fortune 500 elite. Or as Domhoff dubbed them, "Jews, cowboys and maverick patricians." Many traced their roots to the Great Depression, with those difficult years seared into their memory and their political identity fixed in a way that material wealth obtained later in life didn't alter. They were driven by left-wing politics, outsider status, or a sense of noblesse oblige, rather than any desire to advance the self-interest of the wealthy or business classes.

But the rich businessmen Coelho and other Democrats recruited into the party in the 1980s had an entirely different disposition and set of motivations. Many were quite eager indeed to shape the party's ideological cast in a hands-on way that aligned with the interests of capital. Rather than being treated as interlopers, they were welcomed for their sagacity and wisdom. People like Rubin were being asked to get involved in Democratic politics not just as fundraisers or ambassadors but as technicians and policymakers who could guide and enlighten the party on Wall Street's viewpoint.

Coelho was instrumental in building this new culture because he thought it would produce the financial resources Democrats needed to compete with Republicans. He didn't concern himself with appearances or with the possibility that embracing Wall Street's elite could have malign effects on the party. Instead, he claimed this outreach had a higher purpose: party building. Tapping corporate coffers would supply the money to enable Democrats to build the kind of small-dollar, direct-mail fundraising base that the Republican Party had perfected by the early 1980s, when personalized appeals preying on people's fears and resentments generated about 85 percent of GOP funding. Just as Coelho successfully mimicked the Republicans' cultivation of business PACs, so, too, did he hope to emulate their direct-mail fundraising juggernaut to power the Democratic Party cycle after cycle and free it from having to rely so heavily on rich people, organized labor, and even the business interests he himself was aggressively cultivating. "People don't realize what the hell was going on there," Coelho complained many years later, "but I knew what I had to do, and I knew that small donors were critical for our future."

Whether he truly believed it or just said so out of expediency, Coelho presented his pursuit of business money as an unfortunate, but temporary, necessity to buy time for Democrats and stay competitive while he built up a small-donor machine that he believed would eventually become the bedrock of the party. But this required lots of money that had to come from somewhere. "The Speaker's Club and all that gave me the ready cash, because direct mail took time," Coelho said. "And in the meantime I had to build the fucking house, right? And so basically that was the vehicle to get me to where I really wanted to be and create that new party."

History remembers Coelho primarily for the flagrancy of his methods and the Shakespearean nature of his downfall, which became emblematic of a period of tawdry Democratic excess in the mid-1980s. But his diagnosis of the party's vulnerability and his conviction that Democrats needed to cultivate small donors in order to compete with Republicans in the decades ahead was prescient. After Coelho left Washington in disgrace, Democrats across the ideological spectrum continued searching for new methods to build out the party and fund electoral campaigns in a way that wouldn't depend on the whims of particular industries or rich donors. It would take thirty years and the rise of internet fundraising platforms like ActBlue, which has generated billions of dollars from small donors for Democratic campaigns, for that vision to be fulfilled. But ultimately, it was fulfilled. Today, the roles have reversed and Republicans regard the Democrats' small-dollar money machine with envy. It's a particular irony that the great beneficiaries of the new technology piping hundreds of millions of dollars into Democratic campaigns tend to be those politicians who are most explicitly anti–Wall Street—people such as Elizabeth Warren, Bernie Sanders, and Alexandria Ocasio-Cortez.

In different circumstances, Coelho might have survived his procession of scandals. But an even bigger maelstrom was consuming the House. In 1988, the House Ethics Committee opened an investigation into the new Speaker, Jim Wright, and found that he'd received more than $145,000 in improper gifts, including the use of a Cadillac and a luxury condominium, from yet another shady Texas savings and loan operator seeking to fend off federal regulators.

Wright's metastasizing ethics scandal briefly looked to Coelho as if it might provide an opportunity for advancement. It was clear Wright wouldn't survive and Majority Leader Tom Foley of Washington was going to replace him as Speaker, opening up the number two spot in House leadership. But in the end, the fallout from his junk bond deal proved too much. When the Justice Department opened a preliminary criminal inquiry into the purchase, Coelho announced he would leave Congress in the middle of his term. "I want to give my party a chance to move on," he told *The New York Times*.

Coelho resigned from Congress on his forty-seventh birthday, just as he was entering the prime of his career. He didn't stick around Washington for long. Instead, he moved to New York City, summoned all of his drive and personal charm, and soon achieved great wealth and success—this time, as a Wall Street investment banker.

COELHO WAS AN INSTRUMENTALIST, not an ideologue. His pursuit of business money was tactical: it didn't derive from a staunchly held view about the primacy of laissez-faire capitalism or a missionary zeal to deregulate Wall Street. In fact, his voting record put him squarely among House liberals, and he spoke up for entitlement programs Republicans tried to cut because he thought it was good politics. "Once the elderly understand it means cuts in Medicare, cuts in Social Security, they're going to come home to the Democratic Party," he said in 1985. When polls showed that Republicans' biggest electoral vulnerability was the public's perception that they stood for economic unfairness, Coelho encouraged Democrats to campaign as populists. Whatever winning took, he was for.

But he set in motion changes that altered the party's ideological cast and governing agenda. His alliance with business and his cultivation of the finance sector funded Democratic campaigns, just as he'd envisioned. But the people writing the checks wanted to have a say in the party's affairs, and they got it. Robert Rubin became the most influential Democratic voice on economic policy in the 1990s and 2000s, assuming top roles in the Treasury and the White House as Bill Clinton's most important economic adviser. His broad network of protégés—who include Lawrence Summers, Timothy Geithner, Peter Orszag, and Gene Sperling—went on to shape Barack Obama's administration as well and, to a lesser degree, Joe Biden's.

At the DCCC, Coelho produced his own network of business-friendly protégés who assumed high positions in the party: Rahm Emanuel became a congressman, DCCC chairman, and Obama's White House chief of staff; Terry McAuliffe became Clinton's chief fundraiser, DNC chairman, and governor of Virginia; Tom Nides became a deputy secretary of state for Obama and U.S. ambassador to Israel for Biden. Nearly every man in both networks also worked for a time as an investment banker, with Nides rising to managing director at Morgan Stanley in between government stints.

As they arrived at the power positions of the Democratic Party, they changed what it stood for, moving away from the idea of government as direct purveyor of social-democratic goods in favor of a model that borrowed its framework from the private sector and preferred to let the market drive outcomes, relegating government to a supporting position of offering tax credits or other inducements. One influential 1992 book, *Reinventing Government*, by David Osborne and Ted Gaebler, a touchstone for Clintonites, envisioned a government that should "steer, not row." These Democrats continued to see themselves as committed to a liberal agenda, but they redefined what this constituted and how it should be achieved.

The hallmarks of the new Democratic approach reflected its Wall Street lineage: they included fiscal rectitude; scaled-back regulations; the liberalization of trade; the promotion of financial innovation (including consolidation); a disdain, even contempt, for organized labor; and a constriction of liberal ambitions. The idea was to prioritize economic growth, aggressively cut the deficit to persuade the Fed to drop interest rates, reform rather than expand social programs so taxpayers would believe they were a good value, and hope that an economic boom ensued, which would, at some unspecified point in the future, create new possibilities for progressive policy.

This shift is inscribed in the party platform. Beginning in Franklin Delano Roosevelt's presidency, the phrase "full employment" appeared in every Democratic platform, but it vanished in 1992 and didn't reappear until 2016. Opposition to the concentration of big business disappeared at the same time, and it didn't return until 2016 either. On the subject of financial deregulation, the ideological convergence between Democrats and Republicans was especially overt. The 1984 GOP platform said, "Republicans commit themselves to breaking down artificial barriers to entry created by antiquated regulations [to] encourage rather than hinder innovative competition in . . . financial services." That same year, by contrast, Democrats pledged to "pursue cooperation backed by trade, tax and financial regulations that will serve the long-term growth of the American economy." Four years later, they remained committed to "reversing the trend of financial concentration and deregulation." But in 1992, Democrats eliminated that language and replaced it with a ringing declaration: "We believe in free enterprise and the power of market forces."

Looking backward from the aftermath of the 2008 financial crisis, this shift feels jarring and even prophetic. But it didn't feel that way at the time. It fit easily within the broader currents of American society, where traditional hostility toward business was melting away. Between the early 1970s and the early 1980s, the number of college students receiving bachelor's degrees in English fell by almost 50 percent, while the number graduating with degrees in business nearly doubled. MBA degrees doubled over the same period. Corporate CEOs emerged as newly significant figures in popular culture, cast not as cold, hard malefactors of wealth like the Rockefellers and Morgans of an earlier generation but as heroic capitalist icons with important "leadership lessons" to impart to the masses. The bestselling nonfiction book of both 1984 and 1985 was the autobiography of Chrysler's CEO, Lee Iacocca, whose revival of the troubled automaker (with help from a federal bailout) won him global celebrity and mention as a possible future president. Even jeremiads like Oliver Stone's film *Wall Street* (1987) and exposés like Michael Lewis's bestselling memoir *Liar's Poker* (1989) lent an unintended sheen of glamour and excitement to the practitioners of hyperaggressive finance, which helped to recast American political iconography and smooth the path of policy changes in Washington.

It wasn't just money that led Democrats to embrace Wall Street. The financial, cultural, and political indicators were all pointing in the same direction: toward embracing the wisdom of the market. The intellectual consensus for removing financial strictures was so broad that the Brookings Institution and the American Enterprise Institute, respectively the premier think tanks of the left and the right, were compatible enough in outlook to establish a Joint Center for Regulatory Studies in 1998. (It quietly shut down in 2008, amid the global economic collapse.) The few politicians, economists, and journalists who voiced objections were generally ignored. The parameters of respectable debate narrowed to the point that criticizing Wall Street came to be considered unsophisticated.

To understand why Democratic politicians were so blind to the interests of their own constituents in the financial crisis, it helps to step back and consider whom they were listening to and what pressures they were feeling before and after it struck. For the better part of a generation, the leaders of Wall Street financial firms had held outsized influence in policy circles, often cycling in and out of government, as Rubin did, to implement their ideas. They inhabited an insular, close-knit world of almost unimaginable wealth and privilege, one where women, African Americans, and other minorities were practically non-existent as professional peers. Yet here they were, an elect group of mostly older white men, enormously powerful and supremely sure of themselves, steering a party whose voters were quickly becoming more female, Black, and brown.

Democratic lawmakers weren't ignorant about who was electing them, nor did they dismiss their constituents' needs. Instead, they opted to meet those needs in ways that were encouraged by the financial industry, which promised solutions to the knotty problems politicians wrestle with, such as how to make accessible the housing, education, medical care, and so on that ordinary people need to get through life. The answer was to loosen the rules and allow those firms to extend consumer credit to pay for them. It was easy to say yes to finance. Deregulation had few natural enemies. It avoided what political scientists call "coalitional conflict"; it didn't usually upset any vital Democratic groups, or at least none powerful enough to stop it, especially with labor in decline.

The Wall Street approach also seemed to work . . . until it didn't. With no handbook for dealing with the collapse of an economy built on easy credit, Democratic lawmakers turned to the bankers for help and produced a recovery that helped the bankers. When that proved insufficient, when millions of people who'd lost jobs, homes, and a basic sense of security were left to fend for themselves while the financial class was thrown a lifeline, it created an inevitable backlash that finally fractured the elite consensus and opened up new political possibilities. A rising generation of politicians who had had no voice in the old world would emerge in the new one to try to advance them. Elizabeth Warren was the first person to step forward and do so.

7

THE ADVANCING ARMY

Warren had no intention of becoming a politician, at least not at first. What she wanted to do was lead the new consumer protection agency she'd first proposed in a journal article in 2007. Her idea picked up steam in the wake of the financial collapse. When markets finally stabilized and Washington turned to the business of writing new rules, most Democrats thought that making an overt display of protecting consumers from financial predation would be a good idea. As the backlash from angry voters intensified, Warren's proposal became a fait accompli, certain to be included in financial reform legislation.

It made all the sense in the world that Warren would be chosen to lead the new agency. She was a skilled communicator, impeccably qualified. The agency had been her idea! But she was now a celebrity who engendered fierce opposition—not just on Wall Street and among

Republicans, but also among members of Obama's Wall Street–friendly inner circle, who chafed at the notion of an outspoken critic coming in house. Warren wasn't shy, either, about declaring her desire for the job, violating the Beltway custom that candidates for powerful positions behave as silent penitents grateful simply to be considered. Her public interest brought pressure on Obama to nominate her or else anger her growing legions of liberal supporters, which only deepened the resentments of her enemies in the administration.

Obama chose a characteristically cautious middle path. In September 2010, two months after the Dodd-Frank Wall Street Reform and Consumer Protection Act was signed into law summoning the consumer protection bureau into being, he appointed Warren to a temporary position in the Treasury overseeing its establishment. She'd get the agency off the ground, organize its management structure, and hire its staff of five hundred. But he didn't nominate her for the permanent job.

Already, though, a clock was ticking. The law stipulated that the new agency, the Consumer Financial Protection Bureau, would formally assume its regulatory powers the following July. *Somebody* would have to wield them. Warren's interim status raised an obvious question: Whom would Obama choose as the permanent director? It also imbued the decision with ideological significance because it became a proxy battle between finance-friendly centrists and the rising populist left gathering behind Warren, everyone from Jon Stewart and MSNBC personalities to organized labor and progressive Democrats in Congress.

In the Rose Garden ceremony where he introduced her, Obama was flanked by two people, Warren and Tim Geithner, who both stiffly pantomimed a show of team-first mutual collaboration. It was well known in Washington that Geithner vehemently opposed Warren and was instead pushing Michael Barr, an assistant Treasury secretary, as his preferred candidate for CFPB director. But even a temporary appointment provided Warren with a new platform, and she spent much of the next year on a media tour proselytizing for the new agency and, implicitly, for the idea that she should run it.

Warren had her champions. Barney Frank, the Massachusetts Democrat who chaired the House Financial Services Committee and co-authored the financial reform law, pushed hard for her. So did the AFL-CIO, which represented twelve million union members. Editorial boards, consumer groups, the chieftains of the emerging liberal blogosphere, and several hundred thousand petition signers backed her, too, along with eighty-nine House Democrats who sent Obama a public letter urging him to keep her in the role.

Events conspired to make sidelining Warren more difficult than Obama might have wished. In a stunning upset, the Massachusetts Republican Scott Brown won a special Senate election in January 2010 to replace Ted Kennedy, who had died of brain cancer. Brown's victory in a deep blue state instantly derailed Obama's legislative agenda by robbing Democrats of the sixtieth senator necessary to override a filibuster. The upset was widely seen as an expression of anger at the White House for its handling of the economy and its deference toward the big banks. Exit polls showed that voters thought Democrats were too close to Wall Street. This populist tempest jarred members of Obama's inner circle, including Geithner, who had convinced themselves that the public shared their own high opinion of their performance, and now saw clearly that it did not.

The day after Brown's victory, Warren got her first invitation to a high-level private meeting at the White House. It came from Obama's chief strategist, David Axelrod, who lived in the same Washington apartment building as she did. As someone whose job it was to discern political currents, Axelrod was more attuned than his colleagues to the brewing backlash and to the benefit of making inroads with Warren. "After that," a Warren staffer recalled, "we started getting a lot more access."

Axelrod, too, came around to the idea that Warren should lead the CFPB. He understood the power of a populist appeal. With an eye toward the future, he would spend the next two years carefully repositioning Obama as someone who sounded less like Tim Geithner and more like Elizabeth Warren—a makeover that, however insincere it struck true believers, paid off handsomely when Obama wound up squaring off against a rich private equity baron, Mitt Romney, in the 2012 presidential election.

The struggle for the CFPB job carried on across the next year. Some of it played out publicly, thanks to Warren's outspokenness and the noisy activism of the netroots pushing her candidacy. A MoveOn .org petition urging Obama to appoint her garnered hundreds of thousands of signatures, while the progressive blog *Daily Kos* launched a social media campaign. But much of the lobbying took place behind the scenes in factional battles between Democrats and their allied interest groups. Warren tried to influence Obama through these channels, too, sending a message through Axelrod that running the CFPB would be preferable to continuing to torment Geithner as head of the TARP oversight panel. Obama felt squeezed. "Tell her to keep her mouth shut," he messaged back. "She may well be the choice but we can't surface that now."

But when the time came, Obama didn't have the nerve. Even though the national mood was shifting toward Warren's brand of popular discontent, there was a radical disjunction emerging between the outside politics and the inside politics. Opposition to Warren in the financial industry and among its allies in Washington didn't subside. Obama feared running afoul of them. Without anyone saying so directly, Warren came to understand over the summer of 2011 that she wouldn't be getting the job. Obama, ever the pragmatic conciliator, instead gave it to Richard Cordray, a crusading former attorney general of Ohio whom Warren had personally recruited to the CFPB.

WARREN WAS A FAKE POLITICAL candidate before she was a real one. Brown's Senate victory meant Democrats couldn't pass financial legislation alone. Yet almost every Republican publicly vowed to oppose it. Brown was a conspicuous exception, however, because he represented a Democratic state and knew he'd have to run again in 2012 for a full term, during a presidential election. Warren knew it, too.

As early as 2009, a few liberal bloggers had floated the idea of Warren as a Senate candidate. In 2010, the *Boston Globe* opinion page echoed the thought. Warren was initially cool to the idea. At a conference that spring, she told the journalist David Corn that she would rather "stab myself in the eye" than run for Senate. On the other hand, the mere threat of a challenge to Brown would draw enormous attention and pressure him to break with Senate Republicans in order to maintain his viability in Massachusetts. So Warren made herself available to political reporters and pretended to consider a run, even as she privately dismissed the idea and kept angling for the CFPB job. That summer, Brown was one of just three Republican senators to support the Dodd-Frank banking reform. It wouldn't have become law if he'd objected to it.

In July 2011, Obama nominated Cordray, finally slamming the door on Warren's hope of sticking at the CFPB. The Senate suddenly looked more appealing. It was a powerful platform. Massachusetts Democrats were desperate to find a strong challenger to Brown. Warren had a national profile and looked likely to be able to turn her rapturous following into an army of small donors (the likes of which Tony Coelho had dreamed of three decades earlier). It was also clear that she relished the spotlight and had no desire to relinquish her political power by giving it up and returning to Harvard.

The White House, eager to rid itself of a perennial headache, was also on board, which would clear the Democratic primary field of serious challengers and cinch the nomination for Warren. Barney Frank had laid the groundwork some months earlier during a visit with Obama. "I told him that he really ought to appoint Elizabeth to run the consumer agency," Frank recalled. "I said, either she'll get through the Senate and do a great job or the Republicans will stop her, make a hero out of her, and then she can go back to Massachusetts and run for the Senate. And Obama said to me, 'Do you think she really wants to run for the Senate?' And I said, 'Mr. President, I think she might want to run for your job, but she has to start somewhere.'"

Warren entered the race in the fall of 2011. Overnight, it became the marquee Senate contest of the cycle, Democrats' best hope of reclaiming a seat. But it also represented something bigger: it was the first real electoral test of left populism in the aftermath of the financial crisis. And although this was not yet clear, the race was an early example of how the struggle between Republicans and Democrats was increasingly over whether elections would revolve around cultural resentments or class-conscious kitchen-table economics—a struggle that prefigured the central fight in national politics in the decade to come.

Brown's shtick was to present himself as a plainspoken regular guy who crisscrossed the state in a red pickup truck and didn't talk down to people or put on airs. He needled Warren by portraying her as a judgy cosmopolitan Harvard liberal whom he insisted on referring to as "Professor Warren." Brown's campaign centered the issue of Warren's disputed ethnic identity, specifically her past claim of Native American ancestry, which she couldn't prove and thus fueled Brown's charge that she was a phony who had cheated her way into her Harvard position.

Warren had every awareness of the opportunity that the race presented to her, beyond just the chance to land a Senate seat. She wasn't just challenging a Republican; she was trying to prove that a populist message could compete with the neoliberal worldview that continued to dominate the Democratic Party, even after the financial collapse. Against the backdrop of the sluggish economy and Obama's eagerness to strike a deficit-cutting "grand bargain" with Republicans, Warren's insistence that the economy should benefit working people, and her scalding critique of what was wrong with the American economy and who was to blame for it, packed an extra punch. She, too, struck notes that Trump would later co-opt.

"The system is rigged," Warren told the audience at the Democratic National Convention in Charlotte, in the fall of 2012. "Look around. Oil companies guzzle down billions in profits. Billionaires pay lower tax rates than their secretaries. And Wall Street CEOs—the same ones who wrecked our economy and destroyed millions of jobs—still strut around Congress, no shame, demanding favors, and acting like we should thank them." Warren lacked Trump's branding genius in dubbing this self-dealing system "the Swamp." But her description of it resonated all the same. It persuaded a critical segment of the contested working-class voters that Brown had won in 2010—and that Trump would carry in 2016—to return to the Democratic fold and support her candidacy.

In November, Warren defeated Brown 54 percent to 46 percent, a bright spot in an election that yielded mixed results for Democrats.

Obama secured a second term, but Democrats failed to win back the House. Still, Warren's victory hinted at a brighter path ahead if Democrats were to embrace her confrontational brand of populism. A source of great angst inside the party after Brown won Kennedy's Senate seat was that he managed to carry a majority of union households, traditionally a pillar of Democratic strength. Two years later, private polling by the AFL-CIO in Massachusetts found that Warren lured many of them back, winning 61 percent of union households. They responded particularly to the focus of her message: the AFL-CIO found that union voters had an even higher level of antipathy toward Wall Street than the general public.

IT WAS POSSIBLE at that moment to suppose that a broad populist shift in the Democratic Party might be under way. For his reelection campaign, Obama jettisoned the lofty postpartisan platitudes that carried him to the White House and took up many of Warren's favored themes, recasting himself as a warrior for the middle class who would fight the same entrenched Wall Street interests he had rescued from oblivion not long before. In a well-orchestrated bit of political stagecraft, Obama gave a big address in December 2011 in Osawatomie, Kansas, the site of Theodore Roosevelt's famous "New Nationalism" speech in 1910. Roosevelt had attacked Gilded Age excess while vowing to destroy "special privilege" and restore fairness to the American economy. A century later, Obama's speech intended to frame the upcoming election along similar lines and cast the president in the heroic "Roosevelt" role. His rhetoric distilled Warrenism to its essence, even as Obama, characteristically, invoked the Republican Roosevelt as his inspiration.

"For most Americans, the basic bargain that made this country great has eroded," Obama declared. "Long before the recession hit, hard work stopped paying off for too many people. Fewer and fewer of the folks who contributed to the success of our economy actually benefited from that success. Those at the very top grew wealthier from their incomes and their investments—wealthier than ever before. But everybody else struggled with costs that were growing and paychecks that weren't—and too many families found themselves racking up more and more debt just to keep up. Now, for many years, credit cards and home equity loans papered over this harsh reality. But in 2008, the house of cards collapsed." Summoning moral outrage, he listed the malefactors and condemned their behavior: "Mortgages sold to people who couldn't afford them, or even sometimes understand them. Banks and investors allowed to keep packaging the risk and selling it off. Huge bets—and huge bonuses—made with other people's money on the line. Regulators who were supposed to warn us about the dangers of all this, but looked the other way or didn't have the authority to look at all. It was wrong." Now, Obama insisted, the rescue of the middle class from such economic treachery was "the defining issue of our time."

Obama's populist makeover was hardly an accident, and it certainly didn't owe to Warren's example alone. His efforts to heal the partisan divide and usher in a postideological era had failed utterly. A year into his term, Gallup found that Obama was the most polarizing first-year president in U.S. history; the gap between Democratic approval of him and Republican disapproval was larger than anyone before him. To his considerable good fortune, however, it was becoming clear that his opponent was going to be Mitt Romney, a modern-day robber baron whom Axelrod privately considered "the perfect foil." Texas's governor, Rick Perry, one of Romney's Republican rivals for the nomination, plunged in the first dagger, indelibly branding the former

Bain Capital CEO a "vulture capitalist." Then, a month after Obama's Osawatomie speech, a super PAC affiliated with Newt Gingrich, another Republican rival, produced a twenty-eight-minute film called *When Mitt Romney Came to Town* that featured a procession of laid-off workers and painted Romney as a rapacious job killer "more ruthless than Wall Street." Steve Bannon, who would one day run Donald Trump's presidential campaign but at the time was an investment banker active in Tea Party circles, got hold of the film and leaked it to Bloomberg News. For the only time in the primary season, Romney appeared truly damaged. Ten days later, on January 21, Gingrich unexpectedly won the primary in South Carolina, where the textile industry had been gutted by private equity companies. "You could see the beginnings of a populist wave," Bannon later recalled. But Gingrich was ambivalent about the line of attack. Rush Limbaugh and other conservative bigwigs criticized him and leaped to the defense of laissez-faire capitalism. Gingrich wavered. Ten days later Romney beat him in Florida and sailed on to the nomination. Bannon considered it an opportunity squandered: "The people responded, but the politicians didn't." He set off to find one who would.

The lesson wasn't lost on Axelrod. As soon as Romney secured the Republican nomination, Obama's campaign picked up the populist attack. The opening salvo was a brutal ad that depicted Romney as having heartlessly bankrupted a Kansas City steel company in his lust for profits. Thematically, it was a carbon copy of the Gingrich film. A laid-off worker in the ad calls Romney a "vampire." To reporters, Obama's political advisers ceaselessly emphasized the "values" Romney supposedly demonstrated in his business career, implying something untoward or even unethical in his character for having chosen this line of work. The goal was, of course, to redirect the focus of the presidential election away from the slow recovery—the unemployment rate remained above 8 percent all summer—and onto the specific record of his opponent. Yet this required no Machiavellian scheming from Axelrod or any other Democrat because, oddly enough, Romney wanted the same thing.

It was inevitable that Romney's career at Bain Capital—and thus the excesses of the financial industry—would feature prominently in the race because *both* candidates believed that they needed to exploit it in order to win. Romney was eager to de-emphasize his liberal term as Massachusetts governor, so he felt he needed to convince voters that his private equity background imbued him with special skills to fix the weak economy. Obama, presiding over that economy, needed to convince them of just the opposite—that Romney's business skill didn't apply to the presidency. His reelection hinged on discrediting Romney as a viable alternative, which meant going after Bain and the financial industry.

On May 21, a few days after the debut of his "vampire" ad, Obama left a NATO summit in Chicago to address reporters on what he insisted, a touch defensively, was the vital issue of the day—not some weighty geopolitical matter, but Romney's business career. "This is not a distraction," Obama said. "This is what this campaign is going to be about." And so it was. Romney himself bore no small responsibility for the race and its outcome. He invited scrutiny by intentionally mischaracterizing his work at Bain as having been geared in some meaningful way toward "job creation"—he implausibly claimed to have created 100,000—rather than shrewdly maximizing profits for his investors, as was really the case.

But Obama engaged in certain deceptions of his own—a smaller one, about Romney and the menace of private equity, and a larger one, about his willingness to fulfill the Teddy Roosevelt role in a second term. During the campaign, liberals fluent in financial policy mostly kept quiet as Obama heaped the sins of Wall Street on Romney's shoulders. It was good politics. But sometimes the hypocrisy chafed: Obama surrounded himself with Wall Street veterans, gave no prior indication of being troubled by private equity, and made no attempt to change the industry. It didn't factor in the Dodd-Frank banking reforms or pose enough of a threat to worry financial reformers. "It's a predatory business model which is unappealing and undesirable," said Dennis Kelleher, president of Better Markets, a nonprofit that promotes the public interest in financial matters. "But it doesn't pose a systemic threat, and there's no risk of bailouts arising from its activities, so taxpayers are not at risk from it."

The larger deception concerned Obama himself. It was the kind that first-rate politicians routinely deploy—the kind that draws admiring nods from hard-bitten political pros and other cynics, but would strike an ordinary person as classic Washington phoniness. Anyone following the campaign in the newspapers or on television would have settled on an image of the two candidates long before Election Day. Romney, with his patrician mien and expensive homes, was the candidate of Wall Street, the big banks, the financial overclass. He could never outrun Mike Huckabee's deadly quip that he "looks like the guy who fired you." Obama might not have been the savior he was once cracked up to be. Things weren't going great. But as the guy calling out Romney every day, condemning the greed and selfishness of bankers and financiers, and standing up for the little guy, he registered as someone fixing to do something about it if given another term. This broad impression of the candidates was testimony to the effectiveness of Obama's campaign and to the potency of a well-targeted populist message. But it was fundamentally misleading. It didn't reflect Obama's benign view of the financial industry or herald a leftward policy shift or diminish Wall Street's influence on the

Democratic Party one iota. Like their liberal counterparts, Wall Street Democrats mostly kept silent during Obama's attacks because they knew, some of them personally and directly, that these posed very little risk to their livelihoods or even their chance to serve in government. On the same day that his vampire ad rolled out, Obama attended a fundraiser in New York City hosted by a prominent private equity executive.

WHEN A POLITICIAN RUNS as one thing and governs as another, it creates the conditions for unhappiness and frustration. Obama wasn't unusual in campaigning as an economic populist in 2012; by then it was an established tradition among Democratic presidential candidates. Even John Kerry, a rich, prep-schooled windsurfer who ate pizza with a knife and fork, took to the trail to inveigh against "millionaires" and "the overprivileged."

Populist masquerading tended not to cause a big stir after the election, in Kerry's case because he lost, but more generally because there was no populist wing of the party to hold a president to account for his campaign promises and press the cause. Warren's arrival in the Senate changed this.

Outwardly, the Democrats appeared to be singing from the same hymnal. Obama's victory over Romney felt like a referendum on a whole class of moneyed, well-connected financial-insider types in politics. It fit comfortably within a national mood still rife with fury at bankers and their Washington enablers, from Occupy Wall Street on the left to the Tea Party on the right, although the conviction was particularly strong among Democrats. The Pew Research Center found that 91 percent of Democrats thought rich people and large corporations held too much power; 60 percent believed Wall Street did more harm than good. Obama's serene assurances that the "fever" of Republican obstruction would break if he won the election, and the GOP's own existential angst over having lost it—the RNC commissioned an "autopsy" to determine what had gone wrong and how the party could rebuild itself—created the expectation that the great ideological struggle postelection would take place on the political right.

Another thing also seemed to militate against an intraparty clash emerging on the left. The outspoken proponent of the new leftist ideals, Warren, was now a freshman in the Senate, a position freighted with a complicated set of norms and rituals intended to silence (and sideline) newcomers, lest they draw attention away from more senior members. In the patronizing phrase favored by institutionalists, freshmen were to be "seen, not heard." This was doubly true for Warren, because she was a woman and because she was following in the wake of an even bigger female celebrity, Hillary Clinton, who was elected to the Senate from New York in 2000. To everyone's surprise, Clinton proved to be a shrewdly effective senator who navigated the stifling, sexist culture with aplomb. She created a blueprint for leveraging fame that everybody expected Warren to follow.

Well into the twenty-first century, the Senate remained rooted in an earlier time. A vestigial notion of southern gentility, along with the advanced years and feudal powers of its senior members, fostered an atmosphere of sexism that passed itself off as "courtliness" or "fondness for the traditions of the Senate." Female staffers called the Senate "the last plantation." Clinton was deeply unwelcome. Before she arrived, Trent Lott, the Mississippi conservative who was majority leader and who favored a lipstick-and-skirt dress code enforced by monitors informally known as "bench ladies" stationed on the Senate floor, had mused, not unhopefully, that Clinton might be struck by lightning before her swearing in.

Here's how the Senate worked when Clinton arrived in 2001: If you were a freshman set on succeeding—not just on winning reelection, but on gaining a position of power within the institution—you had to submit to being continually judged by the senior members who controlled your fate. You'd summon awestruck words to describe the honor of serving in such an august body and learn to speak in its orotund courtesies ("I rise to second my distinguished colleague"). You'd plow through dull committee work uncomplainingly. At press conferences you'd speak last, patiently observing hierarchy, and nod thoughtfully while the elders bloviated before the cameras. If you were already famous like Clinton, you'd tread very, very carefully, because your presence would threaten to outshine the swollen egos that command the Senate. After a year or so, you might make a floor speech—a modest one only colleagues noticed. After several years, you could hope to assemble a bipartisan group and put your name on a bill that might clear the chamber.

Clinton wasn't anything like what her fellow senators expected her to be: She wasn't pushy or self-righteous; she didn't try to jump the line. She kept quiet and ignored the media horde trailing her through the Capitol. She sought out the Senate's senior Democrat, the operatically self-important, thin-skinned Robert Byrd of West Virginia, by then well into his dotage, and stunned him by asking to become his apprentice, nourishing his vanity with public flattery and deference as she played the role of courtier. Clinton announced that she would heed Byrd's advice to "be a workhorse, not a show horse." (Byrd had said the same thing in 1973 to another ambitious newcomer, Joe Biden—proof that, however well intentioned, advice doesn't always take.) After the 9/11 attacks, Byrd declared himself "the third senator from New York" and steered tens of billions of dollars to the ravaged city.

But Clinton's real conquest involved her old Republican enemies. One by one, she sought them out privately, charmed them with dogged outgoingness—itself a subversion of her caricature—and reversed old impressions. It was no accident that early reports of these meetings included revelatory details that cut against character type, such as her offering to pour coffee for her male seniors. As one of her (male) aides later bragged, "You don't expect the First Lady of the United States to ask if you want two lumps of sugar." Once cast as aloof and hard-edged, Clinton gradually won them over, eventually writing bills with forty-nine Republicans, including many, like Lott, who once numbered among her fiercest critics. Clinton understood what a powerful instrument fame can be and how to use it. In the early 2000s, a reputation for extreme partisanship was still a political handicap. Many of her odd-couple partnerships were rooted in symbiotic benefit: Newt Gingrich, Rick Santorum, and Lindsey Graham (who'd led her husband's impeachment) all made common cause with Clinton as a means of moderating their image. Her genius was in letting them, knowing that it enhanced her own.

In submitting to the institutional culture, Clinton was sublimating her power drive; she wasn't denying it. She showed herself to be a master of cloakroom politics who could work across the aisle, which fortified her political image to such an extent that by 2007, when she launched her presidential campaign, she was widely regarded as the "inevitable" Democratic nominee. "I guess I'm blowing myself up a little," Byrd later said of Clinton, not quite grasping his role, "but I think of her as a pupil of mine."

Clinton's shadow loomed over Warren. It's a measure of the shallowness of U.S. political coverage that when Warren arrived in the Senate as a rough simulacrum of Clinton (female, famous, smart), the collective thinking was: "She had better behave exactly the same way!"

Warren didn't. This fact shouldn't have come as a total surprise. She was more of a crusader than Clinton was, which only heightened the challenge a celebrity senator confronts: balancing one's unique platform and the potential good it can yield against the resentment outspokenness breeds among one's colleagues.

A few weeks into her term, Warren, who had landed on the Banking Committee, attended her first hearing, which happened to be about Wall Street oversight. It was a typically somnolent affair until her turn came to question regulators testifying before the committee. She devoted her allotted five minutes to the seemingly abstruse topic of banking settlements, like the $1.9 billion fine the British megabank HSBC had recently agreed to pay the Justice Department after it was caught laundering money for drug dealers. With a sharpness senators rarely direct at their own party's appointees, Warren admonished the regulators for not being more aggressive in taking big banks to trial. "If a party is unwilling to go to trial, either because they're too timid or because they lack resources," she said, "the consequence is they have a lot less leverage in all the settlements that occur." The problem was most obviously acute with big Wall Street banks. "If they can break the law and drag in billions in profits, and then turn around and settle, paying out of those profits—they don't have much incentive to follow the law." Warren was interrupted by applause from the gallery—something seldom heard at Banking Committee hearings. Then she delivered her coup de grâce in the form of a simple question for the regulators: "Can you identify when you last took [one of] the Wall Street banks to trial?"

Incredibly, none could.

"Anybody?" Warren asked, peering over her glasses.

The exchange reinforced her contention that the swollen financial sector had produced banks that were "too big to jail," even after the great cautionary example of the global financial crisis. "We have not had to do it as a practical matter to achieve our supervisory goals," Thomas J. Curry, the comptroller of the currency, offered limply.

Her showdown with regulators became another entry in the Warren canon, ricocheting across political and news websites. It plainly violated the Clinton doctrine of maintaining a low profile. So did Warren's outspokenness in private caucus meetings, where one Democratic senator noted that she made her points "more loudly than anyone else." On issues ranging from lax oversight to bankers' misdeeds to what she thought were the unconscionable profits the federal government makes from student loans, Warren's approach was to provoke a confrontation in order to draw attention to whatever topic she wanted to highlight and then apply as much pressure as she could by releasing public letters and making a big fuss in the media. As chair of the TARP oversight panel, Warren generated attention but often couldn't get the answers or testimony she sought. As a senator, however, she couldn't be ignored.

Unlike Clinton, Warren didn't make a lot of friends across the aisle. She didn't apprentice herself to any of the old lions of the Senate (Byrd died in 2010 and wouldn't have been a fan). She didn't pour coffee. Her style bred resentment in both parties, although this was usually expressed anonymously through reporters. Republicans likened her prosecutorial zeal to Joseph McCarthy's; Democrats groused that she was upstaging them and compared her with the notorious self-promoter Ted Cruz. She did not follow *The Wall Street Journal*'s suggestion to her to "keep your head down and stay out of the limelight."

Warren's apostasy from conventional wisdom had a simple logic people at the time struggled to see: the Senate had changed. In the twelve years since Clinton's arrival, U.S. politics had polarized so sharply that the incentive structure for ambitious Republicans and

Democrats turned upside down. Republicans no longer cared to cultivate a bipartisan image. Partisanship and obstruction made legislating nearly impossible. This changed the calculus for how someone like Warren could leverage her fame. The old way to influence national politics was to accumulate a record of bipartisan achievement and a reputation for probity, as Clinton had done. The new way Warren pioneered was to have big, loud, messy fights that offered moral clarity and galvanized public sentiment behind a position. Warren used this technique to win a large and vocal grassroots following that gave her an independent base of support and remarkable power for a freshman senator. She used this power to take on her own party.

THERE WAS ONE MORE important difference between Clinton and Warren guiding their behavior in the Senate. Clinton was trying to rehabilitate her reputation ahead of a presidential run. Warren was trying to wrest the Democratic Party from the centrist, finance-friendly powers that had dominated it for the better part of three decades and reorient it toward the working and middle classes. She wanted to advance a class-conscious economic populism that would displace neoliberalism.

This was an audacious, even absurd, ambition for a freshman senator to hold. At the same time, it wasn't inconceivable that voters would respond to someone with different ideas about how to organize the economy to produce a better society. By 2013, the luster had come off Obama, even as he won another term. It wasn't just that his promises of hope and change hadn't materialized and now seemed naïve. Five years after the crisis, most people weren't better off; many were worse off. Since the onset of the Great Recession, wage growth had remained stagnant for white- and blue-collar workers alike, and those with and without a college degree. In fact, real wages had fallen for the bottom 70 percent of the wage scale. Corporate profits, on the other hand, were at historic highs. And prosperity was ever more obviously accruing to those at the very top of the income scale, a distribution of wealth that echoed the early days of industrial capitalism. Historians spoke of a new Gilded Age. As they did in the late nineteenth century, economic conditions generated such anger and alienation that people took to the streets. As the 2012 presidential race unfolded, Occupy Wall Street demonstrations erupted in New York City and spread to seventy more cities, generating concepts such as "the 99 percent versus the 1 percent" that framed popular thinking about economic inequality and provided a tailwind for a politician with Warren's style and message.

Obama had managed to harness some of this energy in 2012 only because Romney was so easily caricatured as the epitome of heartless capitalist excess; the Osawatomie speech happened as the Zuccotti Park protest was in full bloom. But no one in a position of power in 2013, and certainly not Obama, was particularly invested in checking this sort of excess or reversing the growing inequality. And the anemic recovery contributed to a sense that the economic challenges of the middle class didn't weigh heavily on Obama's mind. Young people especially bore the brunt of this dislocation, and it affected their outlook. A Pew poll in December 2011 found that Americans under thirty viewed socialism more favorably than capitalism. So it made sense that people upset about this state of affairs, including people who had voted for Obama without thinking twice, now gravitated to Warren as a means of expressing their dissatisfaction and desire for a different kind of leadership. That was her attraction. T-shirts and bumper stickers declaring "I'm from the Elizabeth Warren Wing of the Democratic Party" became fashionable in activist circles.

Republicans tend to deify their leaders only after they've left the stage, but Democrats like to fall in love, fast and hard. Warren was the first love interest of the party's grassroots since Obama. She built a network of nearly half a million donors and raised $42 million for her Senate race, astounding figures for a new senator. She used this network to help the party: attaching her name to a fundraising appeal brought Democrats more money than anyone not named Obama or Clinton. But in nearly every particular she was different from Obama—strident, not serene, allergic to gauzy nostrums, willing to provoke dispute to advance a cause. Parties rarely conduct their internal soul-searching while they hold the White House, but Warren inflamed internal tensions as a way of forcing change.

One big tension was the party's relationship to Wall Street. An opportunity to relitigate it arrived early in Warren's Senate term, when Larry Summers, Warren's great ideological foe, suddenly and somewhat unexpectedly looked as if he were billeted for the most powerful economic perch in U.S. government, the chairmanship of the Federal Reserve. Summers was everything Warren loathed about Wall Street Democrats: a Rubin protégé and aggressive deregulator, unchastened by the financial crisis, who had enriched himself by working at the hedge fund D. E. Shaw between stints in government. It was an open secret in Washington that Summers had accepted an administration job slightly below his stature (running the National Economic Council) because Obama had promised him the Fed job when Ben Bernanke's term ended.

In her 2014 book, *A Fighting Chance*, Warren tells a story about Summers that's meant to reveal the unsavory way Washington power players wield their influence to benefit one another while ignoring the common good. She recounts how, just after the financial crisis, Summers invited her to dinner at a fancy Washington restaurant under the guise of imparting insider wisdom:

Late in the evening, Larry leaned back in his chair and offered me some advice. . . . I had a choice. I could be an insider or I could be an outsider. Outsiders can say whatever they want. But people on the inside don't listen to them. Insiders, however, get lots of access and a chance to push their ideas. People—powerful people—listen to what they have to say. But insiders also understand one unbreakable rule: *They don't criticize other insiders.*

I had been warned.

Warren presents the tale as a provincial's education in the sordid byways of Washington power, assuring readers she disapproves of that culture. But by 2013, she was an inside player herself, although her network of nonprofit groups, labor interests, think tanks, and allied politicians and Hill staffers occupied the opposite end of the party's ideological spectrum from Summers. Blocking his nomination to the Fed was therefore an important fight for liberal populists to wage—and win—to establish their credibility and influence.

In late July, Ezra Klein, then a journalist at *The Washington Post*, published a short piece stating, apparently based on firsthand knowledge, that Obama was preparing to announce Summers's nomination. Klein's column alarmed liberals for two reasons. Obama's desire to put a Wall Street creature like Summers at the Fed exploded the populist image he cultivated during the campaign: Summers was singularly reviled by liberals. He was so unpopular, in fact, that elite opinion had drifted toward the belief that the Fed's vice-chair, Janet Yellen, would get the job, making her the first woman Fed chair. Klein's column implied she wouldn't be.

Warren already knew this. A few days earlier, after a White House celebration of Richard Cordray's confirmation to the CFPB, Obama had pulled her into the Oval Office to pressure her to support Summers. Warren demurred. Pretty soon, people in her network got a heads-up about Obama's plans for the Fed. Damon Silvers, who served on the TARP oversight panel with Warren, notified his boss, the AFL-CIO president, Richard Trumka, who was no Summers fan. The AFL-CIO aligns itself closely with Democratic leadership, so Trumka couldn't risk putting the full, public weight of the organization behind an effort to stop Summers. Instead, he had Silvers and a liberal strategist named Jeff Hauser run a behind-the-scenes effort to head off the nomination. Digital staffers fed a steady stream of opposition research to reporters and liberal bloggers. Gloria Steinem and Heather Booth, prominent feminists, were enlisted to speak out about Summers's criticisms of women in the academy while president of Harvard University. A trio of left-leaning senators that included Sherrod Brown of Ohio and Jeff Merkley of Oregon, along with Warren, began organizing the Senate pushback.

In a sign of the growing strength of the party's left wing, a broad coalition moved against Summers almost as soon as Klein's column appeared. It represented something Obama hadn't seen before from his party: organized opposition. In the past, Warren was often the lone, or at least the most prominent, public voice opposing her party on some matter of financial or regulatory importance. (Bernie Sanders was not yet nationally known.) But she never spoke publicly against the prospect of Summers's leading the Fed because she didn't have to. A procession of liberal senators from Merkley to Brown, but also Plains-state Democrats such as Jon Tester of Montana and Heidi Heitkamp of North Dakota, went public with their opposition. This left Obama no choice but to court Republicans if he hoped to rescue the nomination. Summers was cooked. In September, he fell on his sword and withdrew from consideration, freeing Obama to nominate Yellen.

"The truth is," Bernie Sanders, another Summers critic, said afterward, "it was unlikely he would have been confirmed by the Senate." That owed partly to Summers's personal abrasiveness. But it also reflected a common orientation among a meaningful bloc of Democrats toward a politics that wouldn't privilege financial markets quite so easily as before.

Warren took every opportunity to highlight this distinction—to show how, even after the financial crisis and Obama's populist reelection campaign, a whole set of norms and behaviors favoring Wall Street continued to shape Democratic governance in ways that quietly undermined the public interest. The following year, Warren went after an Obama nominee named Antonio Weiss whom practically no one had heard of. Weiss was an impeccably credentialed investment banker at Lazard who was tapped to be Treasury's undersecretary of domestic finance and had every reason to expect a smooth confirmation. Lazard had a long lineage of senior partners who had served in top government positions (Felix Rohatyn, Steve Rattner). It wasn't a big Wall Street bank and hadn't needed a bailout. Weiss scrupulously adhered to the process by which Wall Street bankers traditionally move into high positions in Democratic administrations. He donated money to the Center for American Progress, a liberal think tank, which enabled him to burnish his policy credentials by coauthoring white papers on tax reform with such Democratic luminaries as Robert Rubin and Summers. He was a major donor and fundraising bundler for Obama.

The fact that Weiss was unremarkable was precisely why Warren singled him out. She wanted to highlight the values the entire class of bankers-in-good-standing brought into government in order to discredit them and begin rolling back the financialization of her party. She trained her criticism on Lazard's work facilitating international "tax inversions," the practice of U.S. corporations buying foreign companies and then moving their headquarters overseas to escape U.S. taxes, which hollows out the domestic tax base while generating rich fees for Wall Street firms like Lazard. Weiss had recently worked on one of the biggest inversions, helping Burger King slash its tax bill by acquiring the Canadian company Tim Hortons and inverting itself to Canadian ownership. "Enough is enough," Warren wrote in an op-ed explaining her opposition. "It's time for the Obama administration to loosen the hold that Wall Street banks have over economic policy making."

Weiss was quite understandably blindsided by the attack. Not lacking for connections, he summoned a small army of Wall Street heavyweights to call lawmakers on his behalf, including Summers and Secretary of the Treasury Jack Lew, a former Citigroup banker. But the optics were terrible, as Warren knew they would be. A few years earlier, Lazard had moved its own headquarters to the Bahamas to exploit a tax loophole. Few Democrats had the stomach to defend a practice that enriched Wall Street bankers at the expense of U.S. taxpayers. Most found it unseemly. Like Summers, Weiss soon backed out of the job.

Warren's victory didn't make a huge splash. But it marked an important change in Democratic politics, not just because defeating the White House further enhanced her power, but because Warren and her allies broadened the scope of disqualifying financial sins to include standard Wall Street business like tax inversions that hadn't mattered before. That constricted the talent pool Democratic administrations had drawn on for decades to shape economic policy. "One key thing that's changed with Warren is that it used to be that the philosophical piece mattered—if you could demonstrate you're committed to the president's economic agenda, that's what mattered," Ben

LaBolt, a former Obama official, noted after Weiss bowed out. "She's established a new litmus test that you can't have worked anywhere near Wall Street if you're going to a regulatory agency or even an agency that touches on economic policy."

Going after the president's nominees and criticizing his deference to Wall Street upset members of Obama's inner circle, who were accustomed to thinking of themselves as the good guys. They thought Warren's attacks were wildly unfair. But they also sensed, as many Democratic politicians did, that those attacks were working. Voters paid attention to them. This produced a big psychic shift in what people cared about, a kind of consciousness-raising that awakened them to arrangements and behavior they hadn't noticed before but now objected to, a development no Democrat with political ambitions could ignore. Warren liked to point out, for instance, how much influence a single bank—Citigroup—had in the Democratic Party: three of the last four Democratic Treasury secretaries (Rubin, Summers, Lew) had had high-paying jobs there, and the fourth (Geithner) was offered the CEO job but declined. By the time Weiss went down, the notion of Obama's nominating another Citigroup veteran, or any banker, was unthinkable. His own party wouldn't have stood for it. Even the bankers knew it. "I don't think you could have a banker serving in a major role in Washington in the next 10 years," Jamie Dimon, the CEO of JPMorgan Chase, lamented in 2016. "It's just not politically feasible." In the war between Warren and Wall Street, hers was the advancing army.

WARREN'S SENATE STAFF sometimes marveled at the scope of her reach. In 2016, she joined John McCain on a congressional delegation to Pakistan. At one point, they flew by helicopter to a remote, windswept outpost near the border. A Pakistani general emerged to greet them and, spotting Warren, broke into a smile. "I saw that clip of you taking on that banker," the general said. "That was great!" It took Warren a moment to register that he was referring to a Banking Committee showdown she'd had several months earlier with Wells Fargo's CEO, John Stumpf, whose bank had recently settled fraud charges but who couldn't escape Warren's charge that he'd exhibited "gutless leadership"—another viral moment that had evidently reached as far as rural Pakistan. (Stumpf resigned shortly after.)

Her global celebrity imbued Warren with an agenda-setting power. Newspapers routinely referenced "the Warren wing" of the Democratic Party as a distinct entity with its own leaders, issue set, and grassroots following that didn't automatically line up with the White House. She was expert at tapping into the broad discontent in American society—far better than Obama—and giving expression to middle-class grievances. Because she stuck mostly to economic matters, and spurned reporters' entreaties to weigh in on everything else, her words carried extra force: like the old E. F. Hutton commercial, when she talked, people listened. And because she brimmed with moral fervor and made vivid distinctions between right and wrong, Warren's framing of an issue was usually the one adopted by the news media.

But it was the alchemy of her fame, her outspokenness, and—especially—her easy command of the recondite details of banking and finance policy that made Warren a figure of consequence in Democratic politics. Voters in every district knew who she was and cared about what she thought—not true of 99 percent of elected officials. That forced her Democratic colleagues to take positions on issues they'd rather have avoided. "It was uncomfortable for many of them because she was putting questions out there that activists in their state, in their district, were going to demand to know where they stood," said Brian Fallon, a top aide to Senator Chuck Schumer of New York. "Reporters in the hallways of the Capitol were going to ask them about it. [Senators] complained to Chuck behind closed doors all the time, 'She's overdoing it.' Their thought process was, if I lean too far in, it will fray my relationship with the people headlining my donor breakfasts, but if I'm too defensive about what she's pushing, I might wind up in the middle of a social media pile-on and get killed by people back at home."

More often than not, this risk calculus worked in Warren's favor. Especially on high-profile nominations and financial regulatory matters where she chose to weigh in, Warren inverted the usual dynamic between White House and freshman senator; she, not Obama, shaped the Democratic policy debate and gave it a more populist cast. "Democrats are afraid of Elizabeth Warren," Barney Frank declared in 2015. "She has an absolute veto over certain public-policy issues, because Democrats are not going to cross her. . . . No Democrat wants Elizabeth Warren being critical of him."

But unlike some other politicians—Ted Cruz was a leading example—Warren rarely violated the assiduously proscribed interpersonal rules of the Senate. She didn't attack her colleagues, was a willing campaigner for Democrats facing reelection, and was careful not to publicly criticize party leaders (although her views always made it into the press). This won her influence inside the party and, in 2014, a position on Harry Reid's leadership team to reflect her growing stature on the outside.

That made it easier for Warren to advance what not long before would have seemed like a series of quixotic attempts to reshape economic liberalism along lines more favorable to students, workers, and seniors, and slightly less favorable to large financial interests. Her first bill sought to cut the interest rate the federal government charges on student loans to match the much lower rate it charges banks to borrow through the Federal Reserve's discount window. Warren also took aim at the Beltway consensus that favored cutting entitlement programs to balance the budget (and please the bond market). In his failed bid for a "grand bargain" with Republicans, Obama had offered to cut Social Security benefits, an idea popular with the kinds of corporate-funded "blue-ribbon" commissions that provide cover for politicians to do unpopular things like cut funding for seniors. Warren introduced an amendment *expanding* Social Security, an idea considered so outlandish that it didn't factor seriously in Washington debate. Yet when her amendment reached the Senate floor, every Democrat but two felt compelled to vote for it. Warren's ability to present a left-wing economic agenda as plain common sense—Why not ease the "retirement savings crisis" in the news by giving the elderly a bit more money? Why should banks get cheaper loans than students?—put new ideas in play, many of which were quite popular.

No issue better captured the party's growing ideological divide—or highlighted the broader backlash, soon to blow up U.S. politics, against the effects of the neoliberal era—than the fight that developed in 2014 over Obama's signature trade legislation, the Trans-Pacific Partnership. A decade in the making, the agreement between the United States and eleven Pacific Rim countries cut regulation and tariffs on goods and services across an area that generated one-third of world trade. The TPP shared the spirit of the earlier North American Free Trade Agreement in that both were representative of an era that viewed boosting international trade as an unalloyed good. But the decades since NAFTA had illustrated the painful costs of unfettered global commerce, including the hollowing out of entire swaths of the U.S. industrial core as employers chased cheaper labor in Mexico.

These downsides, and the intense emotional energy they generated among those who perceived themselves to be on the losing end of the deal, didn't penetrate elite Democratic (or Republican) thought. Obama saw the TPP as a major legacy item. Hillary Clinton, bidding to succeed him, sought to claim some of the credit for herself. In an infamous speech delivered in Australia while she was Obama's secretary of state, Clinton called TPP "the gold standard in trade agreements."

As with many of the things she championed, Warren wasn't the chief organizer of the opposition or the earliest critic of the agreement but the galvanic figure who became the face of the campaign against it. Unions and environmental groups vehemently opposed the TPP; so did labor-aligned politicians like Bernie Sanders and Sherrod Brown. Activist movements against rampant environmental and economic damage caused by globalization stretched at least as far back as the Seattle street protests against the World Trade Organization in 1999. What Warren did was fit these objections into her broader critique of the bipartisan failure of U.S. political leadership, dramatizing as only she could—until Donald Trump started weighing in—how the regime of free trade had weakened labor unions, shipped U.S. jobs abroad, and let big multinational corporations "rig the rules," as she put it, at the expense of workers and their families. Given the countless interests affected, the draft text of the agreement was kept under literal lock and key: senators had to visit a secure location to read it and were forbidden to share details. Warren invoked this atmosphere of paranoid security to cast sinister allusions, noting that the deal was written chiefly by corporate executives and lobbyists and singling out the U.S. trade representative, Michael Froman—another Citigroup veteran, of course. "No one—no one—was in the room who represented American workers or American consumers," Warren said of the negotiating process, and urged Congress to vote down the deal. For the only time anyone could recall, Obama became so upset that he attacked Warren by name in an interview. "The truth of the matter is that Elizabeth is, you know, a politician like everybody else," he groused. "She's absolutely wrong."

But by then the deal was beyond salvation. To the amusement, and then consternation, of Republicans, Trump was gaining steam in the GOP presidential primaries and attacking TPP along much the same lines as Warren, though with coarser language. Trump called it "a horror show [that's] going to kill all our jobs" and "a betrayal where politicians have sold out U.S. workers" that was "pushed by special interests who want to rape our country." He vowed to withdraw the United States from the partnership if elected (and did so). For Clinton, already on the campaign trail, the wave of antitrade sentiment necessitated an awkward, midcourse correction. In October 2015, feigning ignorance of an agreement she'd helped craft, she turned around and announced her opposition. "As of today," she told Judy Woodruff of *PBS NewsHour*, "I am not in favor of what I have learned about it." Clinton could read the tea leaves as well as anyone. In the end, Congress didn't even bother to vote on TPP.

Warren didn't win all these fights. But even in losing, she guided the future direction of the party. One way to think about her early years in the Senate is that they prepared the ground for a new era of liberalism to come. When Warren first began pushing to expand Social Security benefits, for example, the idea was so far outside the bounds of conventional thought that the *Washington Post* editorial board huffed about "liberalism gone awry." But the combination of moral suasion and fear of a backlash from "Warren wing" voters persuaded the overwhelming majority of Democrats, in a very short period of time, to embrace expansion, such that even as it fell short of becoming law, it ended any future Democratic attempts to cut Social Security, an effect that still endures a decade later. And while Warren's economic populism was invariably described as reflecting the wishes of "the left" or "the far left," it was often true that conservative Democrats also found her ideas congenial. Joe Manchin, the West Virginia senator and liberal bête noire, helped draft her Social Security plan and lobbied others to support it.

The big paradigm shifts in party politics happen during presidential races, when new ideas are tested on a national stage and sometimes catch fire, slingshotting their proponents to new prominence. In 2015, as the Obama era was winding down, the political landscape was ripe for realignment. It was becoming clear that voters were angrier, more disaffected, more impatient with politicians, and more open to populist appeals—although the mainstream media, at that point, did not appreciate the depth of these sentiments or how far voters would take them. Even Clinton, belatedly awakened to the vibe shift, started talking about holding "powerful people's feet to the fire" and so on, though without any real concern that the backlash threatened her. In the insular world of high-level establishment Democratic politics, the presidential primary was viewed largely as a passing of the torch from Obama to Clinton (Vice President Joe Biden's White House ambitions having been quietly spurned), with the main order of business being the minor calibrations in position and tone that Clinton needed to make to fit the popular mood.

But outside that narrow Washington circle, a lot of Democrats—especially state and local party officials in places far from the coasts—had a different view of things. They were eager to raise bedrock questions about what the party stood for and whom it represented, to operate at a higher level of ambition than Clinton seemed to want to pursue. Warren's clashes with bankers and "corporate" Democrats thrilled them because it's invigorating to go into moral battle against such clear-cut villains. It suited their romantic sense of how politics should be conducted. It also raised intoxicating questions about what else might be achieved. But where would the party go? And who would lead it there?

THE OBVIOUS CANDIDATE, of course, was Warren herself. By 2015, she was at the apogee of her political power. A combination of disenchantment with the Obama presidency, trepidation about the prospect of a Clinton renaissance, and longing for the purer, more assertive brand of liberalism she represented made Warren an object of intense interest and constant speculation. A certain type of online, cable-news-obsessed activist Democrat, which included plenty of political and policy staffers, as well as media figures like the MSNBC host Rachel Maddow, held her in awe. She became the object of not one but two campaigns to draft her into the 2016 presidential race.

In late 2014, the progressive group MoveOn.org launched "Run Warren Run" with a budget of $1 million, opening offices and hiring staff in Iowa and New Hampshire. It gathered 365,000 signatures, and the public support of celebrities who included the actors Mark Ruffalo and Susan Sarandon, to urge Warren into the race. At the same time, a different group of activists, some of them veterans of the Occupy Wall Street protests, organized a "Ready for Warren" draft movement. At the Netroots Nation conference in Detroit, the annual gathering of online leftists, Warren was greeted everywhere with chants of "Run, Liz, Run!"

A big part of the attraction was that Warren was already behaving like a presidential candidate; she was at Netroots Nation promoting *A Fighting Chance*, which felt a lot like a campaign book. She'd let herself be drafted into a race before, in Massachusetts. And she already had what amounted to a platform. As two of the Draft Warren-ers pointed out in a letter explaining their rationale, "Signature Warren issues [have] now found wider currency—as when 42 Senate Democrats joined Warren in voting for an expansion of Social Security benefits. On issues from student debt to the TPP, Warren has come to wield the kind of agenda-setting, debate-defining power normally reserved for potential party nominees."

Warren fever was also driven by a powerful antipathy to Hillary Clinton among a segment of the Democratic left fearful that a restoration of the Clintons to the White House would herald the return of neoliberal centrism and the unwinding of the limited gains they had only recently secured in its wake. In this context, Warren loomed as a savior, perhaps the only one who could stop the dreaded Clinton coronation most political observers expected. As another draft leader, a former Obama aide named Christopher Hass, explained, the effort was born out of "the desire for there to be a real, competitive primary in 2016 that will make our party, our eventual candidate, and our country stronger." That was code for "Anybody but Clinton."

At first, Warren was coy about the draft movement, just as she had been in Massachusetts. This supercharged the media coverage and encouraged the belief among her most ardent supporters that she was a selfless public servant about to be called to her greatest duty. It also fed the mythology, which Warren herself promoted, that she wasn't a "real" politician—that she'd entered politics by happenstance, as a by-product of her ideological commitment, and not out of the grasping need and fanatical ambition that many presidential candidates seem to exhibit from an early age. Warren's power derived from the fact that she didn't appear to seek it out.

There were good reasons for Warren to want to run. It would force an intraparty debate, at a level far beyond what she could engineer in the Senate, about the direction of the Democratic Party in a post-Obama world. Clinton, who was being circumspect about her views because she didn't have a real challenger, would have to declare them, and they'd probably shift to the left with Warren in the race. As one presidential historian noted, "Less is known about Hillary Clinton's positions on domestic issues than any other leading candidate since Dwight Eisenhower." And because presidential primaries are strange, contingent affairs, it was always possible Warren would win.

Still, polls showed Clinton in a position of overwhelming strength, broadly popular with Democratic voters. Paradoxically, some Warren partisans viewed this strength as an opportunity. Their thinking went like this: What Clinton lacked in 2008, and still appeared to lack, was an overarching rationale for why she was running for president; casting herself as "inevitable" had flopped once before. Warren didn't have that problem at all. Her power in the Senate, sure to be magnified manyfold in a Democratic primary race, was leading a left-populist movement. If Warren were to enter the race, this line of thinking went, her positions would instantly become, to liberal voters, the benchmark for what constitutes acceptable Democratic policy. Whether or not she won, she'd establish the terms of debate. Clinton would co-opt her message, and that would obligate her to implement at least some of Warren's agenda when she got to the White House. The salient historical comparison wasn't a past primary, but Ross Perot's 1992 presidential campaign. Perot, an independent, didn't win. Yet his popularity made his major policy priority—deficit reduction—a shaping force in the campaign that Bill Clinton took up in the White House.

In the end, Warren opted not to run. She worried that losing would diminish her influence. Some allies agreed. Barney Frank believed her power to strike fear in Democratic colleagues stemmed from the fact that she appeared beyond reproach: she wasn't angling for anything bigger. "But if she were to even hint at being a candidate," Frank warned, "that would be over." Although she didn't advertise it, Warren had also developed ties to Clinton and her campaign that led her to believe she'd have influence in a Clinton administration. Gary Gensler, a former Goldman Sachs executive who'd led the Commodity Futures Trading Commission under Obama and emerged as an unlikely but trusted Warren ally, served as a go-between, shuttling back and forth from Clinton to Warren. And Clinton certainly *sounded* like a populist convert, echoing several of Warren's talking points and making a showy endorsement of her bill to ban "golden parachutes," the big pay-outs Wall Street banks and other private firms often give executives who take positions in the federal government. After years of playing the outside game, Warren decided that she'd have better odds of advancing her agenda on the inside, a choice that would soon go disastrously wrong.

What would have happened if Warren had heeded the calls to run for president? She'd undoubtedly have become the main challenger to Clinton. Her outsider status and scathing critique of establishment politicians would have made for an irresistible campaign narrative. Her fights with Wall Street banks and villainous financiers would have cast Clinton's many ties to that world in a particularly unflattering light. (Clinton was already under fire for having inexplicably given a series of highly paid private speeches to Goldman Sachs and other banks that she refused to release to the public.) As events would soon show, voters in both parties were far more hostile to dynastic politicians like Clinton and Jeb Bush than anyone fathomed in the innocent early days of 2015. Millions of frustrated Democrats, many of whom had already supported Warren's Senate campaign, were yearning to anoint a progressive hero.

So were the disappointed organizers of Ready for Warren and Run Warren Run, who had raised millions of dollars and set up what amounted to a campaign in waiting for a candidate who finally made it clear, in May, that she wouldn't be running. Instead of packing up shop, however, many of them gravitated to a different candidate whose remarkable good fortune it was that Warren bowed out and left him the infrastructure for an insurgent presidential campaign at exactly the moment he was preparing to enter the race.

8

STRAIGHT OUTTA BURLINGTON

The biggest effect of the financial crisis was a loss of faith in U.S. institutions. Initially, and not surprisingly, this loss of faith was concentrated in the financial sector. When Obama was first elected president in the depths of the crisis, Gallup found that confidence in banks had fallen to a historic low. An overwhelming number of Americans (86 percent) cited economic issues as the country's most pressing problem. But as time went on, blame spread. Antipathy toward Wall Street metastasized into antipathy toward the government, which not only struggled to mitigate the effects of the meltdown but also began producing crises of its own, including a debt default scare in 2011 and a shutdown two years later. By 2015, Gallup found, "government" had replaced "the economy" as the top national concern, and the hostility toward bankers that Americans felt in the wake of the crash now extended to the broad governing class. The focus of

Americans' ire shifted from Wall Street to Washington: "poor leader-ship/corruption/abuse of power" was now cited by survey respondents as the primary cause of the country's troubles.

In other words, the electorate was primed for someone who stood outside the party system. It was primed for Bernie Sanders. But voters didn't know it yet, because practically no one outside Vermont knew who he was. A March 2015 poll of Democratic voters showed Hillary Clinton beating Sanders 62 percent to 3 percent in a then-still-hypothetical contest for the nomination, with Joe Biden (15 percent) and Elizabeth Warren (10 percent, though she wasn't running) both well ahead of him. Among the early skeptics was Sanders himself, who had assembled the rudiments of a campaign but was driving his advisers crazy by refusing to make up his mind about whether he was going to get in the race.

One didn't need to see a poll to believe that Sanders was a no-hoper, even absent the Clinton juggernaut. In Washington, he was regarded as a gadfly. Unlike some other colorful politicians who didn't factor heavily in lawmaking, Sanders didn't generate much attention, either. He once held a press conference on Capitol Hill with the AFL-CIO president, Richard Trumka, that failed to attract a single reporter from a mainstream news outlet. So people in Democratic politics didn't think about him as a presidential candidate, because most of them didn't think about him at all. To begin with, Sanders wasn't a Democrat. He was an independent and a self-avowed democratic socialist who caucused with the Democrats. He wasn't particularly well liked. In contrast to the lovable "Bernie" persona that millions of new admirers perceived when he hit the campaign trail, many of his colleagues on the left thought he was a sour, self-aggrandizing purist who couldn't be bothered with the difficult, messy work of legislating. "Sanders's approach is, 'I will say what is the right thing to do and then criticize anybody who doesn't join me.' That's been his mode for twenty-five years," said Barney Frank, the liberal Massachusetts congressman. "He's had the luxury of operating outside the system of collegial and collaborative activities that successful legislators have to conduct," Nancy Pelosi's chief of staff, John Lawrence, complained. "It's been very much about him." Even charitable assessments tended to cast Sanders as a loser. Harry Reid's former chief of staff, Jim Manley, summed him up as "pure of heart, noble of purpose—and destined to fail."

Taken together, Sanders's ideological purity, the "socialist" tag, and his open contempt for big business and Wall Street—to say nothing of his relative obscurity—made him seem a poor bet to raise the tens of millions of dollars a serious candidate would need to run competitively. He had "protest candidate" written all over him. And he would of course be facing an opponent, in Clinton, with practically limitless resources and control of the Democratic establishment, someone whose numerous advantages—including the tacit support of Barack Obama—dissuaded most serious contenders from running. Yet each of Sanders's detractions turned out, remarkably, to work to his advantage once he finally submitted to his advisers' prodding and entered the race in late April.

When Elizabeth Warren bowed out of the running, Sanders moved from understudy to lead actor in a national drama that was already in progress. The 2008 crash and the "jobless recovery" generated a populist left-wing movement with momentum and followers. Warren was its first star, but by 2015 dozens of congressmen and senators reliably lined up with her on policy matters. Journalists referred without irony to the "Elizabeth Warren wing" of the Democratic

Party. Liberal netroots groups like MoveOn.org, which originally formed to oppose the Iraq War, had matured into experienced mobilizing operations that could flood the White House or Congress with thousands of calls and increasingly began focusing their attention on economic and social justice issues. Signs of broad popular dissatisfaction sprouted up everywhere. In 2011, the Occupy Wall Street protests swept the country and made income inequality front-page news. A year later, fast-food workers in New York City launched the "Fight for $15" campaign to raise the minimum wage to $15 an hour, and this, too, spread to other cities, aided by a rejuvenated labor movement. The emergence of MSNBC as left liberalism's cable news flagship and Rachel Maddow as its chief advocate-chronicler also gave shape and direction to the emerging left. ("Such a megaphone," *The New York Times* intoned in 2012, "has never existed before on television.")

What was most noteworthy about all this activity in 2015 was that its participants were now willing, and even eager, to engage with national Democratic electoral campaigns. In the recent past, this often hadn't been the case: activists had opted instead for direct action (the Seattle WTO protests, Occupy Wall Street) or trained their efforts on specific issues such as blocking the Keystone XL pipeline, causes they didn't believe they would be likely to advance by engaging aggressively with the presidential primary process, perhaps because no candidate particularly excited them. Bernie Sanders changed this, producing a gravitational pull that brought them into the electoral process. Once again, Warren had supplied a proof of concept. Her 2012 Senate election campaign, which proved to be a cakewalk, raised a staggering $42 million, far more than any other senator that cycle, Democrat or Republican, with most of it coming from small donors.

What this movement suddenly lacked, once Warren spurned the draft movement, was a popular standard-bearer. "The left was looking for a champion," Mark Longabaugh, a senior Sanders adviser who helped launch the campaign, recalled, "and the left in the Democratic Party had grown tremendously in the decade and a half before then."

Sanders caught fire because a lot more people were open to his message than was commonly presumed. In 2000, about 6 percent of Democrats and Democratic-leaning voters considered themselves "very liberal," and another 21 percent called themselves merely "liberal." When it came to party composition, moderates and conservatives had the clear upper hand. But by 2015, "very liberal" voters had nearly tripled in number and, when combined with the growing "liberal" cohort, now constituted about half (47 percent) of Democratic voters. Hillary Clinton might have been the overwhelming favorite. But it wasn't Bill Clinton's Democratic Party anymore.

Even so, the speed of Sanders's ascent shocked people. It happened in the span of a month. It was most jarringly apparent to the poor souls who rustled up audiences for Sanders before he became a celebrity. One of them, Alex Lawson, organized what might have been the last event before the rocket ship took off—the demarcation point between "Old Bernie" and "New Bernie." Lawson was a young operative who'd done advance work for Sanders before. Sanders was eager to get off Capitol Hill and do a final tune-up for the campaign, so Lawson booked St. Stephen and the Incarnation Episcopal Church, which sits in a polyglot neighborhood a few miles north of the Capitol, for April 22 and started hustling. To drum up an audience for Sanders, he leaned on activist friends at economic justice and senior citizens organizations, then applied a dash of ingenuity. "I squeezed every turnout trick I had to fill that church," he recalled, "seating people diagonally to make the crowd look bigger and moving friends around to fill the empty spots." At the pulpit, beneath a wood carving of Jesus on the cross, Sanders delivered a soon-to-be-familiar stem-winder about the perils of austerity and the government's abandonment of the working class, vowing he'd "be damned if we balance the budget on the backs of the poor." By all accounts, his performance was electric. At the back of the church, his staffers regretted only that a bigger audience hadn't seen him. "And then," Lawson said, "one of them turns to me—I'll never forget this—and says, 'I think when he takes this message outside of D.C., more people are going to be interested.' And from there on, it never stopped."

A week later, Sanders declared for president. His announcement on the Capitol lawn was almost comically perfunctory. There was no crowd, just a hastily assembled group of reporters who'd followed him outside. "Let me just make a brief comment and take a few questions, because we don't have an endless amount of time—I've gotta get back," Sanders said, a bit irritably. He laid out his message: America was facing its greatest crisis since the Great Depression. It stemmed from a broken economic system, rigged by elites, that was failing ordinary workers. He'd met many of them in his travels, he said, and he recounted their complaints: *I'm working longer hours for lower wages. My kid can't afford to go to college. I'm having a hard time affording health care.* How does that happen, while at exactly the same time 99 percent of all new income generated in this country is going to the top 1 percent? How does it happen?"

Sanders's populist outrage succinctly conveyed his campaign's purpose: to make the race a fight over what sort of economic vision Democrats should pursue. "My conclusion," he said, "is that that type of economics is not only immoral, it's not only wrong, it is unsustainable. It can't continue. We can't continue having a nation in which we have the highest rate of childhood poverty of any major nation on earth at the same time as we're seeing a proliferation of millionaires and billionaires. So that's the major issue." Sanders had spoken for less than two minutes. Within weeks, he was drawing crowds of five thousand people, and his campaign was scrambling to book major arenas.

Everybody close to Sanders has a story about when the lightning bolt first hit them and they realized something unusual was happening. For many, the moment came in late May. Sanders had a layover in Minneapolis, so the campaign scheduled a quick rally to take advantage of his time on the ground, booking a small venue near the airport. Right away, the response made clear a bigger one would be necessary, so the event shifted to a local union hall. When RSVPs surpassed a thousand and the union hall would no longer suffice, the campaign moved the event once more, to the American Indian Center in Minneapolis, which held three thousand people. By the time Sanders arrived, the arena was full and an overflow crowd of more than a thousand stretched around the building. "Jesus, what is that?" Sanders mumbled as his car approached. "There's a ballgame going on?" Longabaugh was struck, too. "Five thousand people don't just show up like that," he later recalled. The Summer of Sanders had begun.

In the weeks that followed, Sanders attracted huge crowds everywhere he went: five thousand in Denver, eight thousand in Portland, ten thousand in Madison, while consistently outdrawing Clinton in his swings through Iowa. By standard measures of candidate strength and electability, this made no sense. But Sanders was uniquely equipped to capitalize on the public's growing disgust with politicians and its rising frustration with the winner-take-all economy. He was earnest, cranky, impatient, and blunt—someone who, by the evidence of his appearance and demeanor, was incapable of a politician's typical deceptions. With his Brooklyn accent and a nimbus of flyaway white hair, he was the antithesis of the packaged-and-poll-tested Clinton. He struck people as being angry about the right sorts of things. Gruff authenticity became the hallmark of his appeal.

Sanders's calls for a "political revolution" induced eye rolls in Washington. But less jaded listeners heard plenty to like in what he was saying. Most of his proposals aimed to help working people and curb the political power of the rich: break up the big banks, raise taxes on the wealthy, boost the minimum wage to $15, make college tuition-free (in part by taxing Wall Street), and end what he called the "international embarrassment of being the only major country on earth that does not guarantee workers paid medical and family leave." His animating conviction, delivered in the manic style of Howard Beale, was that a decent living standard should be not a privilege but a right. That message, and his tendency to fixate on economics to the exclusion of almost everything else, gave Sanders's politics a flavor of the 1930s left more than the 1960s left, which further differentiated him from Clinton (who eagerly embraced identity issues in her quest to become the first female president) and most other Democratic politicians as well.

"It doesn't matter what issue comes up—Bernie understands that the fundamental issue for Americans is economic," explained Huck Gutman, an old friend of Sanders's and an English professor at the University of Vermont. "His record on abortion, on gay marriage, on a great number of things has been very good and very liberal, but he never sees those as the central issues. The central issue is: Are people doing O.K., or are a small number of people ripping them off?"

A WHOLE LOT OF PEOPLE in 2015 were feeling ripped off and resentful, which was also made apparent by the surprise insurgent in the Republican primaries: Donald Trump. But Trump's appeal was driven as much by his entertainment value as by his political agenda. Such was his ratings power that CNN routinely cut live to an empty lectern where Trump was scheduled to speak, in giddy anticipation of whatever outrage he would commit next.

Sanders had nothing like Trump's allure for the camera. He'd been saying the same thing over and over again for thirty years, and he disliked the personal attacks that Trump and cable news producers delight in. His drawing power owed instead to his fervent, moralistic attacks on the financial and political establishments, and to his proposing solutions that were outside the ideological boundaries Americans were accustomed to—something that, to people fed up with decades of self-imposed Democratic constraints, was just as transgressive and exciting. Sanders wanted the government to take a much more active role in setting the terms of the economy to improve people's lives, which particularly appealed to those who consistently found themselves on the short end of America's distribution of wealth and opportunity.

Many of those people were young, had reached adulthood amid the financial crisis or the Great Recession that followed, and bore the brunt of the fallout. By 2015, the damage across the millennial generation was apparent in any number of measures. The unemployment rate for people under twenty-five was more than double the overall rate. Job openings were at least 20 percent below their pre-recession peak. Real wages were down 13 percent for recent high school graduates and 8 percent for recent college graduates since 2000. Employers and the government were making life harder, too. The percentage of recent college graduates with employer-provided health insurance dropped by half between 1989 and 2012, to just 30 percent. Over the same period, states and cities cut spending for higher education, causing universities to raise tuition, which doubled the share of households owing student debt and tripled the average size of that debt to $27,000. Younger Americans were also less likely than older ones to qualify for unemployment insurance, food stamps, or the earned income tax credit.

Coming of age during the longest, most severe period of economic and labor market weakness in more than seventy years had an obvious political effect: it pushed young Americans to the left. It was no accident so many of Sanders's rallies were populated with college students and recent graduates. But it was also partly by design. Knowing that an insurgent candidate would be short of resources, Tad Devine, another top strategist for Sanders, scheduled rallies in cities with large college populations in the hope that Sanders would draw big crowds of students, which would in turn produce media coverage and create an impression of momentum. It worked. Sanders didn't just become popular; he became a pop culture phenomenon who spawned memes and social media devotion and messianic followers who saw him as a providential figure.

His enormous appeal stemmed from a kind of anti-charisma, a truculent refusal to indulge the bullshit and euphemism that's the lingua franca of electoral campaigning. Like Trump's, Sanders's métier was the stadium rally, where rolling chants of "Bernie!" from screaming college students preceded a speech that didn't vary much from week to week but brimmed with Old Testament fury and unvarnished contempt—still rarely voiced in mainstream U.S. politics—for the political and financial leaders who had brought the country to its low state.

A rally in Portland, Oregon, on August 9, 2015, as the Summer of Sanders was reaching peak frenzy, drew twenty-eight thousand people to receive the Sanders catechism:

> Brothers and sisters, this country today faces more crises than
> at any time since the Great Depression of the 1930s. And what

we are going to do, and what we understand, is that when problems are caused by DUMB public policy, GOOD public policy will resolve it—and today, we're coming together to develop good public policy.

Today we say, loudly and clearly, that this great nation belongs to ALL of us. Not just a handful of billionaires. . . .

Our country today has more income and wealth inequality than any other major country on earth. And the gap between the very rich and everyone else is worse today than at any time since 1928. . . .

In my view, the issue of wealth and income inequality is the great moral issue of our time—and we are going to inject the issue of morality into politics today.

Without ever intending to, or quite seeming to fully understand it, Sanders generated what amounted to a lifestyle brand for a certain type of earnest, educated young American. As millennials turned one another on to the ecstasies of Sanders's progressive politics, his brain trust saw that an even bigger opportunity to capture the youth vote lay before them than they had initially realized. The Sanders campaign began targeting high school students, including those who were not yet old enough to vote but would be before the caucus or primary date. In a bid to reach this hyper-specific group of seventeen-year-olds, the campaign rented lists from vendors of high school class rings and graduation caps and gowns.

Of course, the economic carnage of the mid-2010s was not limited to the younger generation, any more than concern about wealth inequality or the allure of progressive ideals. Plenty of older people fell for Sanders, too. He quickly captured the minority of Democrats who always support the leftmost candidate in a primary, as well as the larger, overlapping group that disliked Hillary Clinton and was looking for an alternative. In the span of a few months, Sanders erased Clinton's double-digit lead in the early states of Iowa and New Hampshire.

What was more striking than Sanders's poll numbers, though, was the movement that sprang up around him. Almost immediately, he was flooded with volunteers and small donors. This was fortunate because he had forsworn PAC money on principle (and wasn't likely to get much anyway) and his campaign had struggled to put together a staff. "When I'd call up people trying to hire them—mail, polling, advance, press people—they would laugh at me," Longabaugh recalled. "Some of them said flat out, 'I'm not going up against the Clintons, they'll kill me.' And the others said, 'There's no way he's a serious candidate.'" But the popular impression of Sanders shifted dramatically. The influx of money and volunteers, and Sanders's rapid emergence as the main challenger to Clinton, enabled him to spread his message much further and wider than anyone expected; he displaced Elizabeth Warren as the leading advocate and justifier of aggressive economic populism. Some of his new backers were the same activists who had tried to draft Warren into the race and then rebranded "Ready for Warren" as "Ready for Bernie." Others were veterans of Occupy Wall Street. But many more were fresh converts drawn into the presidential campaign by the excitement of a new left-wing movement. Even after his campaign ended, enough of them stayed involved in Democratic politics, organizing progressive groups like the Sunrise Movement and Justice Democrats, that they changed the nature of what the party stood for.

As we've seen, one little-noted by-product of the neoliberal domination of the Democratic Party in the years before 2015 was that leftists and radicals generally opted out of participating in party politics and focused their energies elsewhere. Activists in the anti-globalization movement, the environmental protests at Standing Rock, Occupy Wall Street, and many other causes rarely bothered to try to influence the party platform or the leading candidates for president. Sanders changed this. He was a pied piper who pulled these groups into the process and by doing so added energy and ideological zeal to his campaign. "In the eight years of the Obama presidency, there was a lot of fragmented discontent, especially among young people, that was being expressed through marches, rallies, and sit-ins," said Waleed Shahid, an activist who later joined the Justice Democrats. "That never had a political expression until Bernie Sanders came along. When he said, 'I'm against Wall Street, I'm against the Keystone Pipeline, I'm for the $15 minimum wage,' it created an energy that brought many of them along. He was the Moses figure who brought them into the electoral process."

The groundswell for Sanders was so big that it transformed him from gadfly to major presidential candidate almost overnight. It established beyond any doubt that a left-populist wing would be an enduring part of the Democratic coalition, regardless of Sanders's fate, simply because the support he generated was so enormous—and, by campaign finance standards, unprecedented. In October 2015, the Sanders campaign announced it had raised $26 million in the previous three months, an amount just shy of Clinton's total, despite running a much leaner campaign and relying almost entirely on small donors. A few weeks later, Sanders revealed he had gotten contributions from 750,000 people, surpassing Barack Obama's tally at the same point in his first presidential campaign. Until Sanders came along, political professionals didn't think a serious presidential candidate could sustain a campaign mainly with small donors. Even Obama, who built a powerful network of them, had tapped Wall Street and wealthy bundlers for donations. Sanders dashed those assumptions. ("Money is just bubbling up from everywhere," one campaign finance expert marveled of his campaign.) He went on to raise $228 million, fortified by an army of 5 million small donors, and ended up outspending Clinton during the primary race. Thirty years after Tony Coelho had envisioned a party fueled by small donors and unbeholden to Wall Street—and then proceeded to hoover up as much Wall Street cash as he could in a failed effort to bring that vision to fruition—there was no small irony in the fact that Sanders, a socialist, was the first to demonstrate that such a thing was indeed viable. And if someone as radical and far from the mainstream as Bernie Sanders could build such a well-financed campaign while spurning the corporate money most politicians feel obligated to pursue to win election, then mainstream Democrats would no longer have a compelling reason to indulge the corrupting influence of big business as most of them had been doing for so many years.

This was exciting in the moment because it fueled a belief among Sanders's supporters that he might actually upset Clinton and win the Democratic nomination. By October, he had pulled ahead of her in some polls of Iowa and New Hampshire. On a broader level, it showed that Democrats could, if they wished to, break the ties Coelho and others forged with Wall Street in the 1980s and jettison the ideological commitments that had come with them.

As UNLIKELY AS the rise of Bernie Sanders might have been, his own biography testified to the idea that a stubborn outsider could prevail over long odds, beat the political establishment, and govern successfully, and this added to the frenzy around his candidacy. Sanders was born in Brooklyn just after the Depression, the son of a paint salesman who emigrated from Poland and a mother who stayed at home. The family was not well off and sometimes struggled to make ends meet. But his political awakening came later at the University of Chicago, where he joined the Young People's Socialist League and the Congress of Racial Equality. By his own account, Sanders was an indifferent student more interested in joining local civil rights protests than spending time in the classroom. After graduating in 1964 with a political science degree, he drifted for a bit before marrying and winding up in Vermont, where he became active in local politics. In 1971, representing Vermont's left-wing Liberty Union Party, Sanders ran for the U.S. Senate, lost badly, and then over the next decade ran twice more for Senate and twice for governor, never drawing more than negligible support. During this time, he scratched out a living doing carpentry work, writing freelance articles for local alternative newspapers, and making educational films through a nonprofit he started, the American People's Historical Society, on significant figures in Vermont history (he also made a thirty-minute documentary on his personal hero, the early-twentieth-century trade unionist and socialist leader, Eugene Debs). But he didn't abandon his political ambitions. At a friend's suggestion, he lowered his sights and ran for Burlington mayor in 1981.

The incumbent that year was a five-term Democrat named Gordon Paquette of whom the local populace had grown weary. Paquette didn't take Sanders seriously and so hardly bothered to campaign. Sanders, running a vigorous race as an independent while being perfectly open about his socialist politics, won by ten votes. The local newspaper anointed him "the new radical mayor," although *The New York Times* better captured his essence as "a man of aggressive intellect and careless dress [who] lives in a sloppy one-and-a-half-room apartment and dwells on broad social needs." As a thirty-nine-year-old socialist elected during the Reagan wave, Sanders was a national curiosity. The *Today* show sent Phil Donahue to Vermont to helm a segment titled "Socialism in New England."

Sanders didn't shy away from radical political expression during his mayoralty. At one point he traveled to Nicaragua to meet with Daniel Ortega. But he surprised skeptics by being an effective mayor with a pragmatic streak who oversaw the successful redevelopment of Burlington's waterfront and won the support of the police union. A 1983 poll showed Sanders with a 62 percent approval rating (only 21 percent disapproved of him), and he coasted to reelection three times.

The first reelection race indelibly shaped his view of how left politics could succeed—locally and nationally—and also why the standard Democratic approach so often failed. Sanders knocked on a lot of doors, cultivated the elderly, the poor, and the student population at the University of Vermont, and got many more people to vote than had two years earlier (*The Burlington Free Press*: "Massive Turnout Keeps Sanders in Office"). He convinced people, or believed he convinced them, that a stronger, more activist government was a desirable thing, and the lesson he drew was that overcoming Democratic timidity and stating so forthrightly would activate waves of new voters and transform the political landscape. It became his blueprint for politics. In 2015, he described this formative experience:

> I won in 1981. When I ran for reelection in 1983, we almost doubled the vote turnout. Why was that? Mostly because we paid attention to working-class wards and lower-income people. And those people said, "You know what? Actually, Bernie and the government are doing something for me. [So] we're going to participate." And when we talk about the problems facing this country today, and the dismal, dismal turnout in

the midterm elections last November—I think people are giving up on government, they don't believe government represents their interests. They think, "Why do I want to participate in this charade? Not relevant to me." What we have got to do is make government relevant today and deliver for working people, for lower-income people, for young people. And when we do that, we create this relationship of working together. Voter turnout goes up, and when voter turnout goes up, Democrats win. Republicans win when voter turnout goes down. So I did learn a lot being mayor of the city.

Sanders's presidential campaign was a fully recognizable, souped-up version of his Burlington race three decades earlier, one driven by the same central conviction: Americans were longing for big, transformative social programs supplied by the government but had been cynically denied them by a generation of corrupt neoliberal politicians in thrall to moneyed interests. Millions of disillusioned people who'd lost faith in the political process or never bothered to participate at all stood poised to rally behind a candidate bold enough to promise to deliver them. When Sanders's campaign took off in earnest, this conviction became a critical piece—really *the* critical piece—of the left's understanding of itself in the years ahead.

Like his first mayoral race, Sanders's presidential run was particularly well timed, coming just as another Democratic incumbent was leaving the stage. Sanders managed to capture the pent-up frustrations liberals had swallowed during Obama's presidency. His animating idea of the government aggressively intervening in the economy to help workers held obvious appeal in the wake of a financial crisis and seven years of economic malaise—to young people, who had plainly gotten screwed, but also to blue-collar workers who resided in rural manufacturing hubs and agricultural states and hadn't fared any better. In another stroke of serendipity for Sanders, and not without justification, many of those people blamed the husband of his primary opponent.

THROUGHOUT HIS PRESIDENCY, Bill Clinton was the proud avatar of Democratic neoliberalism, and his years in the White House were bookended by two landmark achievements that advanced this vision. The first was the passage of the North American Free Trade Agreement in 1993, which eliminated trade and investment barriers between the United States, Mexico, and Canada. The second, in 2000, his last major legislative victory before leaving office, was the granting of normalized trade relations status to China, which ended economic restrictions that had been part of U.S. anticommunist policy for decades and cinched China's bid to join the World Trade Organization, opening up its vast market to U.S. trade and investment. Clinton thought that in addition to economic benefits free trade would advance America's foreign policy interests because he believed, along with many other people, that the economic liberalization China was committing to by joining the WTO would inevitably lead to political liberalization. Such was the faith, at that time, in the power of free markets. So over the objection of labor unions worried about competing with cheap foreign workers, Clinton, relying on heavy Republican support, completed the historic deal. *The New York Times* christened it "a stunning victory for the Clinton administration and corporate America." Clinton believed he had cemented his legacy. "This is a good day for America," he said. "In 10 years from now we will look back on this day and be glad we did this. We will see that we have given ourselves a chance to build the kind of future we want."

But almost right away, things didn't go quite as Clinton envisioned, especially for Americans directly exposed to new import competition from China. Within months, dozens of U.S. firms began shifting production to China to take advantage of its lower labor costs. At the same time, Chinese producers rapidly expanded into U.S. markets, showering American consumers with cheap imports. Seeing that they couldn't keep pace with China's labor costs, U.S. producers accelerated their investments in domestic automation. The automotive industry, for instance, became the primary driver of growth in robotics, which eliminated manufacturing jobs.

Yet none of this raised alarm—at least not among people whose lives weren't directly affected by a layoff. Economic theory held that because labor is mobile, displaced workers would simply shift to new industries or relocate to places where jobs were more plentiful. That's what happened in the late 1970s and early 1980s when a surge of Japanese cars and other durable goods hit U.S. markets: most laid-off workers found jobs elsewhere, and net employment levels remained steady. China was different. It became an industrial powerhouse with major effects on the United States that arrived with more speed, scale, and concentrated force than economists anticipated. And this created a disaster for millions of U.S. families and their communities, the effects of which have compounded over time.

Why did this happen? And what were the consequences for the families and communities directly affected? Who came out ahead and whose interests were ignored? The answers had a direct bearing on American politics in 2016. And they can be understood at an unusual level of detail because a group of academics began studying the "China Shock," as they dubbed it, a decade ago and have followed its effects to the present day—not just the economic effects, but the political effects, too.

Starting in 2013, the economists David Autor, David Dorn, and

Gordon Hanson, along with various collaborators, published a series of papers showing that manufacturing employment dropped more sharply in areas of the United States where local businesses faced import competition from China than in areas that didn't. Between 1999 and 2011, they estimated, about a million U.S. manufacturing jobs vanished due to Chinese competition; factoring in ancillary local businesses that withered when plants closed, the cost was somewhere between 2 million and 2.4 million jobs, with the losses concentrated in a geographic area stretching from the Rust Belt to Appalachia to the Deep South. Puzzlingly, to economists, these workers didn't behave the way academic theory said they should. Most didn't find new jobs or move away; they remained out of work, and net employment levels fell. Why did workers recover from the Japan Shock but not from the China Shock? Autor, Dorn, and Hanson, drawing on earlier research, offered several reasons: the Japan Shock was much smaller; the places it hit were wealthier, were more educated, and had additional manufacturers, so local economies were more resilient than the areas affected by Chinese competition and thus better able to absorb displaced workers. China, by contrast, hit lower-skilled industries like furniture making and textiles that tended to be located in rural places with few alternatives for good employment.

A few years after their first paper, the researchers went back and looked at the experience of American workers in labor markets most exposed to Chinese competition. What they found was devastation. The expected adjustment, they confirmed, never happened. Unemployment remained high and wages low; in fact, the drop in per capita income was much larger than quantitative models had predicted. There was no sign of recovery. Many communities were reeling as the economic and social costs piled up. Autor and his colleagues grimly cataloged them: "Labor markets more exposed to import competition

from China experienced more plant closures; larger declines in manufacturing employment, employment-population ratios, earnings for
low-wage workers, housing prices, and tax revenues; and larger increases in childhood and adult poverty, single-parenthood, and mor-
tality related to drug and alcohol abuse, as well as greater uptake of
government transfers"—meaning, more people went on disability.
The 2008 financial crisis compounded the misery. Although imports
from China fell sharply during the subsequent recession, U.S. workers
got no reprieve. Manufacturers continued shedding jobs. And like
rural areas elsewhere, these labor markets were hit harder by the Great
Recession (and were slower to recover) than metropolitan areas; they
also had to contend with a regional "mini-recession" in manufacturing-
and agriculture-heavy areas that hit in 2015, throwing the tepid recovery into reverse:

U.S. Employment in Urban and Rural Areas, 2007–19

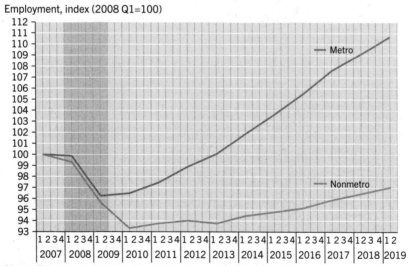

Notes: Data are seasonally adjusted. Shaded area indicates recession period.
Source: USDA, Economic Research Service using data from Bureau of Labor Statistics,
Local Area Unemployment Statistics (LAUS).

One of the saddest findings was that displaced workers hadn't left these depressed regions; they'd simply been left behind and dropped out of the labor force, a condition that increasingly looked to be permanent. "Manufacturing job loss," the researchers concluded in 2021, "translated nearly one for one into declines in the employment-population ratio." These laid-off workers and their communities were casualties not only of the China Shock but of the federal government's neglect in understanding and addressing the effects of globalization. It's little wonder that many felt abandoned and resentful—or that they responded in a way that surprised the politicians, economists, and journalists who had misread their situation from the outset.

Autor and his colleagues didn't neglect to study how these wrenching changes affected local politics. With remarkably good timing, they published a paper, "Importing Political Polarization? The Electoral Consequences of Rising Trade Exposure," in the spring of 2016, just as the presidential primaries were unfolding. Examining congressional elections in the decade after China's entry into the WTO, they discovered that trade-exposed labor markets had undergone a profound ideological realignment. Only it didn't follow the typical pattern of voters ousting Democratic incumbents for Republicans, or vice versa. Instead, they found, "trade exposure abets the replacement of incumbents from both parties with more ideologically strident successors."

It's hard to imagine a better description of the forces at play in the 2016 presidential primaries (even though they didn't factor at all in the paper's analysis). As dynastic politicians and early front-runners, Jeb Bush and Hillary Clinton were functionally incumbents; Trump and Sanders were plainly the most strident candidates in their respective fields, and both were highly attuned to the issue of trade. Voters responded exactly as the paper by Autor and his collaborators suggested they should. Trump won eighty-nine of the hundred counties most affected by competition from China, a *Wall Street Journal* analysis found. Sanders won primaries in sixty-four of the hundred most exposed counties in the Midwest and in northern states; only Clinton's strength among Black voters superseded that pattern in the South. Many of these Sanders voters, particularly in the Midwest, later defected to Trump or opted not to vote, crippling Clinton in the general election.

That the emergence of Sanders and Trump came as a shock to so many people reflected a cultural chasm that had opened up between practitioners of high-level national politics and the majority of Americans who lived and worked outside their direct, personal ambit. Increasingly, on the Washington, D.C., side, this growing distance was apparent only to those whose job it was to try to bridge the chasm. "When I came to D.C. in 1975, there were still chiefs of staff in Congress who hadn't gone to college and that was not unusual," said Michael Podhorzer, political director for the AFL-CIO. "I'm from a working-class background, so I was very attuned to this. My arrival basically coincided with the moment when it switched and you had to be college educated to work in government. That next generation had a lot of people who, like me, had grown up in working-class neighborhoods and still had working-class friends. We were still connected to that world. But the generation that came in after us, almost everyone had grown up in an environment where everyone was college educated, no one was working class, and there was no longer any personal, firsthand connection to how screwed up working people's lives were getting. It marked a great sociological change in the nature of the Democratic Party."

The shift Podhorzer describes in the class background and social connections of congressional chiefs of staff was mirrored in other white-collar professions. More and more, journalists, lawyers, consultants, and businesspeople interacted primarily or even exclusively with members of their own social class. In Washington, this had a distinctive effect that helps explain why the events of 2016 came as such a shock. The staffers and operatives in the power positions of Democratic politics were peers and college classmates of the rising generation on Wall Street, acculturated to the idea that markets were a positive force that could be used in the service of liberal goals. Hadn't Bill Clinton proved that? On a conceptual level, they understood that globalization and shifting patterns of trade produce what the Beltway vernacular bloodlessly terms "winners and losers." But this didn't register as cause for alarm, partly because economic theory held that laid-off workers would simply retrain or relocate to areas where jobs were more plentiful, and partly because those workers were in far-off places and didn't have the ability to lodge complaints through the channels that high-powered Washington policymakers are attuned to. Cut off from the experience of others for whom things were not going as well, the Washington political class didn't anticipate or understand the strength of Sanders's (and, of course, Trump's) appeal. Neither, for that matter, did most journalists.

Even Autor, whose research illuminates so much about the emotional and economic origins of that appeal, didn't sense the earthquake coming. "I don't want to say we could have called it," he said ruefully in the spring of 2016, as Trump and Sanders were becoming major figures. "But we can at least say there's stuff that we missed that had we known, we wouldn't have been as surprised as we have been."

WHEN SANDERS STARTED drawing thousands of people to his rallies in the summer of 2015, it reinforced everything he already believed about politics. By the fall, he was rising in early state polls, despite not having run a single television ad for the first five months of his campaign (Clinton had aired more than forty-eight hundred). At the end of October, he got further encouragement when his internal polling showed that his two central issues—income inequality and the corruption of the campaign finance system—were also the top two issues for Democratic primary voters. Young people were flocking to him. And big-city newspaper reporters filed regular dispatches from West Virginia and other unfashionable locales marveling at Sanders's blue-collar appeal. "Our goal," his campaign manager, Jeff Weaver, explained, alluding to the February 1 Iowa caucus, is "to win by changing the composition of the electorate on caucus night."

Sanders didn't quite win. But he fared much better in Iowa than anybody expected, with Clinton barely edging him 49.8 percent to 49.6 percent. Then he trounced her in New Hampshire eight days later, 60 percent to 38 percent. On the left, his overperformance generated an atmosphere of overwhelming conviction that the revolution was under way, even though the numbers didn't quite bear this out—the 170,000 people who turned out for the Iowa caucuses was well short of the 240,000 that Obama and Clinton had drawn in 2008. Still, Sanders showed he had genuine appeal beyond college campuses. In New Hampshire he carried 70 percent of independents and even beat Clinton among women. With Trump securing *his* first big primary win in New Hampshire (he'd lost Iowa to Ted Cruz), the national media shifted its emphasis to "the working-class fury" roiling the presidential race. Clinton suddenly appeared less than certain to win the nomination.

Sanders had three things going for him that were instrumental to his rise and shifted the future course of the Democratic Party. First, he knew what he was trying to accomplish. "I'm running," he told a gathering of his advisers at an early strategy meeting in 2015, "because I want to move the Democratic Party to the left." Second, he had a blue-print for achieving this, the one he'd developed as Burlington mayor.

The third thing Sanders had going for him was an opponent in Hillary Clinton who, for all her success in the Senate cloakroom, was a remarkably poor presidential candidate who epitomized much of what Americans had come to loathe about the political and financial elite—by 2015, the Clintons were both—yet lacked the self-awareness to see it and adjust. Clinton, for example, kept giving highly paid private speeches to Goldman Sachs and other Wall Street firms (and refusing to release transcripts of them) right until the eve of her presidential announcement. As Mitt Romney was for Obama in 2012, Clinton was the perfect foil for Sanders's populist crusade. And because her team didn't believe he posed a threat, she ignored rather than attacked him, training her criticism on the Republican field, which allowed him to present his vision essentially unchallenged. "When Bernie did his announcement," Brian Fallon, a Clinton strategist, later recalled, "I thought of him as this backbencher who just waves his arms around on the Senate floor and no one gives a shit about his speeches. So the idea that he would tap into something—I was just oblivious to it."

Once Sanders steamrolled her in New Hampshire, Clinton and her team woke up. The entire Clinton family flew to Nevada ahead of the February 20 caucus, and her super PAC flooded the airwaves. From the start, Sanders's Nevada operation was a mess, riven by infighting and an attempted coup (his state director had quit in November). Clinton escaped with a five-point victory. A week later, she won a landslide in South Carolina, 73 percent to 26 percent.

Tad Devine believed that if Sanders won the first four states, it would knock Clinton out of the race. When he didn't manage that, the campaign's strategy shifted to a long slog for delegates that Sanders wasn't equipped to win. Because he wasn't a Democrat, he didn't have ties to state parties and local officials; he also performed poorly with Black voters, who dominate southern Democratic primaries, which allowed Clinton to sweep the South and build an insurmountable delegate lead.

But Sanders didn't fold. He really did have a movement behind him. His activist core of supporters lent itself to the arcane caucus system, where organization and personal commitment, not raw support, often determine outcomes. On March 5 and 6, he won the Kansas, Maine, and Nebraska caucuses by wide margins. And he fared better than expected in the Midwest, especially in places reeling from the China Shock. With double-digit polling leads heading into the March 8 primary states of Mississippi and Michigan, Clinton still expected to deliver a knockout blow. Instead, Sanders pulled off a dramatic upset in Michigan that prolonged the race. It was an ominous sign for Clinton— again, she lost badly among independents and white working-class voters—whose significance was missed because her campaign was focused on delegate math and on convincing reporters that Sanders couldn't win. Nobody in Clinton's circle dwelled much on her obvious vulnerability to a populist critique because they mistakenly thought that by beating Sanders, she was extinguishing the threat of having to face one.

Sanders disliked conflict. He hesitated to personally attack Clinton. Early on, he'd bark at reporters who tried to get him to mix it up. "I am not running against Hillary Clinton," he said to *The Washington Post* in 2015, though of course he was. He famously declined an invitation at an early debate to scold Clinton over the scandal du jour, her flouting of email security protocols while secretary of state, claiming Americans were "sick and tired of hearing about your damn emails." Clinton, beaming like the cat that ate the canary, thanked him. But that reluctance gradually vanished. What lit a fire in Sanders, and led him to behave more like a candidate trying to win a race than an idealist trying to make a point, was his commitment to an economic vision that was, in the context of Democratic politics, the antithesis of what he believed Clinton stood for.

During the primary race, Sanders's economic populism had two components, a positive one and a negative one. He'd begun the campaign focused on the positive—his ambitious policy platform—and mostly avoided the negative, which was to impugn Clinton's many ties to Wall Street and neoliberal trade policy. Once he emerged as a real contender, though, pious abstention didn't seem quite so necessary. So Sanders decided to have it both ways: he didn't attack Clinton's integrity, but his campaign did. The result was highly effective.

Campaign tradecraft follows a strategic arc over the course of a race. Candidates start by running biographical ads to introduce themselves to voters. Then they roll out an issue agenda and follow it up with testimonial or "validation" ads—say, a farmer, a nurse, or a teacher, sometimes a family member, who seems trustworthy and speaks to the bottomless integrity of the candidate. Once a modicum of goodwill is established, campaigns run what are known in the business as "comparative" ads—that is, negative ads—that seek to define the opponent in an unflattering light (these are followed by "closers" meant to cleanse any tinge of negativity and instill warm feelings toward the candidate just before the election).

Sanders's comparative ad went right at Clinton's unseemly relationship with Wall Street, specifically the villainous Goldman Sachs. The ad, called "The Problem," debuted before the Iowa caucus and spotlighted the high fees Clinton collected for her private speeches. "They're one of the Wall Street banks that triggered the financial meltdown—Goldman Sachs," a narrator darkly intones. "How does

Wall Street get away with it? Millions in campaign contributions and speaking fees. Our economy works for Wall Street because it's rigged by Wall Street—and that's the problem. As long as Washington is bought and paid for, we can't build an economy that works for people."

Clinton wasn't named in the ad, but everyone knew to whom it referred. It drew more attention than it might have because of how Clinton's campaign reacted: they pounced. An unshakable piece of political folk wisdom holds that nothing is more risible to voters than a candidate's hypocrisy. "This last-minute sneak attack from the Sanders campaign is clearly meant to plaster the Iowa airwaves in the days before the caucus with negative ads slamming Hillary Clinton, without giving our campaign time to respond," Clinton's Iowa director fumed, essentially guaranteeing that Sanders's ad would have the desired effect. "It's a cynical political ploy in a primary that had until recently been characterized by a respectful back-and-forth about the issues." The ad was so effective that the Sanders campaign repurposed it for other states. It reminded people what they disliked about Clinton, exacerbating her biggest weakness—the widely held belief among voters that she "wasn't honest and trustworthy." It made her constantly vulnerable to populist backlash, like the one that arrived in Michigan.

Winning the Michigan primary helped persuade Sanders to carry on through the end of the primaries, which meant that his criticisms of Clinton's character and economic record were amplified, through all fifty states, by the suffusing force of a presidential primary campaign and all of the attention, advertising, and media coverage it generated— and that the central disputes between Clinton and Sanders would be revived and relitigated during the Democratic convention. This was a blow to Clinton's hopes of unifying the party and focusing on Trump and the general election, far more costly in hindsight than it appeared at the time. But somewhat paradoxically, the extended campaign wasn't great for the left-populist insurgency either, because, although Sanders generated tremendous attention and interest in his ideas and established his influence, his success created pressures that fractured the movement in ways that would become apparent during the 2020 presidential primaries when Sanders and Warren faced off against each other in a bitter struggle to win the Democratic nomination.

ELIZABETH WARREN'S DECISION to opt out of the 2016 presidential primaries was fateful for two reasons. First, it allowed Sanders to get in the race and assume the mantle of leading left populist. Second, this created pressure from the left for Warren to endorse him. After the 2014 midterm elections, Warren accepted Harry Reid's invitation to join the Senate leadership team, a mark of her arrival as a serious Washington player. So Sanders's rise brought into tension her hardwon status as a progressive hero and her growing influence within the Democratic establishment. This was especially tricky for Warren because endorsing Sanders, her ideological ally, would mean sacrificing her ability to influence Hillary Clinton, whom she expected to win and who was known to harbor grudges. It forced a choice on Warren that she didn't want to make.

Warren's choice was to make no choice at all: she withheld her endorsement until it was clear Clinton would be the nominee. In essence, she bet that she had a better chance of enacting her progressive agenda by working through a future president Clinton than by banking on a successful Sanders revolution. Warren's decision shocked her hardcore supporters on the left, many of whom turned against her. "Warren had a chance to help Bernie win when it was still possible—and she declined to do so," said Charles Lenchner, a cofounder of Ready for Warren, who later endorsed Sanders and worked to elect him.

The backlash was palpable, and, to Warren, deeply unnerving. Angry Sanders supporters flooded her Facebook posts with vitriol and charges that she'd sold out. "The feeling on the left was that she lacked courage," said Cenk Uygur, cohost of *The Young Turks*, an influential online progressive news show, "that Bernie's loss could be laid at her feet."

Initially, it looked as if Warren's inside strategy paid off. She nearly managed to maneuver herself into a position of power that would have been inconceivable a few years earlier. When they got together, Clinton and Warren found that they had a good rapport. Warren became a determined campaigner for the nominee. Campaign officials later swore that Clinton seriously weighed naming Warren as her running mate. Warren underwent a full vetting process and was smuggled into Whitehaven, Clinton's Washington home, for an interview. It went well enough that some Clinton advisers were convinced that Warren, with her impeccable populist image, would be the best pick to go up against Trump.

In a memo to Clinton written shortly after the August meeting and obtained by *Bloomberg Businessweek*, Philippe Reines, a longtime adviser, concluded of Warren, "If a crystal ball said she wouldn't antagonize you for four years, it's hard to argue she isn't the most helpful for the next four months to get you elected."

Warren fully understood the symbiotic benefit of such an arrangement and was prepared to accept the job if Clinton offered it. Ultimately, of course, Clinton chose a safe, bland, ticket-balancing male running mate who didn't threaten to outshine her. Yet even so, Warren's influence with Clinton was such that she would have a strong hand in shaping the new Democratic administration, including steering allies into key positions in the cabinet and regulatory agencies. Nearly everything about the campaign and plans for the transition that were already under way augured well for Warren and the leftist cause.

And then Clinton lost.

TRUMP'S VICTORY WAS the great axial shift in American politics that shaped everything that followed in its wake. The left-populist movement that arose in the years after the financial crisis was indelibly altered and diluted by it. Partly this was because Trump's cruelty and racism provoked a moral crisis that seemed to demand a maximalist response from liberals and leftists that didn't limit itself to economic matters, and partly it was because Trump's mutant populism seduced a critical bloc of voters who felt real affinity for Sanders's economic message but not for the Democratic Party or Hillary Clinton.

Sanders was a flawed presidential candidate, but he accomplished a great deal. As an evangelist for a left-populist politics, he far surpassed what Warren had begun, ultimately winning twenty-three states and 43 percent of the popular vote in the primaries. He lost the primary race to Clinton. But by the standard he'd first set for himself—shifting the Democratic Party to the left—he plainly succeeded. This is what his campaign manager, Jeff Weaver, meant by the title of his 2018 memoir, *How Bernie Won*. Sanders reshaped Democratic politics, killing off Clintonian neoliberal supremacy with a big assist from Trump.

But Trump was the immediate beneficiary of Sanders's exit because his hyperaggressive populist resentments appealed to some of the same people who'd been drawn to Sanders. It wasn't uncommon to encounter Trump rallygoers whose second choice was Sanders, or

Sanders fans who liked what Trump had to say. Many of them were clustered in places that were economically depressed and electorally significant, people for whom the China Shock wasn't an academic abstraction but a concrete force in their lives. Trump's accusing Clinton of "unleashing a trade war against the American worker when she supported one terrible trade deal after another" and China of committing "the greatest jobs theft in history" was a way of reaching them. His oft-repeated line that the United States had lost sixty thousand factories since China joined the WTO was the rare Trump claim that was actually true.

As a candidate, Trump didn't garner much respect. But by instinct or calculation, he moved to the center on Social Security and Medicare and vowed to turn the GOP into "a worker's party—a party of people that haven't had a real wage increase in 18 years, that are angry." The big surprise on election night was that his message connected. It was establishment figures like Clinton who'd misread the temper of the times.

Clinton would have been president had she held on to three states Obama won in 2012—Wisconsin, Pennsylvania, and Michigan—and she would have won all three if she'd carried the voters in those states who supported Sanders in the Democratic primaries. She didn't. In all three, the number of Sanders voters who defected to Trump in the general election exceeded his margin of victory. What made them move?

One of the big debates after the election was whether Trump's supporters were motivated by economic distress or racial grievance. Several studies found racial attitudes to be the chief determinant of voter behavior. But it's impossible to measure that sort of thing with psychological precision. Human emotion doesn't sort neatly into polling categories. What's indisputable is that Sanders's message resonated with a group of voters who were willing to cast a vote for a Democrat, but turned elsewhere when one representing their values was no longer on the ballot.

After the election, a Tufts University political scientist named Brian Schaffner, drawing on verified voter data from a gigantic survey called the Cooperative Congressional Election Study, found that about 9 percent of Sanders voters in Wisconsin, 8 percent in Michigan, and 16 percent in Pennsylvania had voted for Trump. Looking deeper into the data, Schaffner sketched a portrait of who these people were. They were not college kids, radicals, or peaceniks. Their average age was fifty-two. They were older, whiter, more conservative, less favorably inclined toward Obama, and less likely than other Sanders supporters to identify as Democrats. "The thing that really stood out to me," Schaffner later noted, "is that a lot of these people who voted for Sanders—and then Trump—don't look like modern day Democrats."

What they looked like were casualties of the financial crisis, people motivated not by political ideology (about half self-identified as "middle of the road") but by economic distress and an understandable dissatisfaction with a Democratic Party that had failed to produce for them, over the previous eight years, a satisfying recovery.

Trump's rise, like Warren's and Sanders's, wouldn't have happened without the 2008 financial crisis. They were all part of the political backlash that followed the crisis like aftershocks from an earthquake. One thing Trump's victory made clear was that the Obama administration's response was more costly than initially assumed. The decision to forgo what Tim Geithner called "Old Testament justice" and concentrate the government's firepower on recapitalizing disgraced banks might have kept the economy afloat. But it also bred a deep resentment. Trump won because he consciously evoked the disgust people had come to feel toward Wall Street and Washington and made himself into an instrument to strike back.

His final ad before the election wasn't about immigration or building a wall. It flashed images of the Federal Reserve chair, Janet Yellen, and the Goldman Sachs CEO, Lloyd Blankfein, and implicated them, along with Clinton, in what Trump called "a global power structure that is responsible for the economic decisions that have robbed our working class, stripped our country of its wealth, and put that money into the pockets of a handful of large corporations and political entities." He added, "The only thing that can stop this corrupt machine is you." It's no surprise this message struck a chord: What was Trump if not the embodiment of a balled fist and a vow to deliver Old Testament justice?

For Democrats, the shock of Clinton's loss raised a pair of urgent, existential questions: Why had voters whom they'd been relying on to win abandoned them? And how could the party reassemble a winning coalition?

9

MOBILIZE

D onald Trump's election had a wrenching, transformative effect on nearly every aspect of Democratic politics, practically overnight. One specific effect it had was wiping out any possibility that finance-centered neoliberalism—or for that matter, Bill and Hillary Clinton—would factor in the future of the Democratic Party. Too great was its culpability for the conditions that allowed Trump to capture the presidency. In this way, his election marked the end of the era Tony Coelho had helped usher in more than three decades earlier, when Democrats began competing unabashedly for the favor of corporate America as a way to finance the party, ignoring or embracing the ideological compromises this necessarily entailed. The cost of such compromise was now fully apparent, not just in the economic damage inflicted by the financial crisis and the Great Recession that followed, but in the disillusion it generated among Democratic voters who hadn't felt enough affinity for Clinton or the party to show their support. But it left wide open the question of who, and what, would come next.

Right away, it was clear the answer wouldn't come from party leaders. When he addressed the White House press corps from the Rose Garden the next morning, Obama's ashen, shell-shocked visage showed that he, too, like everyone else, had failed to recognize what his party was up against and hadn't quite even wrapped his head around what had just happened. It was also clear that the shock of Clinton's defeat to Trump stirred a sudden realization in people all across the country that if the institutional Democratic Party was a spent force, as it appeared to be, then it would be up to them, personally, to rescue the country. How exactly they would do this was unclear. But at a moment in history when it felt as if everything hung in the balance, it seemed important to register their anger and discontent as publicly and forcefully as possible. So one of the first things people did was to pour out into the streets.

In the weeks after Trump's victory, an energetic resistance arose to counter him. It spawned hundreds if not thousands of new activist groups. Most were committedly local endeavors, often made up of neighborhood acquaintances who hadn't been actively involved in politics—or at least not lately—and organized quickly and informally over email, in text messages, or simply through word of mouth. On January 21, the day after Trump's inauguration, many of them joined the Women's March on Washington or attended sister rallies held in cities ranging from Atlanta, Boston, and San Francisco to Ketchum, Idaho. Collectively, these rallies drew more than three million people, many of whom were being pulled into the political system for the first time.

Trump's election was the worst thing many Democrats could imagine. But the political awakening his presidency drove and the great outpouring of energy and activism it produced were the best things that could happen to a party in need of revitalizing. It created a set of conditions that made Coelho's old fantasy about building a party around ordinary working people (rather than wealthy financiers) more plausible than at any point since his 1980s heyday. The challenge for Democrats was how to harness this new energy. They had just learned the painful lesson that antipathy for Trump, by itself, didn't automatically translate to votes. In order to reclaim control of the American government, the countermovement Trump inspired would need to be efficiently directed to the places where it would make the most difference on Election Day. Who would do this? And how?

THERE ARE MANY WAYS to tell the story of the Democratic Party's evolution during the Trump years—how it responded to Clinton's loss, how it reorganized itself and what it stood for, and what its activists and leaders understood themselves to be doing as events were unfolding around them. But the best vantage point to track what was happening inside and outside the party, and to understand the shaping forces, may be the laptop computers of a pair of young men in the Bay Area who awoke the morning after Trump's election as astounded as everyone else—and then, like millions of other people, resolved to do something about it. Although they had little in common with Tony Coelho, they shared the sense Coelho had had after Reagan's victory that the election of a new Republican president marked a historical inflection point and that the Democratic Party was ill-equipped to compete.

Allen Kramer and Alfred Johnson were both happily toiling in the private sector when Trump won. Kramer, twenty-six, who grew up in New York City, was working at Bain & Company in San Francisco, where he had just returned after taking a leave to work on Clinton's campaign. Johnson, thirty-one, was from Washington, D.C. He'd played defensive end on Stanford's football team, then stuck around Palo Alto for business school and a job at a fintech start-up that he had been lobbying Kramer to join. Trump's election jolted them in a new direction. "Alfred and I had a collective realization," Kramer later recalled. "I was helping a large corporation figure out how to sell IT hardware online. Quantitatively, very interesting problem. But I'd just come back from the campaign with the gut-wrenching context of having seen what happened up close."

Kramer and Johnson quit their jobs and moved back east. They were part of a quiet migration that occurred during the chaotic early months of the Trump presidency of committed progressives who left careers or paused their educations to involve themselves full time in electoral politics. Some ran for public office. Others founded activist organizations. Another group, which Kramer and Johnson belonged to, were entrepreneurs, many of them with backgrounds in technology or organizing, who set out to solve a problem that had bedeviled Clinton and other Democrats up and down the ticket: how to identify and turn out more voters, especially among key Democratic-leaning groups that hadn't shown up at the polls for Clinton.

With business school rigor, Kramer and Johnson headed off on a fact-finding mission, quizzing campaign managers, organizers, activists, and data scientists to find the gaps in the system that were causing Democrats to lose winnable races. They were searching for a business idea because drawing on their degrees and experience struck them as the best way they could contribute to the cause. What exactly that idea might be, however, remained elusive for many months. But instinct drew them to the explosion of grassroots energy apparent in the Women's March and events like it. "We kept coming back to the fact that we had millions of people marching in the streets," said Johnson. "But all that energy—the Women's March, the people showing up at airports after Trump instituted the Muslim ban—it was completely undirected. There had to be ways to plug those people into the electoral opportunities that mattered most." (Clinton was also struck by the marchers and, in her memoir, wondered a bit caustically "where those feelings of solidarity, outrage, and passion had been during the election.")

For entrepreneurs with left-leaning political views, there was no better time than the dawn of the Trump era to start a company. Young idealists weren't alone in believing that a generational crisis was at hand. Plenty of rich donors thought the same thing. The feeling was particularly acute among a new breed of fabulously wealthy technologists clustered in Silicon Valley who were newcomers to Democratic politics, but well accustomed to funding start-ups and convinced, not unjustly, that Clinton's campaign and the party establishment undergirding it were wheezing relics of a bygone era no longer equipped for contemporary political campaigns. They were willing to stake millions of dollars to entrepreneurs with convincing plans to modernize the party and take the country back from Trump.

The idea Kramer and Johnson ultimately settled on was a mobile app and web interface that was designed to connect Resistance marchers and other newly politicized activists with nearby candidates who needed volunteer support. They called their company Mobilize-America (later shortened to just Mobilize). Early on, someone cheekily dubbed it "Tinder for the Resistance" and the concept stuck. With seed funding from Higher Ground Labs, a "progressive technology accelerator" backed by Silicon Valley luminaries such as Reid Hoffman and Chris Sacca that had sprung up in the wake of Trump's victory, Kramer and Johnson hired a small staff of engineers and organizers. Then they fanned out across Washington, D.C., Maryland, and Virginia to meet individually with hundreds of Resistance groups, small and large, to try to persuade them to use the Mobilize app to channel their volunteers to the Democratic causes that needed them.

Veteran campaign strategists tended to scoff at the new breed of moneyed interlopers from Silicon Valley with their tiresome sermons about "disruption" and "scalability." But the logic of funding organizing apps and other online tools wasn't just a product of California venture capitalists repeating what was already familiar to them. Trump's victory exposed how poorly Democrats were equipped to compete in the new era of politics he represented. The fact that they were blindsided by Clinton's loss only highlighted how complacent and out of touch the party had become. Trump's shadow loomed over the Democrats' losses. From the outset, he had used his Twitter feed to shape and dominate the race. His campaign exploited Facebook to devastating effect, not only to raise hundreds of millions of dollars and excite legions of new voters, but also by contracting with a shadowy London technology firm called Cambridge Analytica that used the platform's tools to secretly target and discourage Democrats from voting (for instance, by targeting African Americans with Facebook "dark posts"— nonpublic posts whose viewership the campaign controlled so that, as the Trump campaign's digital director put it, "only the people we want to see it, see it").

Technologically, Democrats had fallen behind. And the cost of this failure was most apparent to the young field organizers who crisscrossed the country on Clinton's behalf, toting paper clipboards and relying on methods like door knocking, phone banking, and over-the-air television advertising that would have been familiar to Tony Coelho when he was running the Democratic campaign committee in the 1980s. As any millennial-age field staffer could attest, none of these methods was very likely to reach people their own age. In fact, they tended to miss *two* vital Democratic groups—young people and minorities—both of which were more transient than other groups, which made them harder to reach by traditional methods because they often didn't own landline telephones or pay for cable television. Some Democratic staffers bitterly joked that Trump's campaign had done a better job of reaching these potential Democratic voters than their own side had. "The same people that they don't want to vote are the people we *do* want to vote," a twenty-five-year-old Clinton organizer observed in frustration. By and large, Clinton's campaign failed to reach them. A Tufts University poll taken a month before the election found that just 30 percent of millennials had been contacted by a campaign. In the waning months of the race, a few Clinton field staffers in Michigan became so fed up with these limitations that they went rogue and began surreptitiously organizing voters by text message. (Afterward, they, too, started a company backed by Higher Ground Labs.)

Mobilize, on the other hand, was designed by and for a generation reared on iPhones. At least conceptually, it could solve the problem the Clinton organizers had run into, because everybody—even people who move around a lot and stream TV rather than rent a cable box—has a phone that travels with them to wherever they might happen to reside. If Mobilize could persuade people to download their app, then Kramer and Johnson stood to become the intermediaries who connected the Resistance and the Democratic Party—matchmakers for democracy.

LIKE ALL OF the new political-technology start-ups, Mobilize first focused on Virginia, the only battleground state with elections in 2017. As every political consultant knows, Virginia is an ideal product laboratory because it neatly approximates the country as a whole, with urban and rural areas and a fast-growing immigrant population. The state's profile as America in miniature was further buttressed in 2017 by the fact that Republicans controlled both houses of the general assembly (as they did the U.S. Congress) but not by such large margins that Democrats couldn't envision winning them back.

After consulting with Virginia Democrats, Mobilize selected twelve state house seats held by Republicans that were expected to be competitive in the fall election and then ventured forth to enlist nearby Resistance groups in the effort to flip them. The experiment was candidate agnostic: Mobilize didn't screen for race, gender, or ideology, beyond requiring that the candidate be the Democratic nominee. "The only rules we had were that it had to be a competitive race and had to be within a two-hour drive of Washington, D.C.," said Yasmin Radjy, thirty, Mobilize's Virginia state director, who would go on to become a top official at Planned Parenthood and Swing Left. "The experiment was to see if we could direct scaled volunteer capacity from outside and make a difference on Election Day."

Although Mobilize didn't screen its races, it wound up with a roster of candidates who, had they been handpicked for colorful vitality that contrasted with Trump's Republican Party, could not have been any better. One was a daughter of Vietnamese refugees, another a young working mother of two who stood to become the first Latina elected to the assembly. But the most vivid among them by a mile was Danica Roem, the first transgender woman to run for the Virginia House of Delegates.

If Virginia is a microcosm of America, then the Thirteenth District race between Roem and the twenty-five-year GOP incumbent, a man named Bob Marshall, was like the 2016 presidential election glimpsed in a fun-house mirror: everything was exaggerated even further. Roem grew up in the Northern Virginia district, worked for nine years as a local newspaper reporter, and moonlighted as a singer in a heavy-metal band called Cab Ride Home. She began her gender transition in 2013 and usually wore a rainbow scarf in her hair. Trump's victory pushed her into electoral politics. "What the election taught me," Roem liked to say, "is that there is literally nothing in my background that's disqualifying. That bar is gone."

Her opponent, Marshall, was a kind of ur-Trump who refused to debate Roem or call her by her preferred gender pronoun. Marshall proudly touted himself as "Virginia's chief homophobe" and had the track record to back it up. He was best known for unsuccessfully pushing a state "bathroom bill" that would dictate which restrooms transgender people could use in public buildings. When Roem won the Democratic primary in June, Marshall's Republican backers flooded the Thirteenth District with campaign flyers reminding voters that she had been "born male."

But Marshall was falling out of step with his district, which was increasingly composed of highly educated voters and had gone for Clinton by fourteen points in the 2016 election. Roem, in other words, was exactly the sort of candidate Democrats had to find a way to push to victory, in Virginia and everywhere else, if they hoped to reclaim power.

She wouldn't lack for foot soldiers. Throughout the spring and summer, Kramer and Johnson met with every Resistance organization they could find in the Washington metro area. Evenings were spent pitching groups whose defiant can-do spirit was usually evident in their name: Flip VA Blue, Together We Will NOVA, J Walkers Action Group, Mad Enough to Act, Bagels and Resistance, Turn It Blue DC, and on and on. Most had come together in the heady days after the Women's March, when the surge of solidarity made them feel as if they could accomplish anything. But they soon discovered that effecting political change is trickier than it might at first appear. Outside presidential campaigns, there weren't natural mechanisms to get involved in politics. The District hardly needed flipping, having voted 91 percent to 4 percent for Clinton. Most close-in suburbs were nearly as blue. And practically every group was led by a volunteer who was not a professional political practitioner and did not have easy access to one, either, so guidance was hard to come by.

Mobilize offered a way to channel this activist energy toward a productive cause with a political payoff that wasn't nearly as far off as the next presidential election. For many of the new volunteers, it had the added allure of letting them work on behalf of someone like Roem whose very identity was a rebuke to the open bigotry that distinguished Trump's Republican Party. It packed a deep emotional satisfaction to pile into cars or buses on the weekend and make the hour-long trek from D.C. to Manassas or Gainesville to canvass for Roem or even to spend a few hours textbanking for her campaign. For all her transgressive qualities, Roem was a natural politician with a wry charisma who almost always showed up at events to greet her volunteers when they arrived. Word got around. By the fall, eager crowds of young people, some in rainbow paraphernalia, were turning up on the weekends to knock on doors for Roem and the other candidates. The Mobilize database began to swell.

For all the obvious sociocultural significance of her candidacy, Roem, when speaking with the voters of the Thirteenth District, generally didn't talk about gender identity or Donald Trump or anything having to do with national politics at all. She talked about traffic. In particular, the soul-crushing, gridlocked, six-lane expanse of State Route 28 that is the primary artery running through the district. It was the focus of her campaign. With the country bitterly divided over just about everything and her opponent fanning the culture war flames, Roem stuck to this unifying theme. "Traffic hates everyone," she said. "I just want to fix Route 28."

For people whose primary lens into national affairs is MSNBC or Facebook or Twitter, U.S. politics can often appear to be a neatly delineated Manichaean drama between good and evil. You're either a Democrat or a Republican, an ally or an enemy. But anyone who has canvassed for a politician, especially a local one, knows that real voters are messy, complicated creatures, often brimming with contradictions. The reality "on the doors," as field staffers say, is always and forever unpredictable. Even in the Washington exurbs, the people coming to the door are usually the furthest thing from partisan purists. More often, they're haggard office workers, overburdened parents, and anxious retirees whose cares and concerns rarely map easily onto the issues driving the national political conversation.

One day Radjy was working her way through a block of town houses as a canvasser for Bob Marshall did the same. She watched her counterpart finish up with a man whose pickup truck and Trump lawn sign advertised his Republican loyalties and debated whether she should make an approach. Radjy, possessed of the implacable cheerfulness characteristic of the best canvassers, thought to herself, *What the hell?* and moved in. The man was indeed a Trump supporter and a committed Republican who homeschooled his children. He was also a heavy metal fan and planned to vote for Roem. "We need to do something," he told Radjy, "about Route 28."

By Labor Day, Roem had raised more money than Marshall and become a cause célèbre among local Resistance groups. "The activists and donors loved her," said Johnson. "They wanted to elect the first trans candidate. And she was channeling it all into Route 28 because that's what the voters care about." Across northern and central

Virginia, the other Mobilize candidates, boosted by the surfeit of D.C.-area volunteers who were being directed to their districts, were encountering similar successes. On Election Day, all twelve Mobilize candidates defeated their Republican opponents, including Roem, who beat Marshall by 1,759 votes.

THE BLUE WAVE that swept Virginia electrified Democrats all over the country. But what was the lesson of Roem's victory—that making bold contrasts rooted in personal identity is the key to beating Republicans? Or that kitchen-table issues dictate the outcome of nearly every close race, no matter who's running? Roem thought addressing voters' concerns should always take priority, and deftly directed the attention she got to furthering that goal. But that wasn't how her victory was interpreted in the broader culture.

When the news of it broke on election night, Roem immediately started trending on Twitter. Millions of people were delighted to discover her and share her story. Some of them were famous. A few days after the election, the pop star Demi Lovato flew Roem to Los Angeles to join her at the American Music Awards, declaring herself "just completely inspired" by Roem's story. Lovato obviously wasn't talking about her effort to ease gridlock on Route 28. Nominated for an AMA for a song about bullying, Lovato considered Roem an inspiring example of someone who overcame it. (Even so, Roem gamely plugged her traffic plan while standing beside Lovato on the red carpet, which occasioned a memorable Associated Press story that began, "A dreary, congested Virginia highway has reaped an unexpected measure of fame.") Roem was plainly an inspiring figure. But many people in politics, especially among the rising generation of plugged-in national Democratic strategists, understood the success of Roem and other candidates with nontraditional backgrounds to be evidence in favor of the "bold contrast" approach, something social media virality only reinforced.

This distinction would come to matter a great deal as the 2020 Democratic presidential primaries took shape. But at this early point, it was mostly inside baseball. In short order, it became apparent that most members of the Resistance were less interested in ideological purity than in clawing back power from Republicans, wherever and however they could.

Mobilize's success in Virginia caught the attention of Democratic officials and brought Kramer and Johnson a bevy of new opportunities. One of the first was a March 2018 special election in southwestern Pennsylvania coal country, where Conor Lamb, a square-jawed thirty-three-year-old prosecutor and former marine, was running a self-consciously centrist campaign for an open U.S. House seat in a district Trump had carried by twenty points. Demographically, it was a world away from Roem's constituency of exurban college-educated commuters. And yet this proved no impediment to generating enthusiasm. Lamb, running to represent a district whose residents were older than those of almost any other in the country, hammered away at the specter of Republicans cutting Social Security and Medicare. He raised millions of dollars from small donors nationwide and was flooded with volunteers from outside his district—many of them staunch liberals. On the weekend before the election, Mobilize was arranging thirteen hundred volunteer shifts a day for Lamb.

Trump didn't refrain from involving himself in a race everyone expected Republicans to win. Twice, including on the eve of the election, he flew in to headline rallies to support Lamb's opponent. "The world is watching," Trump declared. "Get out on Tuesday and vote like crazy." Lamb still eked out a remarkable upset win, 49.8 percent to

49.6 percent, leaving Trump to claim that Lamb ultimately had succeeded because he himself was "like Trump." The real takeaway was just the opposite: the Democratic groundswell reached much deeper into Trump country than even the Virginia elections had suggested, and the party was now capable of mustering grassroots activists even on the most challenging political terrain.

ONE THING THE Mobilize brain trust discovered from the groups and candidates it worked with was that even enthusiastic volunteers were often hesitant to download "Tinder for the Resistance." No one, after all, recognized the name "Mobilize"—why would they?—so people sometimes balked when receiving an email that instructed them to download the Mobilize app onto their phone. There was nothing wrong with the technology itself; that much was clear from the race results. But what each campaign and organization really wanted was to be able to equip volunteers with their own branded app, something that Johnson and Kramer realized made intuitive sense. When Roem had collaborated with Funny or Die, for instance, the humor website had first had to run an ad campaign encouraging its fans to download an app "from our friends at MobilizeAmerica"—an added hurdle that was surely a trip point for some number of would-be volunteers. It would be far more efficient, everyone agreed, if Funny or Die and other clients could push their own app.

This was an easy technological fix. Mobilize started letting clients add their own "skin" to its technology—that is, affix their preferred branding to an app or website to give users the reassuring impression that it was their own. Mobilize still designed the technology and ran the back-end functions. But now the company shifted to becoming a customizable platform, which in turn attracted many of the major

Democratic organizations, including the Democratic National Committee, the DCCC and DSCC, and forty-six state parties, along with more than a hundred campaigns and dozens of fast-growing grassroots groups, such as MoveOn, Indivisible, and Swing Left, that collectively claimed twenty million members.

To anyone but lefty tech geeks and professional field organizers, this development would not have registered as consequential, had they noticed it at all. But it marked a pivot point in Democratic Party building because it gave critical mass to the idea that a centralized volunteer database could exist outside a presidential campaign. One reason Democrats had struggled to turn out voters in state and local races was that cutting-edge technology was always developed for—and housed within—campaigns like Barack Obama's that budgeted tens of millions of dollars for it and employed teams of specialists. Down-ballot races lacked the specialized personnel and budgets to make use of it. So when the presidential campaign ended, the tools vanished. A few years later, the process would repeat. "We build the same thing over and over," Betsy Hoover, who ran digital organizing for Obama before helping launch Higher Ground Labs, lamented. "Down-ballot races never really benefit."

But with so many Democratic campaigns and progressive groups signing on with Mobilize, that cycle was finally going to be broken. Mobilize wasn't going to shut down after Election Day. Its database of volunteers would endure and grow. And it wasn't a static repository that put them into hibernation until the next presidential election. Mobilize could, and did, direct volunteers to all sorts of progressive causes and campaigns, which no longer needed to burn through their budgets trying to build organizing tools that were now field-tested and readily available to them. To further establish its utility to Democratic campaigns, Mobilize added the ability to integrate with

ActBlue, the online fundraising software that would direct $1.6 billion to Democratic candidates in 2018, most of it coming from small donors. Almost forty years after Coelho tapped Wall Street in hopes of building a direct-mail system that would draw on small donors to fund the Democratic Party—an ambition that, in its failure, helped transform the nature of what the party stood for and whom it represented—something strikingly similar had come into being. It wasn't by the grand design of one man or even widely recognized as having happened. Nonetheless, it now existed, free from the corrupting entanglements that had enveloped and eventually poisoned the party in the 1980s and 1990s. Its power was, as yet, still largely theoretical. But it was going to be tested in the 2018 midterm elections that were now only months away.

IN THE GRIM PERIOD after Trump's inauguration, Johnson and Kramer had contacted countless Resistance groups and participated in an endless succession of events and rallies, what Johnson liked to refer to as "engagement funnels" that pulled people into the Mobilize system, one by one.

Now they were here, millions of them. It gave Johnson a remarkable, granular view of the Resistance from the inside, one that almost nobody else had. He also had an unparalleled view of the broader horizon. His laptop became something like the command center for a sprawling, far-flung volunteer army of millions stretching from coast to coast. With a few keystrokes, he could call up almost any race and track the movement in real time, with each participant in a rally, house party, phone bank, or canvass serving as another data point in what he could now see was shaping up to be an unprecedented Democratic turnout.

What Johnson saw in his laptop didn't always comport with what other people thought was happening in politics, even people whose business it was to know. When talking with reporters, he'd gently try to correct the misimpression some held that the Resistance was a cauldron of young radicals agitating for left-wing revolution. Certainly *some* members fit that bill. But most did not. The typical Resistance marchers volunteering through Mobilize were older, no-nonsense professional women whom Radjy fondly referred to as "PTA moms"— women who had decided they no longer recognized their own country after Trump's election and stepped forward to take back what they felt they had lost. In 2017, more than 70 percent of volunteers in Virginia were women. In 2018, the number hovered around 65 percent nationwide. And while a surge of participation was indeed evident among younger adults—something Mobilize had originally set out to foster— by Election Day volunteers aged fifty-five and older dwarfed those thirty-four and younger. But what mattered more was that activism was soaring among every age cohort. In the span of four years, midterm voter turnout jumped from the lowest in a century, in 2014, to the highest, in 2018.

Johnson was struck by something else, too. It was impossible to quantify, but he sensed it nonetheless. The women (and men) signing up to volunteer were not ideologues and did not evince the purifying ardor of Bernie Sanders diehards. In fact, the movement floated free from specific ideologies or political leaders—besides, of course, the unifying desire to oust Donald Trump. Johnson thought that for people drawn to the Women's March or to local Resistance groups political organizing had evolved from an activity geared toward a particular race into something broader: a form of community like a bowling league or a book club. "There was something so existentially jarring about Trump's election," he said, "that it created a kind of socialization around politics in a way that we maybe haven't seen since the civil rights movement."

All of the organizing and energy produced the dramatic results Democrats were hoping for. They regained control of the House of Representatives, netting 41 seats. Their particular strength came in the suburbs of fast-growing, traditionally Republican metro areas such as Atlanta, Dallas, Denver, Houston, and Orange County, California. In 2016, Trump had won them narrowly. But Democrats stormed back with help from disaffected Republicans. They also picked up 7 governorships, and flipped 350 state legislative seats and 6 chambers from red to blue. The only blemish was the U.S. Senate, where Republicans maintained control, netting 2 additional seats.

Kramer and Johnson also fared well, establishing Mobilize at the nexus of Democratic politics just as the 2020 presidential race was starting to take shape. A few months after the election, Joe Biden became one of the first presidential candidates to join the Mobilize network. Elizabeth Warren and Bernie Sanders soon followed. Eventually, more than a dozen other candidates would join them.

But the brightest star of the 2018 cycle, who quickly seized Washington's attention, hadn't helped grow the Democratic margin in Congress by flipping a Republican seat. Nor was she about to launch a presidential campaign. Nevertheless, Alexandria Ocasio-Cortez would have an outsized influence on the next chapter of Democratic politics.

10

THE NATURAL

The Democrats' free-market evolution across the 1980s and 1990s didn't go unchallenged by the activist left. In 1999, a meeting of the World Trade Organization in Seattle was shut down, and the National Guard resorted to tear gas, pepper spray, and rubber bullets when thousands of protesters, including many labor union members, brought the city to a standstill to call attention to the low wages and lax environmental standards that accompanied rising globalization and unfettered free trade. A year later, similar protests against the growing neoliberal trade regime and the power of multinational corporations were directed at the annual meetings of the World Bank and the International Monetary Fund in Washington, D.C. In 2004, the Million Worker March, organized by the International Longshore and Warehouse Union, drew an estimated ten thousand people to the

National Mall to demand universal health care, better wages, guaranteed pensions for workers, and an end to the overseas outsourcing of jobs.

But the U.S. invasion of Iraq in 2003 shifted activist energy to foreign policy for the next several years. The months leading up to the war saw some of the largest street protests in recent U.S. history, culminating in globally coordinated marches on February 15, 2003, that drew as many as ten million protesters across six hundred cities. The fracturing of the Western alliance into a "coalition of the willing"—the forty-odd countries including the U.K., Spain, and Poland that supported the U.S.-led invasion—and a group of traditional U.S. allies, including France, Germany, and Canada, that did not back George W. Bush's invasion fed a popular conviction that public attitudes over Iraq were malleable enough that large-scale demonstrations against the war could halt it or at least turn public opinion against it. In Washington and other cities, street protests led by groups such as Code Pink and Veterans for Peace became a regular occurrence of downtown life. Countering the Bush administration's military imperialism became the primary focus of liberal attention and gave rise to a new generation of protesters who established new avenues for organizing and communicating over the internet. What came to be called the netroots began influencing Democratic politicians. Eventually, this younger generation of activists, many of them personally immiserated by the effects of recession, turned their attention back to the domestic political economy. But in the years before the global economic collapse, the Iraq War was the major shaping force in Democratic politics; most notably, the widespread opposition to the war and liberal antipathy to its Democratic supporters carried Barack Obama, who opposed the invasion, past Hillary Clinton, who supported it, to the 2008 nomination.

One of the early signs that the 2008 financial crisis was having a more profound effect on the country and its political alignment than Democratic leaders had anticipated was how a small protest in lower Manhattan in the fall of 2011 suddenly grew into something much larger. Beginning on September 17 and lasting for nearly two months, the Occupy Wall Street protest took up residence in Zuccotti Park, filling the square block dappled with honey locust trees that sits amid gleaming towers in the heart of the financial district. The protest elevated the issue of rising economic inequality to the very center of public attention. It contradicted, in the most vivid way, Obama's assurance that "green shoots" were spreading throughout the economy and producing a recovery of sufficient strength and scope to justify his turning his attention toward reducing the federal deficit.

The two thousand protesters who assembled in Zuccotti Park were responding to a call in the anticapitalist magazine *Adbusters* for a "Tahrir moment," a reference to the recent Arab Spring protests that had toppled governments in the Middle East. Early media coverage was muted. New York City had already seen an anti–Wall Street protest in May, and a group affiliated with the activist collective Anonymous had attempted to occupy Zuccotti Park a month later, in June. Neither amounted to much. But the Occupy Wall Street protest was better planned, and it benefited, at the outset, from the New York City mayor Michael Bloomberg's decision not to intervene and shut it down. After about a week or so, as the protest grew and it became clear people weren't going away, media curiosity picked up.

Occupy Wall Street drew international attention and became the cultural force it did because it achieved things earlier protests hadn't managed to do. Some of this owed to its timing. Its launch coincided with a blast of unexpected bad news about the economy: on September 2 the Labor Department announced that job growth had halted entirely in the prior month, with the unemployment rate still stuck above 9 percent. A few weeks earlier, Republicans' refusal to raise the debt ceiling had shaken global markets and nearly forced an unthinkable catastrophe in which the U.S. government defaulted on its obligations. The near miss led Standard & Poor's to downgrade the federal government's credit rating for the first time in history. It seemed as if the country were coming apart at the seams. A top White House official later called this period "the political nadir" of Obama's presidency.

Occupy had a lights-out marketing pitch. Its famous slogan framing the economy as pitting the 1 percent against the 99 percent injected new terminology into the national political debate, language that was charged with the transgressive frisson of social-class warfare. Obama and a generation of Democrats before him strenuously avoided talking about policy in the stark language of class disparity because it upset the Wall Street contingent in the party. But the slogan resonated with most everyone else. Occupy had a protean ability to absorb and reflect the ambient dissatisfaction even among people who would never march in the streets but were nonetheless pissed off about the general state of things and harbored a lurking sense that they were being victimized by powerful unseen forces. As an anti-austerity movement swept across Europe, the protests spread to hundreds of cities across eighty-two countries.

In addition, Occupy revealed something fundamental about the American condition three years after the crash. It challenged the conventional wisdom about the younger generation that its members were apathetic and disconnected from public affairs. Now, suddenly, they weren't. And because Occupy Wall Street was formally leaderless and advanced no list of demands, and also because it was centered on the media capital of the universe, it invited continuous speculation on the part of the media about "what it all means." That put the protesters themselves in the spotlight. Many were young, vocally disillusioned with the course their lives had taken, and self-consciously inclined to present themselves and their complaints as being generationally representative—an irresistible hook to reporters and producers looking to explain the unexpected drama unfolding in New York City and elsewhere.

"When Obama actually won," a twenty-five-year-old activist explained,

> I remember there was a huge celebration in the streets, on Broad Street in Philadelphia. Everyone was out together. The police cleared it out pretty quickly, but it felt for one moment like we had all come together because we wanted to see something really positive happen in the country. And then of course, we got the disappointments we got. A lot of people are starting to realize that getting Obama elected and all the effort that went into it, it didn't produce. It's compelling people to say, "We tried that, we're not going to waste any of our energy or any of our hope again."

Democratic leaders weren't quite sure how to respond to the demonstrations. Their general instinct was to avoid defensiveness and try to appear as though they were allied with the protesters against an unscrupulous financial system, rather than objects of those protesters' scorn. To shield Obama from criticism, one of his senior advisers, David Plouffe, went on *Good Morning America* and tried to claim moral credit for his boss while rather speciously suggesting that the demonstrators' ire was, or at least ought to be, directed solely at Republicans. "If you're concerned about Wall Street and our financial system, the president is standing on the side of consumers and the middle class,"

Plouffe said, in the canned language of a consultant. "And a lot of these Republicans are basically saying, 'You know what? Let's go back to the same policies that led to the Great Recession in the first place.'"

As if to illustrate that this sentiment was less than pure, the Democratic Congressional Campaign Committee responded to Occupy by using it as a fundraising opportunity, urging supporters in an email to sign a petition backing the protesters. But this drew an immediate backlash from outraged bank executives, who complained to the DCCC's finance chairman, Representative Joe Crowley of New York. Wall Street clients "were livid," one Democratic banking lobbyist reported. "They feel like they're going to be burned in effigy," Anthony Scaramucci, an Obama donor and hedge fund partner who had switched jerseys to support Romney in 2012, explained. Wall Street's anger should hardly have come as a surprise. "Look at the major donors to Obama, look at the major donors to the DCCC," an exasperated banker told *Politico*—they were all bankers!

One group who didn't have to be reminded was the protesters gathered in Zuccotti Park. The hypocrisy they detected in the DCCC and Obama (who had raised more money from Wall Street than his Republican opponent in 2008) was one of the reasons most Occupy activists had lost faith in the political system as a vehicle for social change. It was why they opted instead for direct action—for taking over Zuccotti Park to try to force the changes they thought were necessary.

Any movement without leaders or goals is destined to fail eventually. On November 15, police raided Zuccotti Park and broke up the encampment. The participants scattered. What exactly the occupation had achieved was unclear. It had certainly raised consciousness about income inequality, and that was something. The populist tone Obama struck in his reelection campaign also owed an obvious debt to

Occupy Wall Street. But at the time, there wasn't much tangible that people could point to and attribute to the protests. Some of the repercussions took much longer to see.

Many of the protesters later concluded that there were limits to what they could achieve by a tactical commitment to direct action. Some began to reconsider their abstention from the mainstream political process. And a few started thinking about how they could develop new political leaders who could transfigure the abstractions of the Occupy uprising into concrete policies and get them enacted.

THE PROTESTERS AT Zuccotti Park were not representative of the city or the country they lived in. Most were young, but even among the younger generation of Americans they stood apart in several important regards.

Today, what people would probably notice about them is their "privilege"; they were more likely to be white, male, well educated, and from high-income households than other people their age who lived in New York City or elsewhere in the country. As the occupation was unfolding, a team of academics surveyed hundreds of the Zuccotti Park protesters and came away with a detailed snapshot of who they were. About a quarter of them (24 percent) were students, most in college or graduate school. Among those who had already completed their education, 76 percent had a four-year college degree and 39 percent had a postgraduate degree. By comparison, only 34 percent of New York City residents in 2011 had finished college by the age of twenty-five. As one of the Occupy organizers, a twenty-seven-year-old woman with a master's degree named Sandy Nurse, recalled, "It was the 26 to 29 or 30 crowd that was the strongest in terms of presence—people my age, who maybe had grad school or weren't finding jobs, and had just blazed through college and a Master's program and then were like, 'What the hell is this?'"

The affluence and education level of the protesters should not come entirely as a surprise, because not everyone who is dissatisfied with the economy and their political leaders is able to interrupt their daily responsibilities to join a protest, especially one that stretches for weeks on end. The Occupy participants were what social movement scholars call "biographically available"—meaning they had the time and energy to become activists because they didn't have burdensome work and family commitments that got in the way. In fact, many were already experienced protesters, something that stood out in another figure the researchers collected: 42 percent of respondents reported having participated in thirty or more protest marches or rallies, and 26 percent said they had been arrested for their political activities at some point in the past.

But even this relatively privileged stratum of young Americans had suffered real injuries as a result of the financial crisis and the Great Recession, events that landed with concentrated force on the generation of people who had just graduated from college. Most of the protesters younger than thirty carried student loan debt, some of them crippling sums. Nearly 40 percent had been fired or laid off from a job, and a significant number had been evicted from their homes (10 percent) or foreclosed upon (5 percent) by a bank or mortgage lender. Overcoming these setbacks was proving much more difficult than it might have been under previous circumstances. The surveyors discovered that a particular form of economic precarity was then rife among college-educated millennials: low earning power driven by the maddening vagaries of the busted postcrisis employment landscape. Although some of the protesters were unemployed, many more were *underemployed*, unable to find meaningful full-time work in their trained fields, often juggling multiple unrelated part-time jobs, and falling further and further behind on student loan and rent payments.

Along with their loan debt, underemployment, and weak earning power, the Occupy protesters had an acute awareness that they were being made to pay for the sins of an older generation whose politicians and businesspeople weren't bearing anywhere near the brunt of the consequences of their reckless behavior. No one likes to be collateral damage. When you're also a graduate student and know a thing or two about social thought and political economy, and when you're swept up in a crowd of peers beset by the same injustices, it shapes the nature of the remedy you seek. One of the older Occupy organizers, the anthropologist David Graeber, described his younger counterparts as "forward-looking people who have been stopped dead in their tracks . . . their one strongest common feature being a remarkably high level of education." Not only did this incline them toward the vocal public activism that briefly seized the national spotlight, but it grounded the proceedings in a distinctive form of left-wing politics. That was because, Graeber pointed out, the young participants were "bursting with energy, with plenty of time on their hands, every reason to be angry, and access to the entire history of radical thought."

This ended up mattering more than it seemed when police swept in and broke up the protest. As Graeber's own presence testified, while the crowd mostly consisted of young students and recent graduates, the movement's organizers were mostly experienced activists like himself, people rehearsed in the rigors of radical politics—Graeber was an anarchist—and eager to impart their wisdom to their new collaborators. When the encampment was cleared, these young adepts scattered like spores in the wind, seeding new causes and candidacies. People who had had no previous experience with protest movements or left-wing politics left Zuccotti Park burning with new conviction. As the writer Nathan Schneider, twenty-seven, one of Occupy's most incisive participant-observers, put it, people "came for a protest and arrived at a school."

IN THE FALL OF 2011, Alexandria Ocasio-Cortez had almost all the prime attributes of the people caught up in the Occupy cause (besides, of course, not being white or male). She'd graduated from Boston University in the spring with heavy student loan debt. She was fluent in critiques of laissez-faire capitalism, having double majored in economics and international relations. She had been a popular and outspoken student activist in her time on campus. During her sophomore year, after her father died of cancer, her family had nearly lost their home to foreclosure, a crisis that wasn't uncommon among people she knew. "The financial crisis touched everyone in my neighborhood," she recalled. Two years later, she graduated into a miserable economy. As she applied unsuccessfully for a series of jobs in international relations, she was scraping together the barest semblance of a living waiting tables and tending bar at a Manhattan taqueria.

But Ocasio-Cortez never joined Occupy. In Boston, her activist passions were geared toward women's health (during her junior year, she'd studied abroad in Niger and done volunteer rotations in a maternity clinic) and toward the National Hispanic Institute, a nonprofit that trained Hispanic students for future leadership roles. She wasn't yet disillusioned with mainstream Democratic politics, either. During her freshman year, in 2008, she'd taken a bus from Boston back home to Yorktown Heights, New York, where she was registered, just so she could cast her ballot for Barack Obama in the Democratic presidential primary. Later, she interned for the Massachusetts senator Ted Kennedy. When she moved to the Bronx after graduation, her activism, like that of many people who came of age during Obama's presidency, was directed toward issues such as environmentalism—in her case, fossil fuel divestiture and blocking oil pipelines—that didn't directly intersect with electoral politics.

It took several more years, but eventually the Occupy movement did pull her in. In 2017, when she made up her mind to launch a long-shot bid for Congress, Ocasio-Cortez was still tending bar, and the grinding toll of those years had radicalized her views. During the same period, a loose collection of Occupy veterans was trying, fitfully and without much success, to find and elect candidates who would tout an expansive, confrontational vision of left-wing politics. All of the key people who drafted Ocasio-Cortez to run for Congress and helped shape her campaign emerged from the Occupy protests or the activist diaspora it birthed.

One of the many disputes that arose among the Zuccotti Park protesters was whether the movement should continue to adhere to its spirit of anarchic radicalism or whether it ought to move toward a form of democratic socialism that could exist within—while tempering the excesses of—a capitalist society. Planting his flag firmly in the latter camp, Max Berger, a twenty-six-year-old Occupier, told a *New York* magazine reporter in 2011, "I don't want to live in a fucking commune. I don't want to blow shit up. I want to get stuff done." In the ensuing years, Berger would become a kind of Zelig figure of the socialist left, with a hand in seemingly every group and cause—including, eventually, the effort to elect Ocasio-Cortez. Although he was just one among many activists, and rarely the most prominent or important, he had helped shape the populist cast of the emerging left at several key points along the way. His winding journey illustrates how elements of the Occupy movement gradually developed a foothold in the Democratic Party and pulled it to the left.

When Occupy broke up, Berger and some fellow activists attempted to battle the foreclosure crisis under the auspices of a hastily organized outfit called Occupy Our Homes. They moved into an abandoned home in East New York in the hope that their example would inspire struggling homeowners everywhere to refuse eviction, squeezing the banks and ultimately forcing them to renegotiate the terms of the 2008 bailout. Things quickly went awry. Bank of America, which held the mortgage, found the absentee owner and discharged his debt. The owner told Berger and his friends to leave. A brief standoff ensued. There were awkward race and class dynamics: Berger and the Occupiers were college-educated white socialists, the owner a single Black father. It was December and the house had no heat or electricity. The *New York Post* got wind of the story and ran an exposé with sympathetic pictures of the owner and his young daughters. "It was a disaster," Berger recalled. The protesters soon withdrew.

Berger knew he and his allies needed a better plan for social movement building and training to enact it. A year later, he found his way to a workshop at the James Lawson Institute in Nashville, whose namesake had marched with Martin Luther King Jr. and mentored the Student Nonviolent Coordinating Committee in the 1960s. The next year, he returned. The Lawson Institute brought Berger into the orbit of other young leftist organizers who were trying to figure out how to advance their goals within the political system. Waleed Shahid, who met Berger there and later worked with him at Justice Democrats, remembered it as being a searing emotional experience for everyone because while they were in Nashville, Michael Brown was shot and killed by police in Ferguson, Missouri. Operating under the heavy influence of Bayard Rustin's famous 1965 *Commentary* essay, "From Protest to Politics," which argued that the civil rights movement could achieve its goals only by attaining political power, many of the organizers went on to launch their own groups or take up key positions in them. Berger was an especially energetic launcher of groups. In 2014, he started If Not Now, an American Jewish organization that pressured Israel for greater Palestinian rights. With some fellow Occupy veterans, he also established a training institute called Momentum. Several of its young graduates went on to found the climate group Sunrise Movement.

The following year, Berger and Shahid, along with a dozen or so other activists, formed yet another group, All of Us, that aimed to advance within the Democratic Party a muscular left populism that could counter what the activists considered the damaging austerity pushed by finance-friendly Democrats. An inspiration was a new left-wing populist party in Spain called Podemos. Emerging out of the anti-austerity protests, it was founded by a group of academics, including one Berger knew personally from post-Occupy conferences (and still occasionally texted with) named Íñigo Errejón. In 2015, Podemos won 21 percent of the vote, and Errejón was elected to Parliament. This struck the U.S. activists as incontrovertible proof that college-educated radicals could swiftly gain national political power if they organized effectively behind a bold leftist agenda. To give their insurgency a veneer of professionalism, All of Us followed the time-honored practice of creating a PowerPoint deck with sharp graphics and bullet-pointed goals (for example, "Run a Slate of Progressive Populists in Primaries Up and Down the Ticket"). Berger and some of the other leaders made the rounds of progressive foundations and nonprofits seeking funding and support, but they came away empty-handed. Like many of the budding organizations on the left, All of Us struggled to gain traction.

In the hallowed tradition of left-wing politics, many of the groups that came after Occupy launched with rousing declarations of purpose, but eventually stalled, succumbed to infighting, split up, and formed different groups. Those that did survive often had trouble attracting resources and attention. So while a new generation of activist groups was taking on issues ranging from racial justice and climate change to immigration reform and economic inequality—their common feature being a tendency to demand sweeping, maximalist solutions presented as urgent moral necessities—they remained an atomized, inchoate collection of individual organizations whose marches, social media campaigns, and principled demands weren't having much effect on Democratic politics. In the aggregate, they constituted a sweeping leftist challenge to Democratic neoliberal orthodoxy. But they made little headway until Bernie Sanders entered the Democratic presidential primary in the spring of 2015.

EVEN THOUGH HE wasn't taken particularly seriously at first, Sanders's jumping into the race altered the dynamics of Democratic politics from what they had been throughout Obama's presidency up to that point. Because Obama was widely popular, even revered, among most Democratic voters, leftist political expression during his presidency mainly took the form of protests and issue campaigns, not electoral contests. "In the Obama era," Shahid said, "nobody primaried Democrats. On the left there was a sort of fragmented discontent that mainly channeled itself into social movements and issue campaigns—Occupy Wall Street, the Keystone pipeline, the Dreamers, the $15 minimum wage—until Bernie came along and challenged Hillary."

One result of the pre-Sanders dynamic was that it allowed left-liberal activism to flourish across a broad set of issues, unimpeded by the limitations that electoral considerations, legislative obstacles, and lobbyists all impose on the Washington political debate. Economic populism was one component of the rising leftist vision, as Occupy Wall Street and groups like All of Us attested. But now it shared the spotlight. Whereas economics was the main focus of Elizabeth Warren's efforts once she got to Washington, and the issue that lay at the heart of Bernie Sanders's long political career, it was only a piece in a broader mosaic of causes that animated the new generation of activists Sanders's campaign pulled into the electoral process. His sudden, unexpected success as he shot up in the polls only strengthened the radicals' confidence that an uncompromising, full-spectrum leftist policy agenda would awaken a broad, multiracial coalition that would remake American society.

One of the people Sanders drew in was Ocasio-Cortez. By 2015 she was four years out of Boston University, still bartending, still buried in student loan debt, lucky to clear $200 a day in tips, and losing faith in her future. She had begun seeing a life coach. Sanders's calls for a "political revolution" that would deliver free college, a living wage, and Medicare for All struck a powerful chord. Along with another bartender friend, she started volunteering at Sanders's South Bronx field office between restaurant shifts, organizing routes for canvassers to make sure the campaign was blanketing the right neighborhoods. She was emblematic of the influx of young people to the Sanders campaign in that she had prior grassroots organizing experience, but always for a cause and not a candidate. "Sanders's race," she said, "was one of my first times where I crossed that bridge from grassroots community organizing to electoral organizing." And like many other millennials, Ocasio-Cortez became deeply invested in the campaign, raptly following the coverage on alternative outlets like *The Intercept* and *The Young Turks*, the left-wing political show on YouTube that reliably proselytized for Sanders. It helped her recast her own struggles as being driven less by personal shortcomings than by a broad social deterioration caused by a systemic failure that was as much the responsibility of Democrats as Republicans. "I came of age watching Democratic governance fail me and fail my family," she said later. "I was supposed to be the great first generation to go to college, and I graduated into a recession where bartending, legitimately, and waitressing, legitimately, paid more than any college-level entry job that was available to me. I had a complete lack of hope. I saw a Democratic Party that was too distracted by institutionalized power to stand up for working people. And I decided this is bullshit. No one, absolutely no one, cares about people like me. . . . And I lost hope."

But even in defeat, the hopeful, insurrectionary experience of participating in the campaign seemed to rekindle Ocasio-Cortez's passion for political activism. A few weeks after the 2016 election, she and two friends set off across the country in a borrowed 1998 Subaru on what amounted to a leftist road trip to witness, and participate in, several high-profile protests that were garnering national attention. They drove first to Flint, Michigan, where residents of the heavily Black city were suffering from lead exposure after city officials switched the drinking water supply to the contaminated Flint River in a bid to cut costs. Next, they traveled to the Standing Rock Indian Reservation in South Dakota, where the Lakota Sioux and hundreds of climate activists had been camping out for months to protest construction of the Dakota Access Pipeline, which would carry oil from western North Dakota across tribal lands, potentially endangering the water supply. Finally, they arrived back in New York City in time for Ocasio-Cortez to make it down to the Women's March in Washington.

The road trip features prominently in the lore surrounding Ocasio-Cortez because as she was leaving Standing Rock, she got an unexpected phone call recruiting her to run for New York's Fourteenth District congressional seat—the seat then held by Joe Crowley, the

DCCC finance chairman and presumed House Speaker in waiting who had used the occasion of the Zuccotti Park protest to raise money for the DCCC. Later, after Ocasio-Cortez shocked the political world by upsetting Crowley in the Democratic primary race, this phone call would take on cosmic significance in news stories and profiles as being the moment when fate reached out and put the unsuspecting twenty-seven-year-old on an unlikely path to political stardom.

If that's what it was, Ocasio-Cortez was unusually well prepared to take on a public role. Whether or not she had an inkling that she would pursue public office, the road trip proved to be a sort of trial run. She streamed much of the trip on Facebook Live, narrating her activist experience as she went. These feeds included much more than just her impressions of what she and her friends were seeing and experiencing. In Flint and at Standing Rock, she arranged and conducted interviews with local activists and citizens in the manner of a journalist—or a political candidate on a listening tour. At the Women's March, with the help of a selfie stick to boost the production values, Ocasio-Cortez posted long, searching dispatches on her Facebook page about what the event meant to her. As she marched, she fielded live questions from an online audience that climbed to several hundred people. A few months later, when Crowley's staff tried to get a sense of who their upstart opponent was, a few of them thought that she really was angling for a job on *The Young Turks*. She was a natural performer. As the journalist Charlotte Alter noted of the live-streamed trip, "She was beginning to learn how to think on camera, how to have conversations with people in the comments, how to bring her viewers along for the ride and deliver her opinions in stream-of-consciousness lectures that were at once natural and informative." These skills helped make her the effective politician she was about to become. "It was," Alter noted, "the birth of a social media persona that would define her later political career."

The call Ocasio-Cortez received on the way from Standing Rock was from a new group started by a few staffers from Bernie Sanders's presidential campaign that called itself Brand New Congress. Most of the group's founders—Zack Exley, Saikat Chakrabarti, Corbin Trent, and Alexandra Rojas—had never worked in politics before the Sanders campaign, which helps to explain both the staggering ambition and the naïveté it took to settle on the mission they chose for themselves. The group aimed to replace the entire U.S. Congress by finding and running novice candidates uncorrupted by the business of politics to challenge all 435 congressional incumbents—in Republican and Democratic primaries—all of them running on a single, unified platform focused on the working class. To find these legions of civic-minded amateurs, Brand New Congress put out a call for nominations. One reply came from Gabriel Ocasio-Cortez, who nominated his big sister to run in New York's Fourteenth District race.

Brand New Congress didn't manage to find 435 candidates, which was just as well. The "grassroots-funded machine" that Chakrabarti vowed "would give power back to the people" didn't materialize to the extent he'd envisioned. The group struggled to raise money. But it did generate thousands of nominations that ultimately produced 30 candidates for Congress—all but one of them Democrats. Ocasio-Cortez had no trouble making the cut; she was exactly what the group's founders envisioned: poised, vibrant, fiercely committed, and uncommonly well spoken, but also reassuringly normal with a background rooted in the working class. "We looked at the brother telling the story of a sister who wasn't a giant nonprofit executive, she didn't go work on the Hill for 10 years," Rojas later recalled. "She was someone who watched her family struggle through the financial crisis."

It takes a certain disposition to attempt something as bold as Brand New Congress. You need absolute certainty of conviction—otherwise, why bother? Sanders imbued his followers with a faith that a bold message of radical change could awaken the slumbering masses. Brand New Congress was a test of this proposition. To capture the revolution as it unfolded, the group brought in a documentary film crew. What the cameras captured instead was the painful reckoning that occurs when utopian ideals smack into the hard realities of electoral politics. Every one of the group's candidates lost, except Ocasio-Cortez. "It turned out to be a complete and utter failure," Trent said.

Overnight, though, Ocasio-Cortez became a megastar. And the people who helped her defeat Crowley were greeted not as amateurs whose candidates would go one for thirty in the election cycle but as canny strategists possessed of insights that eluded establishment Democrats—and as harbingers of an onrushing millennial generation whose radical politics would soon reshape the Democratic Party.

The confusion surrounding this sudden new force in Democratic politics owed partly to its complicated lineage, which was byzantine even by the standards of left-wing politics. After Trump's 2016 victory, the prospect of a nonpartisan outfit like Brand New Congress succeeding got even longer. Cenk Uygur, the founder and cohost of *The Young Turks*, convinced Chakrabarti and Exley that an insurgent progressive group made more sense than a nonpartisan one, so together they founded Justice Democrats in January 2017. Trent and Rojas soon joined up, and later Max Berger and Waleed Shahid would, too. "We copied and pasted the exact model of Brand New Congress but just for Democrats," Trent said. Officially, the two groups were allied, and both endorsed Ocasio-Cortez. But by the fall, both were running out of money. So Justice Democrats decided to put all its chips on Ocasio-Cortez, who was deemed to have the best shot at winning her closed primary and made for a compelling spokeswoman for the cause. At that point, Chakrabarti and Trent joined her campaign staff; she was the whole ball game. When she won, they did, too.

BY ANY MEASURE, Ocasio-Cortez ran a remarkable race that was tailored to her district and benefited from shrewd organizing and even technological innovation. Running as a Democratic Socialist, she drew a large, multiracial progressive coalition that overwhelmed an incumbent, in Crowley, who personified the Wall Street–friendly Democrat uninterested in local concerns but assumed to be too powerful to be held to account. In this sense, her victory was a triumph for the brand of politics that Occupy Wall Street had brought to public attention seven years earlier. It consecrated Ocasio-Cortez as the new star of the party's left flank, perhaps even its future.

Her campaign, though, got off to an inauspicious start. In May 2017, the paperwork she filed to enter the Democratic primary listed the wrong congressional district—the Fifteenth, not the Fourteenth—although she campaigned against Crowley from the outset. As a would-be insurgent, she faced two big obstacles, beyond the entrenched incumbent, right out of the gate. The first was time. Working two restaurant jobs left her little opportunity to knock on doors, meet voters, and carry out the rudiments of a congressional campaign. The other obstacle was money. The wave of grassroots donors Chakrabarti had confidently promised a year earlier was nowhere in evidence. By September, the campaign had raised less than $6,000. (Perhaps chagrined, Chakrabarti personally contributed the maximum allowed, $2,700, accounting for nearly half the total.)

On the positive side, Ocasio-Cortez and her inner circle believed deeply in their mission, which is an underrated strength in a grass-roots campaign. While they lacked experience running congressional races, they were skilled organizers and veterans of countless protests. They saw her campaign as a necessary extension of their activism, a theory that Ocasio-Cortez herself, likely knowing she was about to run for Congress, laid out in the Facebook live stream during the Standing Rock road trip. Politics has to be confrontational, she asserted, because leaders only respond to pressure from below. "You're always going to hear: 'Protesters are rabble-rousers, they're troublemakers, protest doesn't do anything, it's ineffective,'" she said. "Protest galvanizes public sentiment, and when public sentiment is galvanized to a certain extent, then that turns into public pressure, and then when public pressure is applied to a certain extent, then we get policy change. That is how protest works." The pressure on Crowley was going to come in the form of her campaign.

Ocasio-Cortez had the good fortune to launch her candidacy in the chaotic early months of Trump's presidency, when liberal alarm was at an apex. In the deeply Democratic Fourteenth District, parts of which were rapidly gentrifying, Trump's election pulled many new people into political activism, and they responded not just by piling into buses and attending Women's Marches but also by paying more attention to what was happening in their own backyards. The challenge lay in conscripting them into the cause of a candidate who didn't appear to have much chance of prevailing. Here, Ocasio-Cortez's doggedness as a campaigner, the limited but necessary support of Justice Democrats, the influence of media outlets such as *The Intercept* and *The Young Turks*, and the creativity of her staff made the difference.

One benefit of a campaign run by millennials without ties to the institutional Democratic Party is that it isn't beholden to outdated methods. As they canvassed the district, Ocasio-Cortez's volunteers were struck by the same limiting factors Alfred Johnson and Allen Kramer were trying to overcome with the Mobilize app in Virginia. Knocking on doors yielded a lousy success rate—particularly in a district full of minorities and transient, mobile-only millennials, groups notoriously difficult to canvass. But the DIY culture of grassroots campaigns allows plenty of room for experimenting. A few Justice Democrats discovered they could use voter registration data to find local residents on social media and serve them digital ads *before* they knocked, which improved the campaign's reception at the door, because voters were now familiar with their candidate.

A bigger innovation was a mobile organizing app not dissimilar to what Mobilize was building. Two early campaign volunteers—Jake DeGroot, a theatrical-lighting designer, and Leo Sussan, a digital marketing specialist—were frustrated by door knocking's obvious limitation: most people aren't at home. Instead of trying to find potential voters off a list, DeGroot and Sussan thought it would make a lot more sense to go where crowds of likely supporters already gathered—bars, churches, subway platforms, and so on—and match them to the list right there. "If we were going to win, we knew it was going to be through grassroots folks on the ground in the Bronx and Queens," DeGroot explained. "We had all these people talking to voters, but we weren't capturing any of the data." A few weeks before the primary, DeGroot pulled an all-nighter and emerged in the morning with a prototype app that contained the campaign's entire voter file and turned it into a searchable, mobile database. It allowed Ocasio-Cortez to ramp up the one thing her team knew it had to do to have a chance of winning: bring more underrepresented people into the system. Despite its late arrival, the app would account for 12 percent of total voter contacts during the fourteen-month-long campaign. And people canvassed via the app turned out at higher rates than those contacted through conventional methods.

The biggest difference maker, however, was the candidate herself. Ocasio-Cortez did everything in her power to contrast herself with Crowley. She spoke Spanish. He did not, instead hauling along a congressional colleague, Representative Luis Gutiérrez of Illinois, to serve rather awkwardly as an unofficial interpreter. Embracing the Democratic Socialist label (after some early trepidation), Ocasio-Cortez countered Crowley's cautious centrism by pushing a platform that included a federal jobs guarantee, Medicare for All, tuition-free public colleges, a $15 minimum wage, ending for-profit prisons, and abolishing the Immigration and Customs Enforcement agency. She also leaned into her deep district ties, criticizing Crowley for pulling his kids out of the local schools and moving his family to Northern Virginia to better accommodate his busy life in Washington.

Most of all, Ocasio-Cortez stressed her working-class background. With less than a month to go, she poured her remaining money into a campaign video she wrote herself that was shot by a pair of socialist filmmakers from Detroit. The ad shows Ocasio-Cortez getting ready for work in an unglamorous apartment, climbing out of the subway, swapping comfortable shoes for nicer ones on the platform, greeting people in the neighborhood not in the stagy way a big-time politician does it but like a normal person who lives there. "I wasn't born to a wealthy or powerful family," she says in the ad. "I was born in a place where your zip code determines your destiny." Calling herself "a working-class New Yorker," as the city rushes by her subway window, she empathizes with the working lives of her future constituents. "Every day gets harder for working-class families like mine to get by—the rent gets higher, health care covers less, and our income stays the same. . . . It's time we acknowledge that not all Democrats are the same, that a Democrat who takes corporate money, profits off foreclosure, doesn't live here, doesn't send his kids to our schools, doesn't drink our water or breathe our air cannot possibly represent us."

The ad conveyed an authenticity about working-class life in the Bronx that sent it ricocheting far beyond its intended audience in the Fourteenth District. Most people's first encounter with Ocasio-Cortez, if they worked in politics and didn't live in New York, was seeing the ad and marveling at its young protagonist. Michael Podhorzer, the political director for the AFL-CIO, who spends his waking hours trying to get voters to care about working people, had never heard of her until a colleague showed him the ad. "I was floored," he recalled. "The best comparison I can make is to the famous Jon Landau line: 'I've seen rock 'n' roll's future and its name is Bruce Springsteen!'"

This burst of attention finally produced the windfall Chakrabarti had been waiting for. In the final three weeks leading up to the primary, Ocasio-Cortez raised more than $135,000, money that funded a vital last-minute organizing push. But Crowley might have caused his own undoing, by deciding that squaring off with a confident, young Latina opponent wouldn't help him be seen as a popular, unifying House Speaker in waiting.

At the second of two candidate debates a week before the election, Crowley didn't show up, sending the former city councilwoman Annabel Palma in his place. The move wasn't just high-handed; it smacked of tokenism, because Palma was a Latina. Afterward, *The New York Times* scolded the incumbent in an editorial that ran under the headline "If You Want to Be Speaker, Mr. Crowley, Don't Take Voters for Granted." The editorial warned that Crowley had "better hope that voters don't react to his snubs by sending someone else to do the job."

To everyone's astonishment, they did.

———

TRUMP'S VICTORY two years earlier and Democrats' losses up and down the ballot left many people in the party bewildered and unsure of how to proceed. Everyone could see that the old neoliberal precepts had failed, generating such enormous alienation and anger that voters had elected a madman. Now another top Democrat had been taken down by populist discontent, this time within his own party. Ocasio-Cortez's victory launched a heated ideological debate about what the upset meant and what lessons it held for the party.

No one could deny that she'd built the kind of cross-class, multiracial coalition that most Democrats knew was central to their party's future. But her campaign's victory had been made possible by factors that weren't easy for others to replicate. Crowley had been caught sleeping; he hadn't been seriously challenged since he was first elected in 1998. One reason his guard was down was that New York's Democratic machine, as a way of protecting incumbents, had created rules that made it outlandishly difficult to vote and run for office. As a result, primary turnout was infinitesimal, which suited most elected officials just fine. But the system had a built-in vulnerability that someone with perseverance and organizing skills could exploit: a challenger who did manage to get on the ballot could win without amassing a huge number of votes. This was one reason Justice Democrats had been eager to back Ocasio-Cortez. The group thought it could find, register, and turn out enough new voters to beat Crowley—and it did.

Crowley was also vulnerable because his district had changed. He'd come out on the losing end of a 2010 redistricting battle, in which one of his political enemies, the assembly leader, Sheldon Silver, had redrawn the district to include a large portion of the Bronx, altering its demographics. By 2018, the Fourteenth District was 48 percent Latino and just 24 percent white, no longer safe terrain for an old Irish Catholic from Queens. No one understood this shift more clearly than Ocasio-Cortez. In the documentary film *Knock Down the House*, which follows Brand New Congress and several of its candidates, including Ocasio-Cortez, through their campaigns, she identifies the weakness in Crowley, the Queens Democratic Party boss, that she would soon exploit. "He can't get challenged by any down-ballot incumbent," she said. "Anybody who wants to keep their job in New York City would never dream of challenging Joe Crowley. It has to come from outside of Queens. It has to come from someone who's new on the political scene that they don't see coming, they can't offer a job or pressure in another way. And it has to be somebody who represents our community in more ways than one. Basically, an insurgent, outside grassroots candidate who's a woman of color from the Bronx."

Thanks to the vagaries of New York's primary system, Ocasio-Cortez was able to build her appeal among a small, very liberal segment of her district's voters—she won fewer than seventeen thousand votes in a primary that drew barely 5 percent of the district's eligible voters—and that was enough for her to prevail. None of this precluded her from becoming a force in the party or invalidated her full-spectrum leftist platform. She played by the rules that Crowley and his cronies had established, and she won.

But even within her winning coalition, there were signs its appeal might have its limits. Ocasio-Cortez's canvassers focused particularly on gentrifying neighborhoods in Queens, where younger, college-educated creative types clustered—the sorts of people who had protested at Zuccotti Park and voted for Bernie Sanders. After the primary, Steven Romalewski, a demographer at the City University of New York's Center for Urban Research, conducted a precinct-by-precinct analysis of the results and concluded that Ocasio-Cortez's success likely owed to this strategy. Some of her staff agreed. "It was the gentrifiers," said Trent. What wasn't clear yet was whether other Democratic candidates could emulate her message and appeal to a broader spectrum of voters.

FROM ONE PERSPECTIVE, Crowley's downfall was a familiar story of a politician's getting arrogant and comfortable, not tending to his constituents, and paying the price for this neglect. But from another perspective, the one favored by Ocasio-Cortez and most of her closest advisers, it represented something much bigger and more consequential: proof that radical ideas about how to reorganize the political economy to engender a better, more equitable society were potent enough to bring down one of the most powerful Democrats in Washington. They wanted her victory to be seen as preparing the ground for a great remaking of the Democratic Party—as an instruction manual for reinvigorating an institution whose appeal had flatlined. As Chakrabarti saw it, Democrats' path to salvation was simple: "Run unapologetically on a bold vision with solutions as radical as the problems our country faces. And then work like hell to make sure everyone hears about it."

Ocasio-Cortez would not have to do this alone. Hip, gentrifying neighborhoods like Astoria, Sunnyside, and Woodside in Queens were home to many young journalists and political staffers who either shared her political ideas or socialized with people who did. Everyone was alert to her message's appeal. As she was winning her race, the 2020 presidential primaries were quietly taking shape. Many of the people working, or about to go to work, for Bernie Sanders, Elizabeth Warren, or one of the other Democratic candidates lived in the

Fourteenth District and had the up-close, visceral experience of the "AOC" phenomenon—not just on Twitter and Instagram, but in real life when, while grabbing coffee or heading into the office, they'd see her iconic purple-and-yellow "¡Ocasio!" posters lining the streets and subways. The excitement surrounding her victory seemed to signal that a new political era might be at hand.

The practical effect of that victory was to widen the aperture of left-wing politics and introduce a kind of conceptual grandeur that others in the party, including many top presidential contenders, soon took up and amplified.

11

A DREAM DEFERRED

The 2020 Democratic presidential primaries took shape in an atmosphere of general agreement that the ideas espoused by Elizabeth Warren, Bernie Sanders, and Alexandria Ocasio-Cortez were in ascendance. In the minds of most candidates and party strategists, the question that the primaries were going to answer was just how far to the left Democratic voters wanted to move.

If we go back to the beginning of our story, in 1978, when the newly aggressive business community was making its first serious incursions into Democratic policymaking by thwarting Jimmy Carter's reforms, the mood in the party was one of anxious decline. The New Deal era was ending. Organized labor, the party's backbone, was losing force. In the midterm elections, Democrats lost seats in the House and Senate, along with six governorships. Ronald Reagan was about to expose the weakness of the party's electoral coalition and usher in an expensive new political era that would lead Democrats to embrace big business. (Among the newly elected governors in 1978 was one who would lead this transition: Bill Clinton of Arkansas.)

But forty years later, after sweeping gains in the 2018 midterm elections, Democratic sentiment was running in the opposite direction—toward the belief that America was on the precipice of another new era, this one auguring a liberal renaissance. A key factor shaping this view was Trump, who was historically unpopular. His unpopularity had just cost his party control of the House. He obviously wasn't going to "pivot" to a saner, more appealing approach. The perception that he was uniquely vulnerable drew the largest Democratic presidential field in at least half a century: twenty-seven candidates would ultimately enter the 2020 primary race.

For all the anguish he caused liberals, Trump's election had an unanticipated effect. It produced a burst of optimism on the left that what had been assumed to be impossible was, in fact, readily achievable. If a supposedly unelectable candidate could defy conventional assumptions as easily as Trump had, then maybe the political constraints that everyone insisted must limit liberal ambitions no longer applied—or had never been real in the first place. More than just Trump's win nourished this suspicion. Things that wouldn't have seemed possible two years earlier were now happening with surprising frequency. Hadn't Ocasio-Cortez (a socialist!) just knocked off the presumed future Democratic Speaker?

The growing agitation for an ambitious left-wing agenda also reflected how Trump had reshuffled Democratic priorities. As he moved cultural issues to the center of national political conflict, race, gender, and immigration eclipsed populist economics as the focus of the liberal insurgency. They also galvanized the Resistance activists drawn into politics by his election. As the political scientist David Hopkins noted, party activists came to view Trump as "a mocking, groping, deporting personification of racism, sexism, and xenophobia." His outrages demanded a response. For many Democrats, a moral imperative to take the maximalist position against Trump on nearly every issue superseded basic electoral concerns. Democratic presidential hopefuls started taking positions that once would have been unthinkable for a serious candidate: abolishing the Immigration and Customs Enforcement agency, decriminalizing migrant border crossings, extending subsidized health insurance to undocumented immigrants, abolishing private health insurance altogether.

But many of the leading Democrats didn't appear to perceive any trade-off—or, if they did, calculated that publicly aligning themselves with the new generation of activists was necessary to establish their credibility. It was often simply assumed that the groups on the receiving end of Trump's ugliest barbs—women, Blacks, Latinos, immigrants—shared the activists' conviction that anything less than the most idealistic response constituted a betrayal, even though voter behavior often didn't bear this out (the gender gap at the polls in 2016, for example, was similar to what it had been before). From certain vantage points the political logic could seem compelling. In 2019, Senator Edward Markey of Massachusetts, a colorless septuagenarian, co-sponsored Ocasio-Cortez's "Green New Deal" climate plan, winning buzz and accolades on the left that turned him into a political celebrity and helped him fend off a primary challenge from an ambitious young upstart, Representative Joe Kennedy III.

It takes a lot of stamina to endure the constant travel, bad food, low pay, and round-the-clock stress of a presidential primary campaign. Consequently, staffers tend to be very young, even in senior positions. Most of the 2020 candidates were surrounded by people not old enough to have been in politics when Bill Clinton was president; some weren't even alive then. Having come of age more recently, they saw themselves as having the sort of elevated social conscience that the older generation of Democrats lacked, and they weren't shy about saying so. Like their activist peers, they were impatient with people who struck them as insufficiently committed to the sweeping social changes they believed Trump's presidency plainly warranted, an outlook that shaped the race from the beginning. From their perspective, Hillary Clinton and her failed campaign were casualties of a changing world. Now enlightened Democrats knew better, and their candidates could finally offer the sweeping changes they were certain voters new and old would respond to. "It's ambitious to expand the electorate," Jane Sanders, Bernie's wife, explained, "but that's what Bernie has always done."

One early sign of the new dynamic came in the fall of 2017, when Sanders introduced a Medicare for All bill that would have vastly restructured the U.S. health-care system. Democratic presidential hopefuls lined up to cosponsor it—not just liberals like Warren, but middle-of-the-party senators such as Kamala Harris of California, Cory Booker of New Jersey, and Kirsten Gillibrand of New York, along with Representative Tim Ryan of Ohio. (Four years earlier, the same bill hadn't drawn a single cosponsor.) Even candidates who stopped shy of Medicare for All felt it necessary to make a show of moving to the left, in Joe Biden's case by adding a public option to Obamacare that would insure millions more people. Taking it all in, Jeff Weaver, Sanders's top aide, crowed that "it was a recognition that the center of gravity in the party has moved in a much more progressive direction."

Along with the party's leftward momentum, those most eager to press revolutionary changes had fewer constraints than outsider candidates in the past. The problem that bedeviled Tony Coelho—how to raise enough money to win elections—was one Warren and Sanders had already solved by showing they could raise huge sums online. The practical challenge of incorporating millions of new people into the political process was one Mobilize had streamlined into an app you could download on your phone. In fact, moving beyond the economic populism that had lifted both Warren and Sanders to prominence and embracing a full-throated leftist platform that excited activists and lit up social media made it even easier to attract money and volunteers. With the Clintons discredited and their worldview consigned to irrelevance, there didn't seem to be any doubt that the primaries would be the crucible in which the future of the Democratic Party was decided. And early on, the energy was all on the left.

WARREN ENTERED THE RACE expecting to take back the mantle of progressive warrior from Sanders. Trump's victory haunted her, as did her decision to pass on the draft movement that had tried to enlist her four years earlier. But she thought his victory was instructive because it showed that voters wanted change on a scale most Democrats didn't fathom. This reinforced her own ambitions. Warren thought Clinton had lost because she was timid. She had focused too narrowly on Trump's behavior instead of offering people a compelling explanation of how she would better their lives. Discouraged voters expressed their disappointment by staying home or by backing her opponent. Trump, on the other hand, had abandoned Republican orthodoxies, made big promises, and won union members, blue-collar workers, and other traditionally Democratic voters in the bargain. Lesson: bigger is better. "Some people think small change, incremental change, is how we will move America in a better direction," Warren said early in the race. "I think big change is easier. It's easier to get more people into the fight, and it's easier to get more people to pay attention to how it would touch their lives. And that's our path to winning."

A few months before she launched her campaign, Warren got an invitation from Klaus Schwab, founder of the World Economic Forum, who was taken with her sweeping moral critique of winner-take-all capitalism and wanted her to speak at the group's annual meeting in Davos. Warren thought she needed an idea big enough for the occasion and landed on an annual "wealth tax" of 2 percent on fortunes over $50 million, slightly higher on billionaires. Her staff calculated it would hit the richest seventy-five thousand people in the United States while raising $2.75 trillion in a ten-year period. That was big, and the revenue could pay for other big endeavors. Warren ultimately passed on Davos. But her wealth tax became the first in a series of sweeping proposals she designed to evoke grand change on the scale of the New Deal or the Great Society: Medicare for All, free college, universal child care, breaking up Big Tech companies, border decriminalization, and much more. "It's all a response to Trump," Barney Frank, the Massachusetts congressman and Warren ally, said. "It's meant to be earthshaking."

Warren intended the wealth tax to shape the Democratic primaries around her economic ideas. Early on, it did. After her first swing through Iowa in January 2019, as she beat the drums against "ultra-millionaires and billionaires," two billionaires known to want to enter the primaries—Michael Bloomberg and Tom Steyer—initially held off. Warren's slashing populist attacks also generated concern in Trump's circle. Steve Bannon, who infused the final stages of Trump's presidential campaign with dark themes of "globalist" Wall Street oppressors holding down the working class, had long considered Warren the most serious threat to Trump's reelection. Knowing his boss's commitment to economic populism was merely rhetorical, Bannon fretted that

Warren would lure away blue-collar voters with a program he described as "populist Democratic nationalism"—a patriotic admixture of pro-worker policies, tax hikes on the rich, and Wall Street crackdowns that would prove to be Trump's kryptonite. In 2017, to blunt her anticipated attack, Bannon quietly lobbied Trump to support a symbolically potent tax increase on incomes over $5 million. When that failed, he devised a plan to steer millions of dollars from the hedge fund magnate Robert Mercer to the 2018 Massachusetts Senate candidacy of a gadfly MIT professor named Shiva Ayyadurai. Bannon intended to use Ayyadurai as a stalking horse to tarnish Warren in her reelection campaign, much as he'd used Mercer's money to tarnish Hillary Clinton ahead of the 2016 Democratic primaries. But Bannon fell out first with Trump and then with Mercer, and the plan never came to fruition.

Almost immediately, though, Warren's presidential campaign ran into a serious problem. Sanders was planning to run, too. Before launching her exploratory committee, Warren invited him to her Washington apartment for a lasagna dinner to hash out where things stood. But neither wanted to defer to the other, so nothing was settled. Worse, at one point in the evening Sanders voiced his doubt as to whether a woman could beat Trump, which Warren heard as his saying that *she* could not beat Trump and took great offense. (The claim later leaked to the press.) Warren's campaign was built on an assumption that Sanders wouldn't be a serious player in the primaries, either because he'd defer to the momentum she expected to have from the very outset or, if ego led him into the race anyway, because she didn't believe voters would support him when a younger, more credentialed, more electable (she thought) progressive was already running and more was at stake than simply casting a protest vote against Hillary Clinton. This assumption turned out to be wrong.

Running on a full-dress liberal agenda of vaulting ambition, Warren positioned herself a tick to the right of Sanders with the aim of isolating him on the socialist fringe. The big differentiator was supposed to be her public avowal that she was "a capitalist to my bones"—discordant with her image as a Wall Street scourge, but sufficient to convince many Clinton and Obama people that she was a safe choice.

But Warren never achieved an air of inevitability thanks to a series of missteps tied to her disputed claims of Native American ancestry. A vocal contingent of Sanders partisans remained implacably hostile to her for not endorsing him in 2016. Had Sanders opted to sit out the race and support her, most of them probably would have come around. Instead, the progressive universe was deeply divided and remained so throughout the primaries. "There is an enormous amount of ill will that was the result of her declining to endorse anyone and deciding not to take a position until after the convention," said Charles Lenchner, the cofounder of Ready for Warren who later endorsed Sanders.

Warren wanted to be seen as the serious figure who could run the White House from day one, in contradistinction to Sanders, whose dishevelment did not connote high-level executive function. As such, she embraced the conceit that she had a "plan" for every issue. To the delight of her fans, her campaign slapped its winsome slogan ("Warren has a plan for that") all over T-shirts and tote bags that began popping up at rallies. Although this strengthened her bond with her college-educated core supporters, Warren could never shake her image as a pinched Harvard professor enough to attract working-class voters, who weren't moved by the claim that she was a literal know-it-all. Warren was trapped as a factional candidate. Even at the height of her campaign in the fall of 2019, when she briefly led the Democratic field, a representative survey found her trouncing Sanders 38 percent to 6 percent among white voters with a college degree, but struggling to appeal beyond that elite group and badly trailing Biden on the question of who was more likely to beat Trump.

What finally sank her candidacy was having to reconcile her belief that voters wanted landmark policy change, on the one hand, with her well-advertised claim to have a plan for everything, on the other. The big policy that shaped the primary race wasn't anything Warren produced, but Sanders's Medicare for All plan. As voters came to understand that "giving everyone Medicare" meant "abolishing private insurance" for 170 million people—whether or not they liked it—the idea lost its luster. Most of the candidates who'd raced to endorse it awkwardly backed away. Warren did not. But this brought public demands, gleefully encouraged by her opponents, to explain how she would pay for such an enormous program. Now she was stuck. Warren did eventually produce a plan shortly before the Iowa caucus: a $20.5 trillion package that not only dwarfed her wealth tax but cost more than all of her other proposals combined. But its bigness turned out not to be a political asset at all. Warren finished third in Iowa, fourth in New Hampshire, lost her home state of Massachusetts on Super Tuesday, and dropped out of the race the next day.

When it came to having an unforeseen effect on Democratic politics, Alexandria Ocasio-Cortez didn't limit herself to ending Joe Crowley's political career. A week after her election, trailed by television cameras, she joined environmental protesters from the Sunrise Movement in occupying Nancy Pelosi's office to demand tougher climate measures. She managed, largely through the force of her political celebrity, to make the Green New Deal a focus of Democratic debate. Her social media fluency made Warren and the earlier generation of online Democrats look like an old analog television set: Ocasio-Cortez routinely live streamed to her millions of Instagram followers as she cooked dinner in her Washington apartment and held forth on the day's issues and controversies. As her fame and influence exploded, her endorsement became a sought-after prize in the primary struggle just then unfolding between Warren and Sanders.

For as much of a splash as Ocasio-Cortez made upon her arrival in Washington, she had more influence in the presidential race than in Congress, at least early on. That owed heavily to the timing of her endorsement, which probably saved Sanders's campaign from a sudden early collapse. During a campaign event in Las Vegas in early October, Sanders felt weak and asked to sit down. Concerned by his uncharacteristic lethargy, his staff took him to an urgent care clinic, and then an ambulance raced him to the hospital. Sanders's campaign was initially circumspect about whether he had suffered a heart attack, aware that, at seventy-eight years old, there were already doubts about his fitness to be president. At the time, Warren still led Democratic primary polls, so there was no reason to assume voters would stick with Sanders once the news of his heart attack inevitably became public.

Warren had spent months methodically courting Ocasio-Cortez through repeated phone calls and a lunch that quickly leaked to political reporters. Aware of her power, Ocasio-Cortez let it be known that Sanders and Warren were the only two candidates getting serious consideration. "Timing is important," Corbin Trent told the *Los Angeles Times* that summer, not knowing how true this would turn out to be. Just days before the heart attack, Ocasio-Cortez had secretly flown to Vermont to meet with Sanders and his campaign team to finalize her endorsement (they were quickly spotted having breakfast at a Burlington diner). While Sanders lay in the hospital, with questions swirling about his future, she called to reaffirm her support. Two weeks later,

Sanders had recovered enough to participate in the Democratic debate in Westerville, Ohio. To maximize the frenzy they knew her endorsement would occasion, Sanders's staff leaked the news to political reporters while the candidates were still onstage. His resurrection was under way.

From the outset, Sanders thought he was the favorite in the race. He differed from the other candidates, including Warren, in believing that the 43 percent of the primary vote he'd carried against Hillary Clinton four years earlier was an indication of the strength of his campaign and his ideas, and not protest votes lodged against the polarizing front-runner. Trump's subsequent defeat of Clinton only underscored how eager fed-up Americans were to embrace unorthodox candidates who were willing to reach beyond the narrow, self-serving strictures of establishment politics. Surely, Democratic voters now recognized this and would rally to his banner.

The key to this race, he believed, would be the same one that had driven his victories going all the way back to his days running for mayor of Burlington: a popular mass mobilization that pulled new voters into the electorate. "It is undeniably true that for Bernie Sanders to win, he needs a mass mobilization of people who have not voted before," his campaign manager said.

But Sanders no longer had the progressive lane to himself. Many of the organizations on the left that supported him in 2016 now had to make a choice about which progressive would make a better nominee. It wasn't automatic. Warren was a ferocious lobbyist, which Sanders was not. The result was a split. In 2016, grassroots leftist groups such as the Working Families Party and the Democratic Socialists of America had all endorsed Sanders. In 2020, the DSA stuck to their guns.

But this time, the WFP decided to back Warren, causing an uproar among Sanders supporters. "If our focus is on victory, we can't be delusional about it," Maurice Mitchell, the WFP's national director, said by way of explaining the group's controversial choice. "You don't defeat the moderate wing of Democrats through thought pieces or pithy tweets, you defeat their politics through organizing."

A few weeks after Sanders's heart attack, however, the intramural battles on the left stopped seeming so important. Ocasio-Cortez's endorsement miraculously revived his campaign. Sanders continued raising more money than anybody else, including Trump. Warren was getting picked to pieces over Medicare for All and falling in the polls. In late October, Sanders made a triumphant return to New York City for a big rally with Ocasio-Cortez in tow. "I am more than ready to take on the greed and corruption of the corporate elite and their apologists," he declared with conspicuous vigor. "I am more ready than ever to help create a government based on the principles of justice, economic justice, racial justice, social justice, and environmental justice." To quiet any doubts about his health, Sanders added, "To put it bluntly, I am back."

What helped make this a reality is that the early part of the Democratic primary calendar was tailored to Sanders's appeal. Iowa and Nevada were both caucus states that rewarded the kind of organizing his supporters excelled at. Everybody knew him in New Hampshire, where he'd romped four years earlier. The chaos that unfolded in Iowa on caucus night, when the app for reporting vote totals failed, briefly seemed like a setback, because Sanders appeared to get the most votes and was denied a televised triumph. But he won New Hampshire and then carried Nevada, too, amassing a big lead in the delegate race.

Still, there were signs of trouble below the surface. Even though he was winning, Sanders wasn't doing so in the way he'd expected, by expanding the electorate to include millions of new voters. In Iowa, caucus turnout was well short of what it had been in 2008, when Obama was running. New Hampshire did see record turnout, but Sanders won less than 26 percent of the vote, down sharply from the 60 percent he'd garnered in 2016. In the moment, this didn't register as a major concern, because winning with modest, rather than gigantic, turnout nets you the same delegate lead.

But it was more fragile than it appeared. Coming out of Nevada, Sanders looked like a sure thing. And then, all of a sudden, he wasn't.

AFTER THE DEMOCRATIC triumph in the 2018 midterm elections, Alfred Johnson and Allen Kramer were in heavy demand. Nearly every Democratic presidential candidate signed on with Mobilize to help organize their campaign, which produced a client roster that spanned the ideological gamut from Sanders and Warren to Joe Biden and Pete Buttigieg. As the 2020 election season got rolling, millions of volunteers for more than twenty campaigns were funneled into Mobilize's platform. This gave Johnson and Kramer a panoptic view of the most committed participants in the Democratic primary process, who they were, and which candidates they were supporting.

Because Mobilize had worked with the Democratic Party committees and hundreds of campaigns in 2018, it had a baseline for what a Democratic wave election looked like from the inside. In a sense, it functioned like a Richter scale: as new data from the primary campaigns poured in, Johnson excitedly watched the numbers exceed what Mobilize had measured in 2018. Some Democrats worried that grassroots energy would dissipate after the party's successful midterm showing. Instead, the opposite was happening; it was growing. Each day, Johnson would pull up charts showing that the aggregate number of people canvassing, phone banking, or hosting gatherings for presidential candidates was eclipsing the record-setting pace of two years earlier.

As was the case then, he also noticed that the attention of the political press tended to reflect the conversations happening on Twitter. When reporters called him to check in, he made sure to balance their interest in Warren and Sanders by pointing out that the surge of volunteer energy was spread widely across the field and not limited to the candidates on the left. In fact, some of the candidates with the most active followers weren't the ones whom the press corps was most eager to write about. Early on, the person whose organization most impressed Johnson was Kamala Harris, who, his data indicated, was about to pull off an enormous campaign launch in Oakland. (More than twenty thousand people turned out.)

As the primaries got under way, nothing in the data pointed to Biden as the likely nominee—at least not directly. He didn't have a particularly active core of volunteers, a large social media presence, or blockbuster fundraising numbers. After disappointing finishes in Iowa, New Hampshire, and Nevada, his campaign was running on fumes. But if you zoomed out, the Mobilize data and other indicators showed that Democrats were searching to fill a role Biden at least had the capacity to inhabit: They wanted someone who could beat Trump. Period.

On one level, that which preoccupied the media and political classes, the primaries were a pitched ideological battle between liberals and centrists that would determine the future course of the party and perhaps the country. But on the level that Johnson and Kramer spent their days and nights puzzling over, that of the neighborhood organizers who are the foundation of every successful party and campaign, the primaries were an unprecedented, mostly unifying exercise in mass civic participation geared toward a single goal. "For Democrats," said Johnson, "there was something so existentially jarring about Trump's election that it created a kind of socialization around politics in a way that we maybe haven't seen since the civil rights movement."

SANDERS CAME OUT of the Nevada caucuses believing he had a clear path to the nomination. As the race moved to South Carolina, with its heavy concentration of Black voters, his campaign expected they would split their support among several candidates, including Sanders, permitting him to maintain a strong delegate position en route to an eventual victory.

That was the theory. In practice, Biden won in a landslide. Sanders and Warren both performed abysmally with Black voters, which came as a major blow and stood as a referendum on the nature of their outreach. Surveying Warren's get-out-the-vote rally on the day before the primary, the *New York Times* reporter Astead Herndon was struck that her crowd was almost entirely white. Warren had worked assiduously, and successfully, to win over racial justice groups, online activists, and prominent scholars, crafting detailed policy proposals that reflected their input. It didn't translate to votes. Summing up the view of local officials, Herndon called Warren's strategy "a case study in the limits of using the language of progressive activists to speak to a black community that is more ideologically diverse."

Sanders, too, had labored to win Black voters since losing to Clinton in 2016. Back then, Black Lives Matter activists frequently interrupted his speeches. He was stung by their criticism and by Clinton's insinuation that his class-focused populism ignored racism ("Not everything is about an economic theory, right?" she'd said at a Nevada rally. "If we broke up the big banks tomorrow . . . would that end racism?"). Afterward, he went on a tour of the South to commemorate the fiftieth anniversary of Martin Luther King Jr.'s assassination and try to build stronger ties with Black voters. Then he went on a popular Black radio show to concede that his movement had been "too white." His 2020 campaign, like Warren's, had faithfully adhered to the language and issue set favored by Black political activists, but he didn't fare much better than she did.

Biden's South Carolina victory set in motion a series of events that rapidly brought the nomination battle to a close. In the days that followed, Pete Buttigieg, Amy Klobuchar, and Tom Steyer dropped out and endorsed Biden (after some behind-the-scenes cajoling from Barack Obama). The race ceased to be an ideological contest and instead narrowed to a choice of who could beat Trump. Voters didn't struggle with the question. Even though Biden's campaign was so short of money that he couldn't travel to many of the Super Tuesday states that voted three days later, he won most of them anyway, effectively locking up the nomination.

Sanders tried to hang on. But within a few days, the fast-spreading coronavirus pandemic shut down schools and workplaces across the country. Biden and Sanders jointly decided to cancel Cleveland rallies that both had scheduled for March 10. That night, Biden swept every county in Michigan's primary—the scene of Sanders's comeback in 2016. And that was it.

IN RETROSPECT, the notion that most Democratic voters would base their choice on anything other than their perception of a nominee's likelihood of beating Donald Trump was probably far-fetched. Casting the primaries as a high-stakes intraparty ideological battle didn't comport with how most people saw the race: they were furious at Trump, wanted him gone from the White House, and were dubious of reformers touting utopian ideas, however appealing those were in the abstract. This posed a particular problem for Warren, because the group that felt strongest that defeating Trump should outweigh personal ideological preferences was also her core constituency: college-educated white women. By nearly a two-to-one margin, Gallup found, they preferred the nominee with the best chance of winning. When Warren faded, many of them moved to Biden, not Sanders.

From the grand, abstract perspective, the primary appeared to deliver a verdict on the appeal of a populist, left-wing politics. Both candidates who fully embraced it (one endorsed by the new Latina congresswoman who was the party's rising star) lost to an elderly white moderate whose Washington political career spanned the entirety of the neoliberal era—and then some—and who campaigned on restoring a gauzy notion of America's past. Given the option to vote for "big, structural change" (Warren) or "revolution" (Sanders), Democrats chose the safer path of moderation and nominated Biden, who won.

And yet the strain of economic populism that arose after the Great Financial Crisis plainly shaped the core ideas of American politics and governance in 2020, even among people who weren't as closely identified with it as Warren, Sanders, and Ocasio-Cortez. The most striking illustration came as the primaries were still unfolding. Trump, with Democratic backing, signed the first of two economic stimulus packages totaling nearly $3 trillion to mitigate the effects of a new financial crisis, this one brought on by the COVID pandemic. They featured an almost point-by-point list of policies Warren had pushed to no avail during the last crisis, measures aimed not at Wall Street but at the general public. These included multiple rounds of direct cash payments to most adults; enhanced unemployment benefits that in some cases exceeded workers' prior wages; a freeze on evictions and student loan payments; and a generous bailout of millions of small businesses contingent upon the continued employment of their workers. It was an effort, on a scale never seen before, to positively affect the lives and livelihoods of millions of American workers and their families and avoid repeating the mistakes of the last crisis. Whether or not Trump was conscious of this, the coherent scheme of aid, and his efforts to keep the economy open—often over the objections of Democrats—helped him to win more votes, including from Black and Latino voters, than in 2016 (his margin improving in seventy-eight of the hundred Latino-majority counties). His protecting people from the economic ravages of the crisis undoubtedly helped Republicans gain seats in the House and Senate, even as he himself lost.

Perhaps this shouldn't come as shocking. When Warren, and then Sanders, began to lose their appeal during the primaries, the major argument against them was that they posed too much of a risk of losing to Trump. But taken on their own, many of their economic ideas were highly popular, not just with Democrats, but with independents and many Republicans. The same surveys that showed voters didn't think Warren was electable also showed that her policy ideas were strongly preferred to Biden's and every other candidate's in the race. Stripped of their association with radical left-wing politicians, populist economic ideas fared well on state ballots, too. In 2020, Arizonans voted to raise taxes on the wealthy to fund teacher salaries, while Floridians voted by a wide margin to raise the state's minimum wage to $15 an hour.

Biden framed the general election, probably wisely, as being a choice between Trump and the turmoil he brings and a familiar, reassuringly moderate alternative who intended nothing more radical than to "restore the soul of America," whatever that pleasant-sounding phrase meant. But Biden wasn't blind to the populist appeal. Nor was he wedded to the market-oriented neoliberalism Democrats had embraced earlier in his career. For much of that period, stretching at least through the bankruptcy battles with Warren in 2005, people in Washington would joke that Biden was "the senator from corporate America." As president, though, he's governed more in the manner of the nickname he seems to prefer, "Scranton Joe."

Biden never got much respect as a politician. Still, throughout the primaries and the fall election, he seemed to have the most perceptive understanding of his own appeal. He didn't try to one-up his competitors with bigger, more radical plans. He didn't employ the abstruse language of the activist class or even seem to comprehend it. He knew his limits. And he found a way to explain what he had to offer and how it might serve to curb the intense economic and political upheavals that have poisoned American civic life over the last fifteen years.

After his string of Super Tuesday victories, Biden held a big rally in Detroit. By then it was clear he was going to win the nomination. Several of the candidates he'd defeated lined up onstage to support him. For Biden, who had been seeking the presidency for much of the last fifty years, it must have been a moment of extraordinary satisfaction. But instead of dwelling on it, he looked ahead. "Look," Biden told the crowd, "I view myself as a bridge, not as anything else. There's an entire generation of new leaders standing behind me. They are the future of this country."

Since taking office, Biden has worked, without anyone quite thinking of it this way, to answer the question: A bridge to what? The broad outlines of an answer can be glimpsed in what he has achieved so far and what might still be to come.

Right away, instead of worrying about deficits, he pushed through another $1.9 trillion COVID package, this time without Republican support, that extended the economic protections already in place while adding new ones. This included hundreds of billions of dollars to support families, an effort that, while it lasted, cut child poverty in half. In a break with past administrations, including Obama's, Biden has begun to remake the political economy along many of the same lines as his populist opponents wished to do, breaking up and preventing concentrations of corporate power, pursuing U.S. industrial policy with an eye toward easing regional economic disparities, and attempting to reduce inequality by seeking to raise taxes on the rich, including through a wealth tax on multimillionaires and billionaires.

Pivoting from the relatively neoliberal free-trade orthodoxies of the Obama era, Biden seems to want to forge a new American moral identity that centers domestic workers and their progress. The toughening of trade policy with China, the reshoring of the semiconductor industry, and hundreds of billions of dollars in green infrastructure investments, much of it spread across rural areas with stipulations that American suppliers should be favored, all paint a rough tableau of a future that has many elements of the patriotic Democratic nationalism Steve Bannon once worried about.

Whether or not Biden succeeds in becoming a bridge to a post-neoliberal Democratic age won't become clear for many years. Projects of that magnitude require more than one term, and probably more than one president, to accomplish. There is great significance in what happens now. The future of the party wasn't settled in the last election. But it may now hinge on the next one.

EPILOGUE

This book has traced the rise of left populism since the 2008 financial crisis and followed three of the major figures who carried it along: Elizabeth Warren, Bernie Sanders, and Alexandria Ocasio-Cortez.

Expressions of economic populism inside the Democratic Party had been all but extinguished by the time the global market catastrophe hit. Beginning in 1978, Democrats, over Jimmy Carter's objection, embraced Wall Street's idea that encouraging "capital formation" was the surest way to revive the moribund economy and set America on a path to broad prosperity. The neoliberal era that spanned the next four decades put this new faith at its center, relying upon market forces rather than the government to set the party's course. Its dominance was so thorough that dissenting voices were eclipsed or ignored, and its Wall Street proponents didn't just guide policy but also financed campaigns and assumed top positions in government. In both Democratic and Republican administrations the prevailing view among the people running the White House, the Federal Reserve, and the Treasury was that prioritizing inflation control, deficit reduction, and financial deregulation should take precedence over social objectives such as promoting full employment and addressing income and wealth inequality.

It took the collapse of the U.S. economy in 2008 and the social upheaval that followed for this way of thinking to lose its grip on American political and intellectual life. When the populist challenge arrived, it came from politicians well outside the Democratic mainstream because that's the only place it could have come from. Warren's attacks on the government's paltry response to the crisis—at least as it pertained to the middle class—resonated so strongly because the lopsided plan that mainly rescued banks symbolized how the political consensus of recent decades had not only failed to universalize prosperity but produced a steady rise in income inequality, with pronounced regional and racial disparities, that consigned millions of people to lives of constant economic precarity. When the economy blew up, they learned just how little they mattered to the people in charge. It didn't sit well. A few years later, Sanders and Donald Trump showed what a powerful political force their collective discontent could be.

In 2016, that backlash put a right-wing populist in the White House. Four years later, a pair of left-wing populists hoped to displace him. That, of course, is not how events played out. But even though the 2020 Democratic primaries didn't produce a populist nominee—an outcome all but assured when Warren and Sanders refused to defer to each other—the influence of the movement they've led, which pulled in Ocasio-Cortez and others, is apparent almost everywhere, not just in Democratic politics.

The clearest measure of this influence isn't the outcome of the 2020 primaries but what happened right in the middle of them. This book has mainly focused on the period of U.S. political history that spans the last fifteen years. The tectonic shift that brought our main characters to prominence was the 2008 crisis. But the narrative of populist influence is bookended by another global market collapse that followed the onset of the COVID pandemic in the spring of 2020 and effectively brought the Democratic primary race to an end. What the response to the COVID crash showed is that elites in both parties understood that this time they had better respond to the needs of the masses or there'd be hell to pay. And they did—to a degree that would have been inconceivable to someone ensconced in the neoliberal consensus of twenty or thirty years earlier.

Long after the 2008 collapse, a former Treasury official who helped implement the government's rescue plan under George W. Bush and Barack Obama reflected publicly on what they had missed and expressed his regret that so many people were left behind. "The biggest mistake we made in 2008," said Neel Kashkari, who oversaw the Troubled Asset Relief Program, was that "we targeted our programs too narrowly." Politicians in both parties worried that spending too much money would enrage voters. Since the 1980s, they'd been conditioned by Wall Street to fear the wrath of "bond vigilantes"—a theoretical group of investors who would punish the government, and wreck the economy, by dumping U.S. Treasury bonds if debt levels were allowed to rise too high. "By applying numerous criteria to make sure only 'deserving' families received help," Kashkari continued, "we narrowed and slowed the programs dramatically, resulting in a deeper housing correction, with more foreclosures than had we flooded borrowers with assistance. The American people ultimately paid more because of our attempts to save them money."

Kashkari issued his mea culpa just as the COVID pandemic was sweeping the globe. It's unusual for prominent figures to hold themselves to public account; Kashkari was by then the president of the Federal Reserve Bank of Minneapolis. But what emerged inter alia in the years before COVID shook global markets was a tacit acknowledgment among political and financial leaders that the populist critics of the Great Financial Crisis had had a point. A generation of Democrats, pushed by left populists, had already begun to rethink the wisdom of unfettered free trade, anti-unionism, and financial deregulation. The Federal Reserve was questioning whether its long-standing practice of managing economic growth by raising interest rates at the slightest hint of inflation was needlessly throttling the American economy and tossing people out of work. And the bond vigilantes never materialized, despite the growing budget deficits and Fed money printing that accompanied the government's crisis response. Inflation didn't immediately spike. The unemployment rate eventually dropped to the lowest level since Dwight Eisenhower's presidency. When COVID generated a new financial crisis, policymakers heeded Kashkari's admonition to learn from the mistakes of the past and "err on the side of helping as many businesses and workers as possible."

Beginning under Trump and continuing under Biden, the government committed trillions of dollars to propping up the economy, most of it aimed at the general public, whether through stimulus checks, unemployment benefits, or rent and eviction moratoriums; private-sector bailouts targeted small and midsized businesses and were conditioned on employee retention. Rather than fret about vigilantes, the Federal Reserve chair, Jerome Powell, encouraged Congress to pursue an aggressive fiscal response, urging House Speaker Nancy Pelosi to "think big" and having the Fed buy up the ballooning government debt to keep borrowing costs low and the economy running smoothly.

Rather than short-circuit the recovery by raising interest rates too soon, Powell and the Fed erred on the side of ignoring inflation for a bit too long.

The staggering scope and scale of the government's rescue of the middle class was reflected in what the chief economist of Goldman Sachs called "the most amazing statistic of this entire period." In the spring of 2020, as COVID shut down entire swaths of the U.S. economy and tens of millions of people were thrown out of work, U.S. household income actually went up.

As with any national emergency response, the programs created to protect people from the effects of the COVID crash had their fair share of flaws—including, in the end, their generosity, which helped cause a temporary bout of inflation. But they also left no question about the power of an aggressive fiscal intervention to alter the basic dynamics of the U.S. political economy in a way that greatly benefited people up and down the income scale, students and seniors, renters and homeowners, workers and business owners alike.

It took a decade after the 2008 crash for the prime-age employment rate (people ages twenty-five to fifty-four, who are the core of the U.S. workforce) to return to its precrisis peak; even then, many industries and geographic regions didn't fully recover. COVID caused a much deeper collapse in 2020. But this time the employment rate recovered to its prerecession peak in under three years while pulling along groups that historically lagged. Black employment reached a new high. The employment rate for women also recovered and then kept on rising, eventually clearing its April 2000 historical peak. For once, wages grew fastest for people at the bottom of the income scale, not the top. The results, and lessons they contain, are nothing short of transformative—if they're put to proper use.

Knowing what we know now doesn't just equip policymakers with better tools to combat the next downturn. It raises broader questions of the sort that populist outsiders like Warren, Sanders, and Ocasio-Cortez have been asking all along: If political leaders can do so much to mitigate recessions and grow the economy, why act only in an emergency? Why not do more for workers and families all the time? What else could be accomplished if politicians took more initiative?

EACH OF THE CHARACTERS in this book arrived on the scene as an outsider. Much of the populist energy that elevated them into national figures and infused Democratic politics came from people who were also outside the party's mainstream or outside the party altogether, from Occupy protesters and climate activists to crusaders for racial justice. The great achievement of Sanders's presidential campaigns was pulling so many of them inside, which helped steer the Democratic Party to the left, even as an aging white moderate, long associated with the corporate wing of the party, became the new Democratic president.

Being an outsider has obvious appeal in politics. You're untainted by the corrupting influence of Washington. Moral purity is always attractive, especially in the wake of sweeping governmental failures, as well as a powerful intoxicant for building reformist movements and campaigns. The outsider who launches a cleansing political revolution is a recurring figure in American history and popular culture who fits people's romantic notion of how politics ought to work in a democracy, on the left and the right.

But politics isn't just a matter of willpower or inspiration. If you really want to reshape the political order, at some point you have to engage with people inside the system or nothing gets done. The activist's dilemma, which Warren, Sanders, and Ocasio-Cortez all confronted, is that you can't float above the sordid mess forever. If you want to use the public support you've built up to advance an agenda, you have to work with people who don't already agree with you—who may not even like you. You have to compromise.

The rise of the populist left was marked by plenty of controversy and infighting—both in the battles against establishment Democrats such as Hillary Clinton and Nancy Pelosi and in the internal battles, between factions on the left. The personal bitterness between Warren and Sanders (and many members of their staffs) broke into rare public view during a January 14, 2020, primary debate, when Warren accused him of having told her in a private meeting that a woman couldn't win the presidency. Sanders angrily disputed the charge.

The critical evolution in the advancement of the left-populist cause, however, was that at several points, especially once Joe Biden had secured the Democratic nomination, the battle lines that had delineated the centrists and the populists wound up not being an impediment to a unified party as the 2020 election drew near. Although it doesn't comport with the gauzy mythology that's risen up around them, Warren, Sanders, and Ocasio-Cortez took steps to ensure that Biden would have the best possible chance to make it to the White House, whereupon he would deliver—they trusted—at least some semblance of their priorities.

Warren was never a true outsider in the sense that the others were, having been brought into the Democratic fold by Harry Reid and Chuck Schumer initially to dispense policy expertise and later to police the TARP bailout. Her electoral career was an accident, prompted by Obama's unwillingness to nominate her to be the permanent head of the CFPB. Publicly, she was willing and eager to joust with establishment figures, including Obama, because it pressured them to do things they wouldn't have done absent the public scrutiny she generated. Privately, however, Warren understood that cultivating influence meant picking her battles and maintaining open channels with the people she criticized. Fateful though it was for her future presidential hopes, her decision not to endorse Sanders in 2016 was a product of this reasoning. Had Clinton won, Warren would have had a strong hand in shaping her new administration. When it became clear Biden would prevail in 2020, Warren dutifully fell in line and enjoyed, if anything, an even stronger hand in influencing the personnel and policy decisions Biden has pursued.

No figure besides Biden loomed larger in the 2020 primaries than Sanders. And nothing Sanders did helped advance his ideological cause more than making an unqualified endorsement of Biden, once his own candidacy faltered, in a joint live stream on April 13. Sanders urged his supporters to vote for Biden in the general election, short-circuiting any possibility of internal revolt. This time, there would be no damaging party rupture, as there had been between Sanders and Clinton supporters four years earlier. Perhaps Sanders simply didn't want to jeopardize the opportunity to oust Trump. Or perhaps after spending much of his career standing in principled defiance against Democratic policies he deemed insufficient, but without achieving much in the way of tangible results, Sanders saw a historic opportunity and acted on it. Biden agreed to let Sanders's allies, including Ocasio-Cortez and Representative Pramila Jayapal, the head of the Congressional Progressive Caucus, help shape the policy agenda for his future administration—something that seemed, at the time, like a meaningless concession from Biden but turned out to matter a lot.

As soon as he was sworn in, Biden signaled just how significantly the scope of Democrats' ambitions had expanded in the years since the last Democratic president was inaugurated. "The way I see it," he said, by way of explaining his $1.9 trillion stimulus package, the American

Rescue Plan, "the biggest risk is not going too big—it's if we go too small. We've been here before." Noting that he'd led the Obama administration's stimulus efforts after the Great Recession, Biden was explicit in his recognition of how it had fallen short: "It wasn't enough." This time, the stimulus not only dwarfed what had followed the 2008 crash; it was an enormous social spending bill dressed up as a COVID response that the entire party, even wayward centrists like Senator Joe Manchin, got behind. A few overheated commentators likened Biden's rescue plan to Franklin Delano Roosevelt's response to the Great Depression. A more useful historical point about Biden's achievement would focus on Sanders, who shifted the basic orientation of the Democratic Party away from financed-centered neoliberalism and toward the beginnings of a social democracy that, while hardly Scandinavian, is far more concerned with improving the lives of the kinds of people mostly left out of the social bargain before—and especially after—the 2008 crash.

But this shift couldn't have happened without Biden or someone like him, which carries its own lesson. The 2020 primaries showed the limitations of what politicians who code as "radical left-wingers" can achieve, whether they're socialists like Sanders or liberal capitalists like Warren. It took a nonthreatening moderate who didn't excite anybody to finally bring major elements of the populists' agenda into being.

OCASIO-CORTEZ CAME OF AGE in the teeth of the Great Recession, and it affected every aspect of her life, from her family's brush with foreclosure to her struggles with student loans, health insurance, and the grim labor market. It's no wonder she was drawn to activism in the years after the crash: her generation suffered the most harm and had the least to gain from maintaining the political and social status quo. "We were all children of the recession," said Waleed Shahid of Justice Democrats. "There's an overwhelming sense that the economic and political system in our country is rigged." Replacing it, or at least forcefully reordering its priorities, was a cause Ocasio-Cortez embraced.

From the moment she arrived in Washington, Ocasio-Cortez was the center of controversy. Initially, that appeared to be her goal, a way to draw attention to her causes and put public pressure on her fellow lawmakers. Occupying Pelosi's office with activists from the Sunrise Movement was just the start. In the early weeks of her term, Saikat Chakrabarti and Corbin Trent, whom Ocasio-Cortez hired as her chief of staff and communications director, respectively, became notorious for ignoring congressional decorum and taking to television and Twitter to criticize Democratic members of Congress, including Pelosi, often in bluntly personal terms. In a promotional video for Justice Democrats, Ocasio-Cortez endorsed the idea of running primary challengers against her new Democratic colleagues. Chakrabarti, who also appeared in the video, explained that staying "true to the movement" and "fighting unapologetically on the inside" were necessary to achieve the radical solutions they wanted.

Along with three other women of color—Representatives Ilhan Omar of Minnesota, Rashida Tlaib of Michigan, and Ayanna Pressley of Massachusetts—Ocasio-Cortez gained notoriety as a member of "the Squad," a cohort of outspoken House freshmen who became lightning rods for scrutiny. She drew steady criticism, much of it anonymous, from colleagues put off by her confrontational approach. Pelosi criticized her publicly, pointing out that the Squad wasn't influencing Democratic policy. "They're four people, and that's how many votes they got," she sniped to *The New York Times*.

By July, Pelosi was fed up and summoned Ocasio-Cortez to a private meeting. It served to extinguish what might be called the activist phase of her congressional career; shortly thereafter, Chakrabarti and Trent left her staff, and Ocasio-Cortez toned down her public criticism of Democratic colleagues. "She found out that antagonism toward your colleagues is not an effective way to legislate," Drew Hammill, a top Pelosi staffer, explained. "You had a lot of people making it very clear to her that this is not the way to get results."

Good politicians adapt. Ocasio-Cortez was no exception. In the year after, she found more productive methods for advancing climate and other goals, learning when to go on the attack and when not to. Her relationships with other House members improved. As Warren had done early in her career, Ocasio-Cortez became a confident and prepossessing star of oversight hearings, deftly engineering showdowns that generated headlines and public pressure. It became not uncommon to hear positive comments from colleagues surprised and enchanted that the diligently prepared woman with whom they established productive working relations wasn't the socialist firebrand her public image suggested.

As she began learning how power operates in Congress, Ocasio-Cortez adapted in ways that sometimes ruffled her old allies. In 2020 a group of prominent leftists, touting the activist slogan "Power concedes nothing without a demand," pressed her and other progressives to threaten Pelosi's speakership unless the House held a vote on Medicare for All. Ocasio-Cortez noted that support fell far short of a majority. "So you issue threats, hold your vote, and lose," she replied on Twitter. "Then what?" It would be more productive, she explained, to pursue policies where a large coalition really did exist: "You can use leverage to push for things that *can* happen and change lives—ie a $15 min wage vote in the first 100 days (doable), elevating longtime progressive champions to important positions of leadership (also doable). That's the opportunity cost to weigh."

Ocasio-Cortez often seems trapped in an image that doesn't recognize the evolution she's undergone in Congress. Occupying Pelosi's office made her an icon for a generation of young activists and sympathetic journalists, who still write about her with awestruck admiration. Her first weeks in Congress provided what activists, journalists, and Republican opponents love most: an exciting new figure righteously denouncing her own party's compromises and shortcomings. The Green New Deal resolution, a staggeringly ambitious and unrealistic climate and jobs bill, briefly became a Washington obsession. But fairly early in her tenure, Ocasio-Cortez came to see that direct action and righteous demands don't, on their own, produce the outcomes many activists imagine they will. For all its attention, the Green New Deal was a nonbinding resolution that lacked legislative detail and even in the form of a vague messaging bill couldn't draw the support of a majority of Democratic members.

Today, the important development for the future of the Democratic left is still largely invisible, hidden behind the laudatory headlines that routinely mischaracterize its young star as a political supernova bending Washington to her will (as one magazine put it, "AOC Has Already Changed D.C. It Hasn't Changed Her Much"). But Washington *has* changed Ocasio-Cortez, in a way that's entirely conducive to achieving progressive goals. She's dropped tactics like occupying the Speaker's office and making broad threats to oust Democrats. Instead, she's used her influence to shape Biden's agenda while also working to elect a steady stream of multiracial progressive allies whose presence in Congress will gradually expand the horizon of what the left can hope to achieve in the years ahead.

A sign of this sophistication was how she dealt with Biden. As the

Democratic primaries began, she made clear she was no fan. "In any other country, Joe Biden and I would not be in the same party," she said, "but in America, we are." Implicit in her statement is a recognition that in America's two-party system social-democratic goals can be realized only through the Democratic Party. When Biden prevailed, Ocasio-Cortez supported him and resisted the strenuous efforts of the political press corps to bait her into criticizing a nominee whom everyone knew she hadn't wanted.

In activist circles, moving from outsider to insider is often viewed as a betrayal. But being on the inside isn't the same thing as selling out. It means your interests are represented. You get a say in what happens. Politicians, even those backed by corporate dollars, aren't cartoon figures. They respond to incentives. The ones who have been around for a while, like Joe Biden, understand that for Democrats to win, they must be what Adlai Stevenson once called "the party of everyone"—a broad coalition that includes a younger generation closer in outlook to Ocasio-Cortez than Biden.

Traditionally, when a Democrat locks up his party's presidential nomination, he or she pivots toward the center to appeal to the broadest group of voters. But after Biden won the 2020 primary, he turned to the left—because he felt he had to. On the campaign trail, he spoke approvingly of the Green New Deal, calling it a "crucial framework" (without fully endorsing it). As part of his deal with Sanders, he appointed Ocasio-Cortez to a task force to help develop climate policy. Two years later, in August 2022, Biden signed the Inflation Reduction Act, which for strategic reasons wasn't pitched as an environmental bill, but delivered the largest climate investment in U.S. history, $370 billion over a decade.

Ocasio-Cortez still gets covered mainly through the lens of "the Squad." It must get tiring. But among the rising generation of Democratic staffers and strategists who will soon run the party, she's come to be seen as a significant figure in her own right, the rare activist turned politician who—regardless of whether she one day runs for president—has channeled her movement's priorities into the central arteries of a party that previously showed little concern for them. "You can see her pointing a path toward the future in a way that none of the other Squad members are doing," says a Warren adviser. "She's the one really marking the future for the left in the post-Biden era."

AT SOME POINT in the not-too-distant future almost every major figure in Democratic politics today will depart the stage. Elizabeth Warren, Bernie Sanders, Joe Biden, Nancy Pelosi, and Chuck Schumer, as well as the great unifier of Democrats, Donald Trump, are all in their seventies or eighties. Retirement or defeat—or in Trump's case, possibly prison—awaits them all. When they're gone, the question of who will lead the Democratic Party and what it will stand for will be more wide open than at perhaps any time since the 1940s.

U.S. politics has been consumed by issues of culture and identity ever since Trump's rise. Trump himself, of course, has been the chief driver of this trend, stoking racial grievances and raising alarm over "migrant caravans," critical race theory, and the like. Prosecuting the ever-more-esoteric battles of the right-wing culture wars has become the primary objective of contemporary popular conservatism, whether the issue is school book bans, gender transition, or one of the countless permutations of "wokeness," and whether the aggressor is Donald Trump, Ron DeSantis, or someone else. The gravitational pull of these conflicts has shaped the political opposition.

Trump's victory over Hillary Clinton traumatized a generation of Democrats, who explained it to themselves by imbuing him with mystical powers to manipulate voters. How else could someone so manifestly unfit have landed in the White House? How to respond to Trump's relentless focus on culture and race has divided Democrats nearly as much as it has divided Republicans. The central conflict in Democratic politics right now is between people who want to elevate specific identity groups like racial minorities and women that have come under his direct attack and other people who favor an approach laser focused on winning back the white working-class voters who were once the foundation of the Democratic coalition, until Trump came along and lured them away.

But framing the political choice as a simple binary between race and class isn't likely to lead Democrats to the promised land of a durable governing majority that will enable them to do big things. Trump's grip on our collective consciousness obscures another, more important driver of the anger, resentment, and distrust coursing through American society—he's more symptom than cause. The bigger villain in the story is the shift in the U.S. political economy from its post–New Deal industrial focus, which enabled middle-class stability, to its post-1970s focus on unleashing the power of markets through deregulation while shrinking the welfare state. This shift might have raised per capita GDP. But it also produced rising inequality, pronounced racial and regional disparities, and a justified sense among millions of people that they'd been left behind, yanked out of an era when America was great—at least for people like them, at least compared with now—and consigned to a worse one marked by constant upheaval and economic precarity. Long before Trump rode down his golden escalator and into the presidential race, Black people, rural denizens, white factory workers, and many others had all seen their life situations deteriorate as a result of this shift. What Trump did was exploit their grievances for political gain. He didn't reinvent politics.

Progressives, especially the ones featured in this book, have plenty of visionary proposals for remaking society. What's missing is a coalition that could turn them into reality. If a Democratic president could wave a magic wand and bring into being the Green New Deal or Warren's "big, structural change," it might well produce a higher level of political and social contentment, perhaps even enough to usher in another era of long-term Democratic control of government like the one that followed the New Deal. But lacking a wand, Democrats face a much tougher challenge. The constitutional structure of the Electoral College and the Senate gives Republicans a built-in advantage by favoring sparsely populated rural states and the preferences of voters who live there. Any enduring Democratic governing coalition will have to appeal to them. It's the keyhole through which every ambitious plan must pass.

Over the last decade, the Democratic Party has become less appealing to working-class voters, many of whom defected to Trump and the Republicans. Some liberal analysts write them off as irredeemable racists. But the move in recent elections of more Blacks, Asians, and Latinos to the Republican column—a trend that appears to be driven mainly by working-class voters—vitiates the notion that this out-migration is motivated chiefly by racial bigotry (as does the fact that many white working-class Trump supporters voted for Barack Obama). Over the same period, Democrats' support among white college-educated voters has shifted just as dramatically, an advantage that put Joe Biden in the White House. To succeed in the years ahead, Democrats will have to remake the political economy once more, this time to serve the interests of people of all races and classes, including people who don't currently support Democrats.

Economic issues are always at the center of American politics, even if they're eclipsed by cultural disputes that are more viscerally thrilling on cable news and social media. Rather than fear the Republicans' culture wars—or respond to them by racializing policies that benefit everyone—Democrats should take the opportunity to reestablish the party as serving the interests of working people of every race and ethnicity. Under Trump, Republicans have gone all in on betting their future on working-class voters, but without doing much to improve their material circumstances. Attacks on "wokeness" won't suffice forever. Democrats can win them back.

If we go back to the beginning of our story, when the New Deal era was reaching its tumultuous end and Democrats were grasping at new ideas like "capital formation" to keep the party afloat, what we can see, along with the genesis of the party's turn to Wall Street, is the importance of addressing the economic disruptions that periodically upend American life and fall hardest on the working and middle classes. In the late 1970s, Democrats didn't do that. Instead, they embarked on building a new economic regime that disfavored the mechanisms that protected their own voters: unions, trade restrictions, industrial policy, a strong social safety net, rules to curb the predations of big banks. Losing sight of the welfare of their own constituents eventually carried a steep cost: a series of terrifying economic shocks and social upheavals that culminated in the election of Donald Trump.

It took the backlash to the 2008 financial crisis to persuade Democratic policymakers that governing in the interest of financial markets isn't always wise. And it took the emergence of a left-populist faction to steer them back toward the party's historic concern with the economic lives of ordinary people. At the same time, the advent of modern organizing and fundraising technology makes this focus a plausible basis for running competitive elections. Democrats don't need to go hat in hand shaking down big banks and corporations, as Tony Coelho did in the 1980s, not when small donors excited by honest candidates can generate billions of dollars to support them and then organize themselves to get those candidates elected.

An underappreciated aspect of Biden's presidency is how fully he appears to have absorbed these lessons and rejected, or at least loosened, his party's embrace—financial and intellectual—of Wall Street and Silicon Valley. This is apparent in his aggressive actions to break up concentrated corporate power, his support for industrial policy, his folding of "care workers" into the category of people to whom that policy should apply, and his being more attuned to the home-front costs of globalization than any of his predecessors. What recent Democratic president would tweet, as Biden did, "I proposed a minimum billionaire tax because no billionaire should be paying a lower tax rate than a schoolteacher or a firefighter"?

Democrats are at the beginning of a new era that is still largely undefined. Pushed by the populists in his party, Biden has started to give shape to what it might look like. But nothing guarantees it will resemble what he's begun or that the next generation of Democrats will prioritize the same things—or that a post-Trump Republican Party won't wake up and realize that it had better address the needs of its working-class constituents if it hopes to hold on to them.

Warren, Sanders, and Ocasio-Cortez pulled the Democratic Party back toward its roots, toward the still unrealized dream of a broad multiracial coalition of the working, middle, and upper classes and a political economy that works for everyone, not just the privileged few at the top of the income scale. We don't know yet whether history will remember them as harbingers of a new Democratic age or insurgents who ultimately didn't change the party as they'd hoped.

But today, as their concerns are being revived, it's worth remembering why this vision is so important and what it will take to see it fulfilled.

ACKNOWLEDGMENTS

One afternoon in January 2010, I was sitting in Treasury secretary Timothy Geithner's ornate corner office conducting a final interview for a long magazine profile. I'd followed him through the depths of the financial crisis, watching up close as the Obama administration raced to contain it. Almost everyone I'd spoken to in the months prior, from Lawrence Summers to Robert Rubin to Jerome Powell, considered the government's response to have been a heroic success. The economy was growing again, the stock market booming. But Geithner was shaken. Three days earlier, Massachusetts voters had delivered a jarring rebuke, electing a Republican to fill Ted Kennedy's Senate seat in a special election that looked as if it might bring Obama's agenda grinding to a halt. The populist backlash had arrived.

In the years that followed, that backlash became the shaping force in U.S. politics. Watching it unfold and writing about its effects became a significant part of my job as a journalist. The early inkling in Geithner's office that something profound was shifting in Democratic politics put me on a path that led to this book.

Much of my initial reporting on the financial crisis and my three main characters was conducted for magazine pieces, first in *The Atlantic* and then in *Bloomberg Businessweek*. At *The Atlantic*, I was blessed to work closely with two talented editors, Scott Stossel and Corby Kummer, who fostered and encouraged my early interest in the political effects of the crisis and its major players.

Special thanks as well to my *Bloomberg* bosses, Mike Bloomberg, John Micklethwait, and Reto Gregori, for allowing me time to work on this book, even as I was covering many of the politicians and events in real time. Joel Weber cheerfully pushed me to write more about liberal populism and always found space to publish it. I'm also deeply indebted to several current and former Bloomberg colleagues for their editorial insights and subject matter expertise. My beloved editor, Wes Kosova, sharpened my thinking and writing at every stage and continues to serve as a trusted sounding board, even now that he's no longer editing. Robert Schmidt was a peerless guide to understanding the hidden ways in which Wall Street influences political Washington. Joe Weisenthal helped me better understand the inner workings of the postcrisis economy and the psychology of bond vigilantes.

Robert Kuttner and Damon Silvers were incredibly knowledgeable tutors on the political economy of the late 1970s and the 1980s. So was Michael Podhorzer, who read and critiqued drafts of several chapters. Along with several of Kuttner's books, Stuart Eizenstat's memoir of the Carter administration and Judith Stein's economic history of the 1970s were particularly valuable resources. I'm also deeply grateful to the archival staff at the Jimmy Carter Presidential Library and Museum. Tony Coelho graciously took time to explain the many challenges he faced in the 1980s and how he met them. I'd also like to thank Steve Bodow and Hillary Kun of *The Daily Show*.

Writing a book like this one can sometimes feel like having an extended conversation about politics and history. I benefited enormously from the insights of friends, fellow writers, and political strategists who were always game to talk. They include Paul Glastris, Justin Slaughter, Aaron Ament, Jeff Hauser, Ken Baer, Chris Wilkinson, Ganesh Sitaraman, Alfred Johnson, Yasmin Radjy, Lee Sachs, Jake Siewart, Dan Geldon, Mark Longabaugh, and Max Berger. None was more valuable or better company than the late John Homans, whom I miss dearly. Every page benefited from the wisdom he imparted to me.

I was fortunate to have a strong editorial team behind me every step of the way. First on the list is Xan Mandell, a gifted researcher who turned up every obscure document and journal article I asked for and has such a sharp eye that he also made a habit of including material I hadn't known about—which was often the most valuable. Ingrid Sterner's contributions went far beyond copyediting. As he was on my last book, Scott Moyers, my editor at Penguin Press, was a joy to work with at every step of the process. So was Helen Rouner, whose careful reading and deft editorial suggestions immeasurably improved the final text. I'm also grateful to Ann Godoff, Elisabeth Calamari, Matt Boyd, and Lauren Lauzon.

My agent, Gail Ross, was instrumental in putting this project together, as well as a steady source of support throughout the writing process. So was my sister, Abby Green, and my parents, Gary and Priscilla Green, who talked me off the ledge at several difficult points. My in-laws, Mark and Susie Woodard, graciously took in my family to give me time alone to write.

Finally, the love and support of three people in particular contributed more than anything else to helping me write this book: Alicia, Chloe, and Nick. No words can express my gratitude to them or my happiness at being back in their company.

A NOTE ON SOURCES

This book was germinating long before I ever realized I was going to write it. For some time, I'd wanted to do a book about the recent history of the relationship between Wall Street and Washington and had begun talking to historians and poking around in archives—and then, boom, the financial crisis hit and it suddenly became apparent that that history was unfolding all around me.

Some of the interviews I conducted during the crisis and its immediate aftermath became the seeds of this project. I've also drawn on conversations and reporting for subsequent *Businessweek* features and news stories. While I was researching the book, several sources provided me with emails, strategy memos, polling data, and private notes, some of which are quoted or described herein, and some of which were shared on "deep background"—meaning that they could inform my writing and analysis but couldn't be quoted or cited. Wherever I've drawn on the work of other journalists or authors, I've tried to include a citation, either in the text or in an endnote. Quotations that are not cited there are drawn from my own reporting. Any mistakes I've made are, of course, my own.

NOTES

PROLOGUE

2 **I told the story:** Joshua Green, *Devil's Bargain: Steve Bannon, Donald Trump, and the Storming of the Presidency* (New York: Penguin Books, 2018).

4 **Gary Gerstle:** Gary Gerstle, *The Rise and Fall of the Neoliberal Order: America and the World in the Free Market Era* (New York: Oxford University Press, 2022).

CHAPTER 1: THE THREE-MARTINI LUNCH

9 **a young aide:** Stuart E. Eizenstat, *President Carter: The White House Years* (New York: Thomas Dunne Books, 2018), 4.

10 **Carter had a favorite illustration:** Clyde H. Farnsworth, "Carter Said to Seek a Deductibility Lid for Business Lunch," *New York Times*, Sept. 5, 1977; John Kifner, "Business-Lunch Curb Decried by Rohatyn," *New York Times*, Sept. 30, 1977; Joseph Thorndike, "A Cultural Tax History of the Three-Martini Lunch," *Forbes*, Jan. 21, 2021.

10 **"You're taught there's virtue":** Deborah Rankin, "No More 'Free Lunch'?," *New York Times*, Nov. 6, 1977.

10 **"Who are these people":** Kifner, "Business-Lunch Curb Decried by Rohatyn."

11 **"We're in a hyper-tense, high-pressure business":** Rankin, "No More 'Free Lunch'?"

11 **"I don't care if it brings in revenue":** Robert Kuttner, *Revolt of the Haves: Tax Rebellions and Hard Times* (New York: Simon & Schuster, 1980), 234.

12 **"Tax reform is so screwed up"**: Eizenstat, *President Carter*, 316.

12 **wish he'd counseled**: Eizenstat, *President Carter*, 278.

13 **"a walking encyclopedia of tax law"**: "Taxes: Taking Aim at a 'Disgrace,'" *Time*, July 4, 1977.

13 **"Jesus in the wilderness"**: Interview with Hendrik Hertzberg, Dec. 3–4, 1981, 115, Project on the Carter Presidency, Miller Center of Public Affairs, University of Virginia.

13 **"My advice hadn't been sought"**: Eizenstat, *President Carter*, 317.

14 **"Stu, I will never do this again"**: Eizenstat, *President Carter*, 299.

14 **"We are left now with accumulating criticism"**: Judith Stein, *Pivotal Decade: How the United States Traded Factories for Finance in the Seventies* (New Haven: Yale University Press, 2010), 179–80.

15 **a jowly, pin-striped**: Elizabeth Drew, "Charlie," *New Yorker*, Jan. 9, 1978, 32.

17 **"I got phone calls"**: Kuttner, *Revolt of the Haves*, 244.

17 **"Within a relatively short period"**: Kuttner, *Revolt of the Haves*, 246.

18 **dropped dead of a stroke**: Art Pine, "Lawrence [*sic*] Woodworth, Expert on U.S. Tax Laws, Dies at 59," *Washington Post*, Dec. 8, 1977.

18 **"They were braced for an attack"**: Kuttner, *Revolt of the Haves*, 243.

18 **bombarded investors with mail**: Kuttner, *Revolt of the Haves*, 243.

19 **made the cover of *Time***: "Tax Revolt!," *Time*, June 19, 1978.

19 **"Any resemblance between this bill"**: Samuel Francis, "Update on the Revenue Act of 1978," Issue Bulletin, Heritage Foundation, Aug. 22, 1978.

19 **"I think the story"**: Laura Kalman, *Right Star Rising: A New Politics, 1974–1980* (New York: W. W. Norton, 2010), 244.

20 **snippet of doggerel**: *Congressional Record*, House of Representatives, Oct. 14, 1978, vol. 124, part 28—Bound Edition, 95th Cong., 2nd Sess., 38638.

21 **"The unpleasant facts we have to face"**: Memo from Eizenstat to Carter, Oct. 14, 1978, Stuart Eizenstat's Chronological Files, container 91, 10/8/78–10/14/78, Jimmy Carter Library and Museum, Atlanta.

21 **without fanfare**: Eizenstat, *President Carter*, 319–20.

22 **"the Great Compression"**: Claudia Goldin and Robert A. Margo, "The Great Compression: The Wage Structure in the United States at Mid-century," *Quarterly Journal of Economics* 107, no. 1 (Feb. 1992): 1–34.

22 **"Carter and his advisers vacated"**: Stein, *Pivotal Decade*, 200.

CHAPTER 2: DEMOCRATS FOR THE BUSINESS CLASS

28 **"I would get rid of government"**: Randall Rothenberg, *The Neoliberals: Creating the New American Politics* (New York: Simon & Schuster, 1984), 126.

28 **"They have joined in the clamor"**: Arthur Schlesinger Jr., "The Democratic Party After Ted Kennedy," *Wall Street Journal*, Dec. 7, 1982.

29 **"You have to respect"**: Charles Peters, quoted by Randall Rothenberg, "The Neoliberal Club," *Esquire*, Feb. 1982.

30 **"Our proposals"**: Paul E. Tsongas, "Atarizing Reagan," *New York Times*, March 1, 1983.

31 **Examining the distribution of gains:** "The Distribution of Household Income, 2016," Congressional Budget Office, July 2019.

32 **Even mild criticisms:** Noland D. McCaskill, "Bernie Sanders Questions Obama's Leadership," *Politico*, Feb. 11, 2016; Kyle Cheney, "Bernie Blurbs for Book on How Obama 'Let Progressives Down,'" *Politico*, Jan. 30, 2016; Brett LoGiurato, "'That Is a Low Blow': Democratic Debate Derails After Hillary Torches Bernie over Past Obama Criticism," *Insider*, Feb. 11, 2016.

32 **stopped seeming so scary:** An excellent history of how corporations made peace with government oversight in mid-century America is Nicholas Lemann's *Transaction Man: The Rise of the Deal and the Decline of the American Dream* (New York: Farrar, Straus and Giroux, 2019).

32 **"The public is hardly unaware":** Richard Hofstadter, *The Paranoid Style in American Politics, and Other Essays* (New York: Vintage Books, 1965), 212.

33 **advancing consumer rights:** Paul Sabin, *Public Citizens: The Attack on Big Government and the Remaking of American Liberalism* (New York: W. W. Norton, 2021).

33 **Wall Street donors:** Campaign finance data from the Center for Responsive Politics show that Obama received a record $17.3 million in contributions in 2008 from the "securities and investment" industries, while McCain received $9.7 million.

34 **"Harry Hopkins role":** David Dayen, "The Most Important WikiLeaks Revelation Isn't About Hillary Clinton," *New Republic*, Oct. 14, 2016.

CHAPTER 3: THE SERMON

35 **"Who's this?":** Reid, interview with David Axelrod, "The Axe Files Podcast," CNN, Oct. 12, 2019, transcripts.cnn.com/show/af/date/2019-10-12/segment/01; Alex Seitz-Wald, "A Cold Call from Someone She Never Met Changed Elizabeth Warren's Life. It Was Harry Reid," NBC News, Sept. 29, 2019.

37 **more than sixty military veterans:** James Dao and Adam Nagourney, "They Served, and Now They're Running," *New York Times*, Feb. 19, 2006; Ari Berman, "Fightin' Dems," *Nation*, Feb. 8, 2006.

37 **coauthored a book:** Elizabeth Warren and Amelia Warren Tyagi, *The Two-Income Trap: Why Middle-Class Mothers and Fathers Are Going Broke* (New York: Basic Books, 2003).

39 **credit card industry's great champion:** Due to its corporate-friendly laws and courts, Delaware issues roughly half of all U.S. credit cards—along with a steady stream of politicians like Biden eager to champion the industry. See

Claire Tsosie, "Why So Many Credit Cards Are from Delaware," *Forbes*, April 14, 2017.

40 **"Senator, if you're not going to fix":** The Warren-Biden exchange occurred during the Feb. 10, 2005, hearing of the Senate Judiciary Committee in the Dirksen Senate Office Building, Washington, D.C. See www.youtube.com/watch?v= InVvVzprIxQ.

40 **As Warren lamented:** Elizabeth Warren, "The Changing Politics of American Bankruptcy Reform," *Osgood Hall Law Journal* 37 (Spring/Summer 1999).

41 **threatened the financial institutions:** Arvind Krishnamurthy, Stefan Nagel, and Dmitry Orlov, "Sizing Up Repo," *Journal of Finance* 69, no. 6 (2014): 2381–417; Adam Tooze, *Crashed: How a Decade of Financial Crises Changed the World* (New York: Viking, 2018).

43 **total value of credit default swaps:** Figures from the Corporate Finance Institute.

43 **70 percent of new U.S. mortgages:** Tooze, *Crashed*.

44 **loosen its "net capital rule":** Peter Gowan, "Crisis in the Heartland: Consequences of the New Wall Street System," *New Left Review*, Jan./Feb. 2009, newleftreview.org/issues/ii55/articles/peter-gowan-crisis-in-the-heartland.

44 **buried deep within:** Edward R. Morrison and Joerg Riegel, "Financial Contracts and the New Bankruptcy Code: Insulating Markets from Bankrupt Debtors and Bankruptcy Judges," *American Bankruptcy Institute Law Review* (Winter 2005).

45 **"An increased rate of home ownership":** Alan Greenspan speech at the Ninth Annual Economic Development Summit, Greenlining Institute, Oakland, Jan. 10, 2002, www.federalreserve.gov/boarddocs/speeches/2002/20020110/default.htm.

47 **"This is like waking up":** The former regulator is quoted in Andrew Ross Sorkin, "Sale Price Reflects the Depth of Bear's Problems," *New York Times*, March 17, 2008.

47 **stuffed stock certificates into briefcases:** Timothy F. Geithner, *Stress Test: Reflections on Financial Crises* (New York: Broadway Books, 2014), 196.

48 **"What made the crisis":** Barney Frank, foreword to *On the Brink: Inside the Race to Stop the Collapse of the Global Financial System*, by Henry R. Paulson Jr. (New York: Grand Central Publishing, 2011), ebook.

48 **"couldn't keep using duct tape":** Paulson, *On the Brink*.

49 **"It is a matter of days":** Paulson, *On the Brink*.

49 **"Nancy, we're racing to prevent":** Paulson, *On the Brink*. Additional details from Andrew Ross Sorkin, *Too Big to Fail: The Inside Story of How Wall Street and Washington Fought to Save the Financial System—and Themselves* (New York: Viking, 2009).

50 **"Decisions by the Secretary":** Author's copy of memo.

50 **one in eight mortgages:** Geithner, *Stress Test*.

52 **"Too many borrowers":** Phillip Swagel, "The Financial Crisis: An Inside View," *Brookings Papers on Economic Activity*, no. 1 (2009): 15.

52 **"We have to position this":** Paulson, *On the Brink.*

53 **totaled nearly $7 trillion:** Tooze, *Crashed.*

CHAPTER 4: ORDINARY PEOPLE

56 **confidence in banks:** Justin McCarthy, "Americans' Confidence in Banks Still Languishing Below 30%," Gallup, June 16, 2016, news.gallup.com/poll/192719 /americans-confidence-banks-languishing-below.aspx.

56 **an overwhelming majority:** R. J. Reinhart, "More in U.S. Say Government Is the Most Important Problem," Gallup, June 15, 2017, news.gallup.com/poll/212 426/say-government-important-problem.aspx.

56 **"The market was deteriorating":** Paulson, *On the Brink.*

57 **"The U.S. and the global":** "Questions About the $700 Billion Emergency Economic Stabilization Funds: The First Report of the Congressional Oversight Panel for Economic Stabilization," U.S. Government Printing Office, Dec. 10, 2008, 3, fraser.stlouisfed.org/title/questions-700-billion-emergency-economic -stabilization-funds-5006.

58 **"taught me that the squeeze":** Elizabeth Warren, *A Fighting Chance* (New York: Metropolitan Books, 2014).

59 **"We are here to investigate":** "First Report of the Congressional Oversight Panel," 3.

60 **"While the Fed staff":** Swagel, "Financial Crisis," 21.

60 **redlining and denial of credit:** Kriston McIntosh et al., "Examining the Black-White Wealth Gap," Brookings Institution, Feb. 27, 2020, www.brookings.edu /blog/up-front/2020/02/27/examining-the-black-white-wealth-gap/.

60 **"Spending public money":** Swagel, "Financial Crisis," 21.

61 **"pro-growth Democrat":** David Axelrod, *Believer: My Forty Years in Politics* (New York: Penguin Press, 2015).

61 **"During the Bush administration":** Hennessey quoted in Joshua Green, "Inside Man," *Atlantic,* April 2010, www.theatlantic.com/magazine/archive/2010/04 /inside-man/307992/.

62 **"You would not want them exposed":** David Barstow and Mike McIntire, "Calls for Clarity in New Bailout for U.S. Banks," *New York Times,* Feb. 9, 2009.

62 **In January, news broke:** Charles Gasparino, "John Thain's $87,000 Rug," *Daily Beast,* Jan. 22, 2009, www.thedailybeast.com/john-thains-dollar87000-rug.

63 **multimillion-dollar Super Bowl party:** Megan Chuchmach et al., "Bailed Out Bank of America Sponsors Super Bowl Fun Fest," ABC News, Feb. 1, 2009, abc news.go.com/Blotter/WallStreet/bailed-bank-america-sponsors-super -bowl-fun-fest/story?id=6782719.

63 **the insurance giant AIG:** Edmund L. Andrews and Peter Baker, "AIG Planning Huge Bonuses After $170 Billion Bailout," *New York Times,* March 14, 2009.

63 **"How do they justify"**: Obama quoted in Jeff Mason and David Alexander, "Outraged Obama Goes After AIG Bonus Payments," Reuters, March 16, 2009.

63 **"do everything we can"**: *The Tonight Show with Jay Leno*, season 17, episode 50, March 19, 2009, www.imdb.com/title/tt1375261/.

63 **73 percent of Americans:** "Obama at 100 Days: Strong Job Approval, Even Higher Personal Ratings," Pew Research Center Report, April 23, 2009, www.pewresearch.org/politics/2009/04/23/obama-at-100-days-strong-job-approval-even-higher-personal-ratings/.

64 **"People are angry"**: Elizabeth Warren opening statement at Congressional Oversight Panel Hearing, Dirksen Senate Office Building, Washington, D.C., April 21, 2009.

65 **"Are you saying"**: Warren-Geithner exchange, Congressional Oversight Panel Hearing, April 21, 2009.

68 **a staggering $78 billion:** Duff & Phelps valuation reported in "Congressional Oversight Panel February Oversight Report: Valuing Treasury's Acquisitions," U.S. Government Printing Office, Feb. 6, 2009.

69 **"In a sense, this had to be the opposite"**: Swagel, "Financial Crisis," 52.

70 **history seminar:** "Learning from the Past: Lessons from the Banking Crises of the 20th Century," hearing before the Congressional Oversight Panel, March 19, 2009.

70 **"main source of influence"**: Diana B. Henriques, "Bailout Monitor Sees Lack of a Coherent Plan," *New York Times*, Dec. 1, 2008.

CHAPTER 5: THE MEDIUM IS THE MESSAGE

74 **"home for piano-playing cats"**: EW staff, "The 100 Greatest Movies, TV Shows, Albums, Books, Characters, Scenes, Episodes, Songs, Dresses, Music Videos, and Trends That Entertained Us over the Past Ten Years," *Entertainment Weekly*, Dec. 11, 2009, 74.

75 **"She could see that blogs"**: Marshall quoted in Joshua Green, "Elizabeth Warren Has a Radical Plan to Beat Trump at His Own Game," *Bloomberg Businessweek*, July 25, 2019. See also Jack Bohrer, "'It Is a Pleasure to Blog with You': Elizabeth Warren's Early Years Online," NBC News, Jan. 6, 2019, www.nbcnews.com/politics/politics-news/it-pleasure-blog-you-elizabeth-warren-s-early-years-online-n954961. Warren and her students actually created an entire sub-blog within *Talking Points Memo* called "Warren Reports: On the Middle Class" that continued publishing until she joined the Congressional Oversight Panel in 2008. While she mostly stuck to policy matters, Warren, like a true blogger, sometimes just riffed on *New York Times* stories or took the occasional swipe at a politician. In March 2006, Warren (or a conspicuously lousy speller blogging under her name) attacked Joe Biden as being part of "a bi-partisan coalition to prefer powerful corporation [*sic*] over hard-working families." She went on: "For years,

Senator Joe Biden vied with Republican Senators Charles Grassley and Oren [*sic*] Hatch for head cheerleader for this bill. Even as he tried to position his national image as a strong supporter of women, Senator Biden was twisting arms to get the bankruptcy bill through Congress."

75 **powered by hundreds of millions:** Joshua Green, "The Amazing Money Machine: How Silicon Valley Made Barack Obama This Year's Hottest Start-Up," *Atlantic,* June 2008.

76 **"White House and Treasury officials":** Charles Duhigg, "Fighting Foreclosures, F.D.I.C. Chief Draws Fire," *New York Times*, Dec. 11, 2008.

76 **Warren's first YouTube video:** "Elizabeth Warren Introduces the First Report of the Congressional Oversight Panel," Dec. 11, 2008, www.youtube.com/watch?v=X-C4c2rGbIc.

79 **"He meets with bankers":** Ron Suskind, *Confidence Men: Wall Street, Washington, and the Education of a President* (New York: Harper, 2011).

80 **a can of Pepsi:** "At One Dollar, Citi Share Worth Just a Soft-Drink," *Economic Times*, March 6, 2009.

80 **abruptly pulled Santelli:** Santelli was replaced by another CNBC personality, Jim Cramer, a *Daily Show* fan who evidently expected a warm reception but walked into a wood chipper. Stewart's on-air evisceration of him, Cramer complained, "made me into a buffoon." See Peter Lattman, "Jon Stewart's Wall Street Corner Man for Tonight's Cramer Battle," *Wall Street Journal*, March 12, 2009; Zev Chafets, "Jim Cramer Hits an All-Time High," *New York Times Magazine*, May 11, 2011.

80 **"like an astronaut":** Warren, *Fighting Chance.*

81 **"Why not liquidate":** *The Daily Show with Jon Stewart*, season 14, episode 50, April 15, 2009, www.cc.com/video/ecpfjd/the-daily-show-with-jon-stewart-elizabeth-warren-pt-1.

82 **a journal article proposing:** Elizabeth Warren, "Unsafe at Any Rate," *Democracy: A Journal of Ideas*, no. 5 (Summer 2007).

84 **a *Time* magazine poll:** James Poniewozik, "Jon Stewart, the Fake Newsman Who Made a Real Difference," *Time*, Feb. 5, 2015; Bill Carter and Brian Stelter, "In 'Daily Show' Role on 9/11 Bill, Echoes of Murrow," *New York Times*, Dec. 26, 2010. See also Sophia A. McClennen and Remy M. Maisel, *Is Satire Saving Our Nation? Mockery and American Politics* (New York: Palgrave Macmillan, 2014).

84 **couldn't help but patronize:** The canonical example came in 2017, when the Republican Senate majority leader, Mitch McConnell, used an obscure rule to silence Warren from finishing a scathing speech about Trump's attorney general nominee, Jeff Sessions. "She was warned," McConnell explained. "She was given an explanation. Nevertheless, she persisted." *The Washington Post* dubbed the silencing "the move that launched a thousand tweets." Warren later printed up T-shirts and turned "She persisted" into a campaign slogan.

85 **"was better at impugning":** Geithner, *Stress Test.*

85 **"We're with Barack"**: Alex Thompson, "'Why Are You Pissing in Our Face?': Inside Warren's War with the Obama Team," *Politico*, Sept. 12, 2019.

88 **"By happy coincidence"**: Jeffrey Toobin, "The Professor," *New Yorker*, Sept. 17, 2012.

89 **"We were way ahead"**: Toobin, "Professor."

89 **Warren, Westbrook, and Teresa Sullivan published**: Teresa A. Sullivan, Elizabeth Warren, and Jay Lawrence Westbrook, *As We Forgive Our Debtors: Bankruptcy and Consumer Credit in America* (New York: Oxford University Press, 1989).

90 **"The first book says"**: Toobin, "Professor."

90 **"It's our job"**: Warren and Tyagi, *Two-Income Trap*.

91 **"It is impossible to buy"**: Warren, "Unsafe at Any Rate."

92 **the U.S. poverty rate actually fell:** "Income and Poverty in the United States: 2020," U.S. Census Bureau, Report No. P60-273, Sept. 14, 2021.

95 **"These were very capable people"**: Green, "Inside Man."

97 **a *Time* cover touting:** *Time*, Feb. 15, 1999.

102 **The final cost:** "Troubled Asset Relief Program Monthly Report to Congress: July 2021," U.S. Department of the Treasury, Aug. 10, 2021.

103 **"My administration is the only thing"**: Eamon Javers, "Inside Obama's Bank CEOs Meeting," *Politico*, April 3, 2009.

104 **"With the world economy"**: Barack Obama, *A Promised Land* (New York: Crown, 2020).

106 **"Here were the two of us"**: Warren, *Fighting Chance*.

CHAPTER 6: FOLLOW THE MONEY

111 **thin white envelopes:** Brooks Jackson, *Honest Graft: How Special Interests Buy Influence in Washington*, rev. ed. (Washington, D.C.: Farragut, 1990).

111 **"created an atmosphere"**: Jackson, *Honest Graft*.

112 **"I said I could raise"**: Jackson, *Honest Graft*.

112 **"The guy is beautiful"**: Dudley Clendinen, "New Center Moves Democrats from Machine Age to TV Age," *New York Times*, Feb. 7, 1984.

114 **"I have a job"**: The story of Coelho's relationship with Hope is drawn from Jackson, *Honest Graft*. Also author's interview.

115 **In the 1981–82 cycle:** Gary C. Jacobson, "Party Organization and Distribution of Campaign Resources: Republicans and Democrats in 1982," *Political Science Quarterly* 100, no. 4 (Winter 1985–86).

116 **Between 1974 and 1983:** Robert Kuttner, *The Life of the Party: Democratic Prospects in 1988 and Beyond* (New York: Viking, 1987).

116 **an advisory opinion:** Federal Election Commission, Advisory Opinion 1975-23, Nov. 24, 1975, www.fec.gov/files/legal/aos/66709.pdf.

117 **Membership was gained:** Martin Tolchin, "For $5,000 a Year, Welcome to the Speaker's Club," *New York Times*, March 24, 1983. Also, Jackson, *Honest Graft*.

117 **A Texas businessman:** The story of Devlin is drawn from Gregg Easterbrook, "Washington: The Business of Politics," *Atlantic Monthly*, Oct. 1986.

120 **"It never even occurred":** Jackson, *Honest Graft.*

120 **a rich California lawyer:** David Menefee-Libey, "Embracing Campaign-Centered Politics at the Democratic Headquarters: Charles Manatt and Paul Kirk," in *Politics, Professionalism, and Power: Modern Party Organization and the Legacy of Ray C. Bliss*, ed. John C. Green (Lanham, MD: University Press of America, 1984).

121 **"We have to have the dollars":** Jackson, *Honest Graft.*

121 **"All of those boys":** Jackson, *Honest Graft.*

122 **"The party tried to sell its soul":** Easterbrook, "Washington: The Business of Politics."

123 **reaped $3 million:** Irwin Ross and Alison Bruce Rea, "In Demand: Wall Street's Liberals," *Fortune*, April 27, 1987.

125 **a three-way standoff:** The tripartite battle to influence and eventually repeal Glass-Steagall is described in Sandra L. Suarez and Robin Kolodny, "Paving the Road to 'Too Big to Fail': Business Interests and the Politics of Financial Deregulation in the United States," *Politics and Society*, June 2010.

125 **"After 1982," they concluded:** Eric Keller and Nathan J. Kelly, "Partisan Politics, Financial Deregulation, and the New Gilded Age," *Political Research Quarterly* 86, no. 3 (2015).

126 **"We are not interested":** Andrew Taylor, "Bankers' Opposition Stalls Glass-Steagall Rewrite," *Congressional Quarterly Online*, Oct. 21, 1995.

126 **In 1987, the Fed:** Nathaniel C. Nash, "Bank Curb Eased in Volcker Defeat," *New York Times*, May 1, 1987.

127 **There were dissenting voices:** Stephen Labaton, "Congress Passes Wide-Ranging Bill Easing Bank Laws," *New York Times*, Nov. 5, 1999.

127 **"taxpayer exposure to potential losses":** Sanders House floor speech, July 1, 1999, www.youtube.com/watch?v=0YYNg2wJ3I4.

128 **"The concerns that we will":** Labaton, "Congress Passes Wide-Ranging Bill."

128 **"Special interest is not":** Ruth Shalit, "The Undertaker," *New Republic*, Jan. 2, 1995.

129 **Coelho was caught using:** N. R. Kleinfield, "He Had Money, Women, an S.&L. Now Don Dixon Has Jail," *New York Times*, March 17, 1991; "Ex-Owners of Vernon S&L Convicted of Fraud," Reuters, Dec. 21, 1990; Sara Fritz, "Congressional Income: Pay Is Tip of Iceberg," *Los Angeles Times*, Dec. 19, 1988.

130 **"Their liberalism tends":** Kuttner, *Life of the Party.*

131 **People like Rubin:** Drawn from Kuttner, *Life of the Party.*

133 **"I want to give":** Michael Oreskes, "Coelho to Resign His Seat in House in Face of Inquiry," *New York Times*, May 27, 1989.

133 **"Once the elderly understand":** Shalit, "Undertaker."

135 **The hallmarks of the new:** See David Osborne and Ted Gaebler, *Reinventing Government: How the Entrepreneurial Spirit Is Transforming the Public Sector*

(Reading, MA: Addison-Wesley, 1992); Kenneth S. Baer, *Reinventing Democrats: The Politics of Liberalism from Reagan to Clinton* (Lawrence: University Press of Kansas, 2000); J. Bradford DeLong, "Robert Rubin's Contested Legacy," *American Prospect,* Jan. 16, 2004.

135 **This shift is inscribed:** Text of the party platforms was drawn from the American Presidency Project at the University of California, Santa Barbara: www .presidency.ucsb.edu/.

136 **the number of college students:** Figures drawn from Barbara Ehrenreich, *Fear of Falling: The Inner Life of the Middle Class* (1989; repr., New York: Twelve, 2020); David Vogel, *Fluctuating Fortunes: The Political Power of Business in America* (Washington, D.C.: Beard Books, 1989).

136 **The bestselling nonfiction book:** Robert D. McFadden, "Lee Iacocca, Visionary Automaker Who Led Both Ford and Chrysler, Is Dead at 94," *New York Times,* July 2, 2019.

CHAPTER 7: THE ADVANCING ARMY

141 **Warren had her champions:** Suzanna Andrews, "The Woman Who Knew Too Much," *Vanity Fair,* Nov. 2011.

142 **"Tell her to keep":** Axelrod, *Believer.*

143 **As early as 2009:** "Draft Liz Warren for Kennedy's Senate Seat," Truth/Slant, Sept. 16, 2009; "The Woman Democrats Need," *Boston Globe,* Jan. 24, 2010.

143 **"stab myself in the eye":** David Corn, "Elizabeth Warren Won't Rule Out a Senate Bid . . . Kinda," MotherJones.com, March 11, 2010.

144 **"I told him that":** Toobin, "Professor."

146 **the AFL-CIO found:** AFL-CIO Political Department memo on the Massachusetts Senate race, Nov. 6, 2012.

147 **"the perfect foil":** Axelrod, *Believer.*

148 **got hold of the film:** I was the grateful recipient of Bannon's leak after bumping into him at a New Hampshire hotel. See Joshua Green, "Gingrich-Allied Attack Film Shows Romney as 'Ruthless' Rich," Bloomberg News, Jan. 11, 2012.

149 **His reelection hinged:** Joshua Green, "Obama's Bogus War on Bain," *Bloomberg Businessweek,* May 25, 2012.

149 **"This is not a distraction":** "Remarks by the President at NATO Press Conference," May 21, 2012, Obama White House Archives.

151 **The Pew Research Center found:** "Public Views of Inequality, Fairness, and Wall Street," Pew Research Center, Jan. 5, 2012.

152 **a blueprint for leveraging fame:** Clinton Senate details drawn from Joshua Green, "Take Two: How Hillary Clinton Turned Herself into the Consummate Washington Player," *Atlantic Monthly,* Nov. 2006.

156 **"more loudly than anyone":** Noam Scheiber, "Hillary's Nightmare?," *New Republic,* Nov. 10, 2013.

156 **"keep your head down"**: Victoria McGrane, "A High-Profile Newcomer Keeps a Low One, for Now," *Wall Street Journal*, Dec. 26, 2012.

158 **real wages had fallen**: Heidi Shierholz and Lawrence Mishel, "A Decade of Flat Wages: The Key Barrier to Shared Prosperity and a Rising Middle Class," Economic Policy Institute, Aug. 21, 2013.

158 **A Pew poll in December 2011**: "Little Change in Public's Response to 'Capitalism,' 'Socialism,'" Pew Research Center, Dec. 28, 2011.

160 **In late July**: Ezra Klein, "Right Now, Larry Summers Is the Frontrunner for Fed Chair," *Washington Post*, July 23, 2013.

161 **Digital staffers fed**: Matthew Yglesias, "The Extremely Effective Leak Campaign Against Larry Summers," *Slate*, July 24, 2013.

162 **"The truth is"**: Zachary A. Goldfarb and Ylan Q. Mui, "Larry Summers Withdraws Name from Fed Consideration," *Washington Post*, Sept. 15, 2013.

163 **"Enough is enough"**: Elizabeth Warren, "Enough Is Enough: The President's Latest Wall Street Nominee," *Huffington Post*, Nov. 19, 2014.

164 **"I don't think"**: "Jamie Dimon Q&A: From His Biggest Mistakes to Future of Finance," *Bloomberg Markets*, March 1, 2016.

166 **"Democrats are afraid"**: Ryan Lizza, "The Virtual Candidate," *New Yorker*, May 4, 2015.

169 **"The truth of the matter"**: Obama interview with Matt Bai, Yahoo News, May 9, 2015, www.yahoo.com/news/why-obama-is-happy-to-fight-elizabeth-warren-on-118537612596.html.

169 **"As of today"**: Clinton to Woodruff, *PBS NewsHour*, Oct. 7, 2015.

172 **"Signature Warren issues"**: Public letter from Ilya Sheyman and Charles Chamberlain, June 2, 2015, www.politico.com/magazine/story/2015/06/elizabeth-warren-run-warren-run-campaign-118514/.

172 **"the desire for there"**: Maggie Haberman, "Ex-Obama Aide Makes Warren-2016 Push," *Politico*, Dec. 11, 2014.

173 **"Less is known about Hillary"**: Mike Dorning, "Hillary's Mystery: Where Clinton Stands on Issues Dividing Her Party," Bloomberg News, March 17, 2015.

CHAPTER 8: STRAIGHT OUTTA BURLINGTON

178 **Americans' ire shifted**: Gallup surveys on "Most Important Problem Facing the U.S.," Feb. 12, 2009; Jan. 15, 2014; Sept. 17, 2015.

178 **A March 2015 poll**: CNN-ORC International poll, March 18, 2015.

180 **"Such a megaphone"**: Brian Stelter, "The Anti-Fox Gains Ground," *New York Times*, Nov. 11, 2012.

181 **In 2000, about 6 percent**: "Liberals Make Up Nearly Half of Democratic Voters," Pew Research Center, Jan. 17, 2020.

183 **"Jesus, what is that?"**: Margaret Talbot, "The Populist Prophet," *New Yorker*, Oct. 12, 2015.

184 **"It doesn't matter":** Talbot, "Populist Prophet."

185 **damage across the millennial generation:** Job openings 20 percent below prerecession peak from Jesse Rothstein, "The Lost Generation? Scarring After the Great Recession" (working paper 27516, National Bureau of Economic Research, July 2020); falling wages from Heidi Shierholz, Natalie Sabadish, and Nicholas Finio, "The Class of 2013: Young Graduates Still Face Dim Job Prospects" (EPI briefing paper 360, Economic Policy Institute, Aug. 10, 2013); health insurance figures from Heidi Shierholz, Alyssa Davis, and Will Kimball, "The Class of 2014: The Weak Economy Is Idling Too Many Young Graduates" (EPI briefing paper 377, Economic Policy Institute, May 1, 2014).

190 **"Money is just bubbling up":** Jeff Stein, "Bernie Sanders's Campaign Is Still Raising Far More Money Than Hillary Clinton's," *Vox*, March 23, 2016.

191 **"new radical mayor":** "Sanders Takes Over Today," *Barre Times-Argus*, April 6, 1981; Dudley Clendinen, "It's New Politics vs. Old in Vermont as Mayor Strives to Oust Alderman," *New York Times*, Feb. 28, 1982.

192 **"I won in 1981":** Sanders to David Axelrod, "The Axe Files Podcast," Sept. 28, 2015.

194 **"a stunning victory":** Eric Schmitt and Joseph Kahn, "China Trade Vote: A Clinton Triumph," *New York Times*, May 25, 2000.

195 **a surge of Japanese cars:** Katherine Eriksson et al., "Trade Shocks and the Shifting Landscape of U.S. Manufacturing" (working paper 25646, National Bureau of Economic Research, March 2019).

196 **a series of papers:** David H. Autor, David Dorn, and Gordon H. Hanson, "The China Syndrome: Local Labor Market Effects of Import Competition in the United States," *American Economic Review* 103, no. 6 (Oct. 2013); David H. Autor, David Dorn, and Gordon H. Hanson, "The China Shock: Learning from Labor-Market Adjustment to Large Changes in Trade," *Annual Review of Economics* 8 (Oct. 2016).

197 **workers got no reprieve:** David H. Autor, David Dorn, and Gordon H. Hanson, "On the Persistence of the China Shock" (working paper 29401, National Bureau of Economic Research, Oct. 2021).

198 **"trade exposure abets":** David H. Autor et al., "Importing Political Polarization? The Electoral Consequences of Rising Trade Exposure," *American Economic Review* 110, no. 10 (Oct. 2020).

199 **a *Wall Street Journal* analysis:** Bob Davis and Jon Hilsenrath, "How the China Shock, Deep and Swift, Spurred the Rise of Trump," *Wall Street Journal*, Aug. 11, 2016.

200 **"I don't want to say":** Autor, interview on *Marketplace*, April 26, 2016, www.marketplace.org/2016/04/26/theres-reason-trade-divisive-election-issue/.

201 **filed regular dispatches:** Andy Kroll, "The Bernie Revolution: What's So Appealing About a Grumpy 74-Year-Old?," Yahoo News, Dec. 3, 2015; David Weigel, "In Rural America, a Startling Prospect: Voters Obama Lost Look to Sanders," *Washington Post*, Oct. 5, 2015.

201 **the national media shifted:** Patrick Healy and Jonathan Martin, "Donald Trump and Bernie Sanders Win in New Hampshire Primary," *New York Times,* Feb. 9, 2016.

205 **"This last-minute sneak attack":** Ken Thomas, "In Iowa Push, Sanders Expands Criticism of Clinton's Record," Associated Press, Jan. 28, 2016.

207 **"If a crystal ball":** Memo quoted in Joshua Green, "Elizabeth Warren Has a Radical Plan to Beat Trump at His Own Game," *Bloomberg Businessweek,* July 25, 2019.

209 **His oft-repeated line:** Census figures show that 59,794 U.S. manufacturing establishments closed between 2001 and 2015.

209 **racial grievance:** An excellent source is John Sides, Michael Tesler, and Lynn Vavreck, *Identity Crisis: The 2016 Presidential Campaign and the Battle for the Meaning of America* (Princeton, NJ: Princeton University Press, 2018).

210 **"The thing that really stood":** Jeff Stein, "The Bernie Voters Who Defected to Trump, Explained by a Political Scientist," *Vox,* Aug. 24, 2017.

CHAPTER 9: MOBILIZE

215 **Allen Kramer and Alfred Johnson:** Background details drawn from Joshua Green, "Can Democrats Harness the #Resistance?," *Bloomberg Businessweek,* Nov. 2, 2017.

217 **"where those feelings":** Hillary Rodham Clinton, *What Happened* (New York: Simon & Schuster, 2017).

218 **targeting African Americans:** Joshua Green and Sasha Issenberg, "Inside the Trump Bunker with 12 Days to Go," *Bloomberg Businessweek,* Oct. 27, 2016.

221 **"Virginia's chief homophobe":** Chris L. Jenkins, "Marshall Admits No Doubts About Marriage," *Washington Post,* Nov. 4, 2006.

224 **"just completely inspired":** Lovato quoted in Meg Swertlow, "Demi Lovato Hits 2017 AMAs Red Carpet with History Making Transgender Lawmaker Danica Roem," *E! News,* Nov. 19, 2017.

224 **"A dreary, congested Virginia highway":** Matthew Barakat, "Road Made Famous by Transgender Candidate Not a Simple Fix," Associated Press, Dec. 17, 2017.

CHAPTER 10: THE NATURAL

233 **a blast of unexpected bad news:** On Sept. 2, the Bureau of Labor Statistics announced that zero new jobs had been created in August and the unemployment rate remained above 9 percent. Bureau of Labor Statistics, "The Employment Situation—August 2011," news release, Sept. 2, 2011, www.bls.gov/news .release/archives/empsit_09022011.pdf.

234 **"the political nadir"**: Dan Pfeiffer, "Messaging Economic Progress to an Angry Public," Substack, Nov. 21, 2021, messagebox.substack.com/p/selling-economic-progress-to-an-angry.

234 **an anti-austerity movement**: Sophie Tedmanson, "Wall Street Protests Turn Global," *Times* (London), Oct. 15, 2011.

235 **"When Obama actually won"**: Philadelphia protester quoted in Ruth Milkman, Stephanie Luce, and Penny Lewis, "Changing the Subject: A Bottom-Up Account of Occupy Wall Street in New York City" (conference paper, XVIII ISA World Congress of Sociology, July 2014).

235 **"If you're concerned about Wall Street"**: Plouffe appeared on *Good Morning America*, ABC, Oct. 11, 2011.

236 **Wall Street clients**: Robin Bravender and Anna Palmer, "Wall St.: Dems Can't Have It Both Ways," *Politico*, Oct. 18, 2011.

237 **white, male, well educated**: Demographic data of protesters and Nurse quotation from Milkman, Luce, and Lewis, "Changing the Subject."

239 **"forward-looking people"**: David Graeber, "On Playing by the Rules—the Strange Success of #OccupyWallStreet," NakedCapitalism.com, Oct. 19, 2011.

240 **"came for a protest"**: Nathan Schneider, *Thank You, Anarchy: Notes from the Occupy Apocalypse* (Berkeley: University of California Press, 2013).

240 **"The financial crisis touched everyone"**: David Freedlander, *The AOC Generation: How Millennials Are Seizing Power and Rewriting the Rules of American Politics* (Boston: Beacon Press, 2021).

241 **didn't directly intersect**: This point was made by Ryan Grim in his deeply reported recent history of the left, *We've Got People: From Jesse Jackson to Alexandria Ocasio-Cortez, the End of Big Money and the Rise of a Movement* (Washington, D.C.: Strong Arm Press, 2019).

241 **"I don't want to live"**: Berger quoted by John Heilemann, "2012=1968?," *New York*, Nov. 23, 2011.

242 **"It was a disaster"**: Candice M. Giove, "'They Took My Place!': Single Dad Trying to Take Back Home Occupied by OWS," *New York Post*, Jan. 15, 2012.

245 **"Sanders's race"**: Charlotte Alter, "'Change Is Closer Than We Think.' Inside Alexandria Ocasio-Cortez's Unlikely Rise," *Time*, March 21, 2019.

246 **"I came of age"**: Astead W. Herndon, "Democrats, Pushing Stimulus, Admit to Regrets on Obama's 2009 Response," *New York Times*, March 16, 2021.

246 **"I was supposed to be"**: David Remnick, "Is Alexandria Ocasio-Cortez an Insider Now?," *New Yorker*, Feb. 14, 2022.

247 **"She was beginning to learn"**: Charlotte Alter, *The Ones We've Been Waiting For: How a New Generation of Leaders Will Transform America* (New York: Penguin Books, 2020).

248 **The "grassroots-funded machine"**: Chakrabarti quoted in *Knock Down the House*, directed by Rachel Lears (Atlas Films, 2019).

248 **"We looked at the brother"**: Alter, "'Change Is Closer Than We Think.'"

250 **the wrong congressional district**: Grim, *We've Got People.*

250 **Perhaps chagrined**: Federal Election Commission, "Alexandria Ocasio-Cortez for Congress—Individual Contributions," May 17, 2017—Sept. 1, 2017.

251 **"You're always going to hear"**: Charlotte Alter, "Alexandria Ocasio-Cortez's Facebook Videos of Her Trip to Standing Rock Reveal Her Political Awakening," *Time*, Feb. 19, 2020.

252 **A bigger innovation**: Organizing data and DeGroot quotations from Joshua Green, "AOC's Organizing App Is Spreading to Democratic Socialist Campaigns," *Bloomberg Businessweek*, March 26, 2019.

253 **an unofficial interpreter**: David Freedlander, "The 28-Year-Old Progressive Hoping to Unseat One of the Top Democrats in Congress," *New York*, June 25, 2018.

253 **a campaign video**: The ad ("The Courage to Change") was released on May 30, 2018. See youtu.be/rq3QXIVR0bs.

254 **raised more than $135,000**: Federal Election Commission, "Alexandria Ocasio-Cortez for Congress—Individual Contributions," May 30, 2018—June 26, 2018.

254 **The editorial warned**: New York Times Editorial Board, "If You Want to Be Speaker, Mr. Crowley, Don't Take Voters for Granted," *New York Times*, June 19, 2018.

255 **portion of the Bronx**: District demographics and primary turnout from *Cook Political Report.*

256 **"He can't get challenged"**: Lears, *Knock Down the House.*

256 **a precinct-by-precinct**: The Romalewski study is cited in Zaid Jilani and Ryan Grim, "Data Suggest That Gentrifying Neighborhoods Powered Alexandria Ocasio-Cortez's Victory," *Intercept*, July 1, 2018.

257 **"It was the gentrifiers"**: Grim, *We've Got People.*

257 **"Run unapologetically on a bold vision"**: Jilani and Grim, "Data Suggest."

257 **many young journalists**: Sean McElwee of Data for Progress famously held a weekly happy hour that drew Democratic Socialists, activists, journalists, and candidates, including Ocasio-Cortez.

CHAPTER 11: A DREAM DEFERRED

260 **largest Democratic presidential field**: "2020 Presidential Candidates: Tracking Which Democrats Ran," NPR, Jan. 31, 2019.

261 **"a mocking, groping, deporting"**: David A. Hopkins, "How Trump Changed the Republican Party—and the Democrats Too," in *The Trump Effect: Disruption and Its Consequences in U.S. Politics and Government*, ed. Steven E. Schier and Todd E. Eberly (Lanham, MD: Rowman & Littlefield, 2022).

262 **"It's ambitious to expand"**: Eliza Collins, "Sanders Campaign Says Winning Democratic Nomination Requires New Voters," *Wall Street Journal*, Oct. 23, 2019.

262 **"it was a recognition"**: Joshua Green and Tyler Pager, "Democratic 2020 Candidates Inch Away from Medicare for All," Bloomberg News, Aug. 3, 2019.

263 **"Some people think"**: Edward-Isaac Dovere, "Elizabeth Warren Has Momentum. Can She Build a Movement?," *Atlantic*, July 21, 2019.

266 **a representative survey**: Quinnipiac University Poll, Oct. 14, 2019.

268 **"Timing is important"**: Janet Hook, "Alexandria Ocasio-Cortez Dangles 2020 Endorsement: Bernie Sanders or Elizabeth Warren?," *Los Angeles Times*, June 11, 2019.

268 **secretly flown to Vermont**: Paul Heintz, "AOC, Sanders Dine at Burlington's Penny Cluse Café," *Seven Days*, Sept. 29, 2019.

269 **"It is undeniably true"**: Collins, "Sanders Campaign Says Winning Democratic Nomination Requires New Voters."

270 **"If our focus"**: Astead W. Herndon, "Working Families Party Endorses Elizabeth Warren. Here's Why It Matters," *New York Times*, Dec. 6, 2019.

272 **eclipsing the record-setting pace**: Joshua Green and Tyler Pager, "Democrats Rally to 2020 Candidates on Surge of Anti-Trump Energy," Bloomberg News, Feb. 1, 2020.

273 **"a case study in the limits"**: Astead W. Herndon, "Elizabeth Warren Has Won Black Activists. She's Losing the Black Vote," *New York Times*, Feb. 28, 2020.

274 **"too white"**: Troy L. Smith, "Bernie Sanders Admits 2016 Presidential Campaign Was 'Too White,'" Cleveland.com, March 5, 2019.

275 **By nearly a two-to-one margin**: "Electability of Democratic Nominee Outranks Issue Stances," Gallup, June 25, 2019.

EPILOGUE

281 **"The biggest mistake"**: Neel Kashkari, "What the 2008 Rescue Package Can Teach Us About Today's Relief Bill," *Washington Post*, March 27, 2020.

281 **"bond vigilantes"**: For history and origin, see Joe Weisenthal and Tracy Alloway interview with Ed Yardeni, "The Inventor of 'Bond Vigilantes' Explains Why They Just Showed Up in Italy," *Odd Lots* (podcast), June 11, 2018.

282 **The Federal Reserve was questioning**: A good overview of the shift among economic policymakers is Matthew Boesler, "The Covid Trauma Has Changed Economics—Maybe Forever," Bloomberg News, June 1, 2021.

282 **"think big"**: Nancy Pelosi, weekly news conference, March 26, 2020, pelosi .house.gov/news/press-releases/transcript-of-pelosi-weekly-press-conference -today-56.

283 **"the most amazing statistic"**: Boesler, "Covid Trauma Has Changed Economics."

286 **"The way I see it"**: Joe Biden, "Remarks by President Biden on the State of the Economy and the Need for the American Rescue Plan," Feb. 5, 2021.

288 **"We were all children"**: Alter, "'Change Is Closer Than We Think.'"

288 **"true to the movement"**: Eli Okun, "Politico Playbook Power List 2019: Saikat Chakrabarti," *Politico*; Laura Barrón-López and Heather Caygle, "Group Aligned with Ocasio-Cortez Prepares to Take Out Democrats," *Politico*, Jan. 16, 2019.

288 **"They're four people"**: Maureen Dowd, "It's Nancy Pelosi's Parade," *New York Times*, July 6, 2019.

289 **"So you issue threats"**: Alexandria Ocasio-Cortez (@AOC), Twitter, Dec. 11, 2000, twitter.com/AOC/status/1337619367857713154.

291 **"In any other country"**: David Freedlander, "AOC Has Already Changed D.C. It Hasn't Changed Her Much," *New York*, Jan. 6, 2020.

296 **"I proposed a minimum billionaire tax"**: Joe Biden (@JoeBiden), Twitter, May 8, 2023, twitter.com/JoeBiden/status/1655653545977208870.

INDEX

INDEX